# COMPUTING WITH MINI COMPUTERS

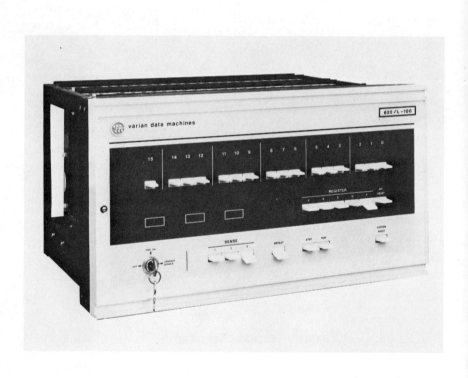

# COMPUTING WITH MINI COMPUTERS

Fred Gruenberger

School of Business and Economics
California State University, Northridge

David Babcock
*Popular Computing*
Woodland Hills, California

Melville Publishing Company

Los Angeles, California

The jacket design is by John Gruenberger,
using a pattern from the problem
described in Section 15.5.

 Copyright © 1973, by John Wiley & Sons, Inc.

Published by **Melville Publishing Company**
a Division of John Wiley & Sons, Inc.

*Library of Congress Cataloging in Publication Data:*

Gruenberger, Fred Joseph
  Computing with mini computers.

  (Computer science series)
    1. Miniature computers—Programming.    I. Babcock,
David, joint author.    II. Title.

QA76.6.G78        001.6'4'04        73-4793
ISBN 0-471-33005-1

Printed in the United States of America

10 9 8 7 6 5 4 3 2

To Fran and George

*The Way to Learn Computing
Is to Compute*

# PREFACE

Starting in 1967, a breed of computers now categorized as minis appeared. By 1972, there were several dozen manufacturers making such machines, and they had reached such a degree of uniformity that they can be described as follows:

1. Their Central Processing Units (CPUs) sell for between $3000 and $20,000.
2. Their word length is either 12 or 16 bits (most often 16).
3. Their main frames measure $19 \times 11 \times 21$ inches (usually designed to be rack-mounted).
4. Their internal operating speeds are from 1 to 4 microseconds per full word addition.
5. They have markedly similar instruction sets, particularly in their schemes for addressing large amounts of core storage (ranging from 2048 to 65,536 words) within the constraint of their short word length.
6. Some of them offer microprogramming capability through the addition of electronically alterable read-only storage.

The mini computers in their early stages of development were marketed almost exclusively to the Original Equipment Manufacturers (OEM). That is, the machines were sold in large lots to the makers of other equipment, typically the makers of key-to-disk equipment. In this atmosphere, the mini maker produced a bare CPU, with little or no software beyond a simple assembly language and some diagnostic utility programs. Use of minis as free-standing computers, to be sold to end users and to function as general-purpose computers was carefully avoided.

Starting around 1970, some of the mini makers began to offer such pieces of software as a Fortran compiler, a BASIC language interpreter, an RPG (Report Program Generator) program, editing routines, more sophisticated assemblers, and operating systems. Attention now focused on use of minis as the heart of complete computing installations.

This notion seemed to run counter to the general trend in computing;

namely, to centralize and concentrate computing power in larger and larger machines. There is no question that as computers get larger, the cost of each executed instruction falls significantly. Thus, it is reasoned, by replacing many small machines with one large machine that absorbs the work load of the small machines, the total cost of computation can be lowered. This line of reasoning is called the "economies of scale" argument. A crude analogy is found in the transportation of people: The cost per mile per person is much lower in a bus than in individual cars.

A parallel argument urges that computing power be furnished to the small user via time-shared use of a large machine. The person who needs only a small amount of computing, or who needs computation at widely spaced time intervals, will be better off economically, the argument goes, by buying a small time slice of a large machine, rather than by having his own dedicated machine.

To a large extent, these arguments rest on a deep fear that unless computing power is concentrated, some computer might stand idle. Here the analogy is always made to the generation of electric power, where few users can afford to operate their own generators, and all users are better off by having electricity generation concentrated in a relatively few installations.

There are few devices in our technological society that are required to function continuously. Large jet planes are one, and household refrigerators and freezers are another. Nearly every other device built by man has as its chief function, if we judge by usage, to sit and rust. We use our personal cars, for example, on the order of 4% of the time, and the 96% of idleness does not disturb us unduly. The desk calculator in our office is utilized much less than 1% of the time, but the university does not schedule people to absorb the 99+% of the idle time. And so it goes with device after device; we expect them to sit idle most of the time, since this idleness adjusts them to our needs and desires, rather than the other way around. Those who advocate economies of scale most avidly would balk at a centralized, time-shared pencil sharpener; they seem to enjoy the convenience of having small, inefficient units in their offices.

Consider the other end of the electric power generating network that is so often cited as proof of the value of centralization. True, we all enjoy the benefits of centralized generation of electric power and the low costs that accrue from it. But to the **user** of electric power, the analogy breaks down. A typical home today may have 40 electric motors, totalling perhaps 6 horsepower, but seldom having more than 1 horsepower in use. The parts of the home that need physical power could be run, in theory, with one 3 horsepower motor and a lot of shafts and belts and power takeoffs. The industrial world saw how silly that was at the turn of the century. It has been universally concluded to put the power where it is used, even though the total available power is then much greater and most subunits will be idle most of the time.

Now, analogies are tricky and dangerous, and it remains to be decided whether the **use** of computing power corresponds to the generating end of the electricity analogy or to the home-use end. The rise in the use of mini computers is an obvious expression of the belief by someone that computing use is analogous to the use of electric power in the home.

The argument is strengthened by another fact of life. When computing power is centralized and concentrated, it becomes economically necessary to minimize idle time of the CPU; just as with large jet planes, the total investment must be protected by driving the large computer continuously. This means that elaborate mechanisms must be created to feed an endless stream of problems to the large machine, and complex communications links must be set up to move the problems from the end users to the machine and move the output back to the user. Moreover, complicated control and bookkeeping systems must be set up to keep the whole mess straight, and these systems themselves absorb a significant amount of the computing power that is available. Big computers are intrinsically more efficient than small computers, but they tend to defeat the main purpose, which is to deliver computing power to those who wish to use it. Large computers have a nasty way of inducing users to serve the machine, instead of having the machine serve its users.

The attempt to bring the economies of the large machine to the small user via time-sharing can also be attacked. There have been few studies of the true cost of operating a time-shared terminal, but the commercial vendors of such terminals agree that they must realize upwards of $1000 per month per terminal to stay in business. Figured over 5 years (which is about the life of a computer these days), this amounts to $60,000. It is possible to acquire a complete computing installation for well under $20,000. There is an imbalance here—something is wrong. The raw costs neglect, of course, the ancillary requirements for operating one's own installation (and these are severe), but the case for cost-cutting via time-sharing is surely not clear-cut.

In any event, a mini computer can certainly function as a free-standing general-purpose computer and can do a creditable job equivalent to any other machine.

Among the vendors of minis who foster the free-standing environment and furnish general-purpose software, the current leaders, in terms of number of machines installed, include Digital Equipment Corporation, Varian Data Machines, Hewlett-Packard, Inc., Microdata Corporation, and General Automation, Inc.

The technical material in this book is based on a Varian 620/L. We found the Varian machine perfectly suited to our purpose, which was to put together an introductory text in computing. Such a text, we believe, must proceed from the bottom up, working from the machine itself toward the high levels of sophistication and symbolism. To that end, the logical design of the Varian machine is most satisfying; the operation repertoire contains all necessary commands, plus a rather elegant structure for the types of addressing needed by a mini. The electronics of the Varian 620 CPU is solid (and this is true of all the minis), needing no attention whatsoever through months of operation. Indeed, the computing power, in terms of throughput capability, compares favorably with that of an IBM 704, which was at one time the giant machine of the field.

The Varian mainframe, with 16,384 words of core storage, plus a Model 33 Teletype, † plus a photoelectric paper tape reader, constitutes a modest computing installation, suitable for learning a great deal about the art of computing, and capable of supplying the needs of several classes of beginning students. It is our belief that such an installation provides an efficient and effective avenue toward learning.

This is an introductory text in computing, designed for a one-semester college-level course. It is based on the assumption that many schools will use a mini computer as a general-purpose machine and specifically as a machine with which to learn computing.

The approach is from the bottom up, starting with a brief exposure to the machine language of a typical mini, followed by the use of assembly language, and then Fortran and BASIC. All the fundamental topics, such as sequencing, address modification, looping, and subroutining, are covered.

The student is assumed to have had high school algebra and some familiarity with trigonometry.

One hundred exercises are scattered through the book. Some of these are time-honored problems for the learning of the computing art; some are new problems; and some are both new and challenging. Those exercises that are considered essential to the understanding of some concept in computing are so indicated. The student is encouraged to read the discussions (for selected exercises) that appear in Appendix 3, whether or not he works on a particular exercise.

Particular emphasis is placed throughout the text (and in detail in Chapter 16) on the concept of adequate validation of programs.

It is a pleasure to acknowledge the gracious cooperation of Varian Data Machines through its President, George Vosatka, and the help of their Customer Engineer, Richard Guise. Critical comments on the manuscript from Rick Kerns of Varian Data Machines, William Lane of California State Uni-

† Trademark of Teletype Corp., Skokie, Ill.

versity, Chico, and Richard Andree of the University of Oklahoma, all resulted in significant improvements to the text.

Throughout this book, we have tried to stick to the idea of "This is one of the ways it has been done," and avoid any suggestion of "This is the way it should be done." The most obvious fact about all machine computation is "There is always a better way—and a still better way after that."

We find computing endlessly challenging and fascinating. Our goal with this text is to pass along some of that feeling to those who are new to the game.

Northridge, California

*Fred Gruenberger*
*David Babcock*

# CONTENTS

xiii

# 1

# PROLOGUE

## 1.1 Introduction

The subject of this book is computing. To those who are not experienced in the use of computers, the notion of "computing" may be unclear; following are four common misconceptions about the subject:

1. "Computing is what is done with an adding machine or a desk calculator, only faster and automatically." Yes, we can have a computer do those things, and at speeds up to a billion times as fast. But computing differs from hand calculation by more than speed and automatic operation.

2. "Computing consists of writing instructions for a machine to execute (in other words, computing is "programming")." True, to compute we must instruct the machine and hence we must be able to "program." To drive a car we must be able to steer, and yet steering is not the essence of driving.

3. "Computing is the study of the electronic makeup of a computer." Again, knowledge of how a computer is constructed is useful, and some of it is necessary, but computing involves more than that.

4. "Computing is what goes on to produce paychecks, or department store bills, or airline reservations, or the control of an oil refinery." This is the school of thought that says computing is some specific application. There must be general principles that apply to all applications, and these should be of paramount concern to the beginning student.

1

## 1.2 What Computing Is

The discipline called computing consists of five interrelated subjects:

1. *How to compute.* This is the mechanics of the subject: the logical organization of the machines; sequencing and address modification (these technical terms will be explained later); looping and subroutining; coding (the writing of instructions); problem analysis and flowcharting; assembly and compiler languages.

2. *What to compute.* What are the characteristics of problems that lend themselves to computer solution? When is the computer **not** the proper tool to apply to a given problem? What are the alternative tools that can be used when the computer is not the proper tool? How can we detect problems that are impossible (or not feasible) with the equipment we have access to?

3. *How to compute right.* How can we certify the results we obtain from a computer? This is the subject of program validation (or program testing), which will concern us in detail in Chapter 16. For the moment, let's put it this way: If you have not established, in some methodical way, that the results you produce are correct, then they are probably wrong, or, worse, garbage.

4. *How the computer computes.* This is the engineering side of the subject, and includes the study of electronic circuitry, storage devices, and communications. There have been only a few variations to the basic design of a computer laid down by John von Neumann in 1946, but each variation has its effect on the art of computing. For example, nearly all computers now in operation are binary machines. In the early 1960s, decimal machines were quite popular (there were about 13,000 of them at one time), and the presence of decimal capability built into the hardware† of the machine makes quite a difference in the way the user goes about his work.

5. *The implications of computing.* There is a philosophy of good computing, and there are specific characteristics of bad computing. Computing has social implications (such as in the invasion of personal privacy and the impact of public computing systems on the welfare and well-being of the populace).

Some aspects of computing are well-defined and precise; specific rules can be stated for these parts. Other parts resemble art more than science, and each student must go through the experiences of all other students in order to gain some "feel" for the art. In one sense the computer is the ultimate in precision equipment, each of whose functions is rigidly defined. In a broader sense, the functions of a computer are quite mysterious, even though we have great confidence that the machine will carry out the instructions we compose—faithfully, unerringly, and fast.

† Is the term "hardware" familiar? As each new word appears in the text, make it part of your computing vocabulary. Appendix 1 is a brief glossary of many such terms.

## 1.3   The Need for Speed

It is assumed throughout this book that the reader has access to a mini computer; there is little difference in principle between one mini and another. One characteristic they all have in common is speed. None of the existing minis operates below 250,000 executed instructions per second, and some of them reach top speeds of 2,000,000 instructions per second. A little figuring shows that even the slower machines can execute a billion instructions† during a class period.

It would seem, then, that whatever we can get our computer to do will be done so fast that we will be hard-pressed to keep it busy. You will have that feeling right up to the time you get your first nontrivial program operating. And perhaps then it will become clear that a difference in degree of sufficient magnitude adds up to a difference in kind. A tool that can perform in a few minutes more arithmetic than a man could perform in a lifetime (even aided by a desk calculator) offers a new dimension in computational power.‡

The term just used was "arithmetic." The computer is much more than an arithmetic device, although it is that. Everything that a computer does is done by manipulating numbers — usually arithmetically. But the computer is a logical device. The **solution** to a problem is always expressed in numbers, since all the information contained in a computer is in the form of numbers, but the **problems** that are solved need not involve numbers at all. Indeed, many of the more interesting problems handled by computer (chess playing, for example) do not involve numbers.

The earliest electronic machines operated at speeds of a few thousand executed instructions per second. At the time when operating speeds got up to tens of thousands of instructions per second (around the mid-1950s), computer people talked wistfully of the true microsecond machine; that is, one capable of executing a million instructions per second. Today, the largest and fastest machines have top speeds of 100,000,000 instructions per second, and the dream now is of the true nanosecond machine (i.e., the billion-per-second machine), which should arrive around 1978.

What is the big rush? Why do we seek ever faster machines? And couldn't we achieve the same effects simply by building more of the slower machines? The difference between 1973 equipment and 1953 equipment (in raw computing power) is a factor of 6000. This implies that a full year's work of a 1953 machine, around the clock, can be done in 90 minutes on a

---

† It is hard to make the number "1 billion" vivid. A billion seconds is 31 years. A billion grains of table salt weighs 300 pounds and occupies 8 cubic feet. A billion IBM cards would make a stack 100 miles high.
‡ Another way to look at it is this: All the arithmetic performed by everyone from the time of the cavemen up to World War II could be repeated in a few hours on any computer made after 1956.

1973 machine (in both cases, the largest and best of the day). In fact, the mini that you are using probably has more throughout power than the best machine of 1953 — at $1/300$ of the cost.

There are several reasons for constantly striving for more and faster machines:

1.  Familiar problems get bigger. It was once considered remarkable to solve a system of eight simultaneous equations. Today it is considered routine to solve a system of 100 equations, and that represents on the order of 200 times as much arithmetic. Moreover, the $8 \times 8$ case took minutes, and the $100 \times 100$ case now takes a few seconds.

In every area to which computers are applied, the problems have grown: There are more variables and more cases to consider, and situations that used to have to be approximated can now be handled precisely. The world is getting somewhat complicated.

2.  This complicated world is getting conditioned to numbers. When the Social Security Act was passed in 1935, the tax rate for it was set at 2%, probably because few firms were equipped to calculate with any number more complex than 2. Now the rate can be 4.625% with impunity; it is expected that anyone can handle that kind of arithmetic.

Numbers are all around us; every adult is registered under many identifying numbers. Everything we do seems to involve numbers. Computers are needed to manage all that numerical information.

3.  No matter how fast a machine can process a given problem, someone may want it still faster and be willing to pay for that speed. Sometimes higher speed, which implies lower response time, is absolutely vital if the job is to be done at all. Control signals for an orbiting vehicle cannot be delayed, for example. Even in the prosaic world of airline ticket sales, customers will be calm and patient for a minute or so, and then they will mumble and grumble and go to seek another airline. This last example is circular, to be sure; the computer created the situation that it then solved, which created a new situation, and so on. Nevertheless, modern living has created many situations in which we demand a very low response time from computers — and that means faster machines are needed, and always will be.

4.  There are more problems to be solved. Computers are usually obtained to handle some specific problem (in business, for example, the first uses of the machine are for payroll, accounts receivable, billing, and inventory control). After the tasks for which the machine was obtained are running smoothly, it is only natural to look around for more things to do, and there are always plenty of tasks to be done.

It is said that work expands to fill the available computer time. Consider the situation in college computing classes. At one time, the total access to a computer that could be offered a student amounted to about ten minutes in a semester course. Today it is common to offer virtually unlimited access to a machine to every student, to run whatever he wishes. Computing centers on college campuses process several thousand student submissions per day at each college, and this is not considered excessive. Only a fraction of these runs are for the purpose of learning computing; students in widely varying disciplines run problems relating to their fields of study. The situation is the same in the industrial and scientific world; there is simply more to do, and the computer is the common element.

5.   Many problems are serial in nature; that is, each stage in the problem depends on the preceding stage, so that the problem solution must proceed in order. For such problems, there is no advantage in having two computers to work with; the solution is not speeded up with two computers, or with all the computers in the world. If the problem is serial in nature, and the solution is too slow, then we must either seek a faster machine, or improve the method of solution, or both.

You probably need little convincing that computers are fast devices, and we have tried to establish that they will be made to operate even faster in the future. Yet all this computing power is useless without some direction. The important thing is the man/machine interface, which is presumably why you are learning computing. Raw speed in a machine is desirable, but for most problem situations, the critical factor is that of getting a workable solution, and for that purpose any computer functions much like any other.

## EXERCISES

*It is not uncommon in computing to number things, like lines of code, by tens, to allow for later insertion of other lines. The exercises in this book were originally numbered by fives, and later insertions bear the in-between numbers.*

**5.**   Calculate the cost of using the computer you have access to. Find out its purchase price, the length of its useful life, the number of hours it operates per month, and its effective speed. You will probably find that it furnishes in excess of 10,000,000 executed instructions per dollar (for many of the minis, the figure exceeds 100,000,000 per dollar).

**10.**   Whatever figure you arrive at for Exercise 5, it is safe to predict that by the time your installation gets its next machine, the figure will be significantly higher, perhaps by a factor of ten. What are some of the implications of the fact that computing power becomes ever cheaper?

**15.** At this point, you are probably just beginning your study of computing. List, for future reference, your notions of (*a*) a trivial computer problem; (*b*) a really large computer problem; (*c*) a numerical problem that is impossible to solve by any computer; (*d*) a numerical problem that would strain the capabilities of the machine you are using; (*e*) a business problem that would be suitable for your machine.

# 2

# APPROACHING THE COMPUTER

## 2.1 The Transition

If the reader is not familiar with the operation of a desk calculator, it would be a good idea to get to one† and observe it in action. Examine the action of such a machine while it performs single additions and subtractions, repetitive additions, multiplication by shifting, sequenced multiplication, division by repeated subtraction, and programmed (sequenced) division. In particular, observe what happens when the machine is cleared to 0 and then the number 1 is subtracted in the unit's position (namely, a string of 9's all across the accumulating counter).

Suppose, now, that we wish to use such a machine to calculate values of

$$Q = \frac{A + \dfrac{B}{C}}{C - \dfrac{A}{B}}$$

for all integer values of A, B, and C between 1 and 10 (which will produce 1000 values of Q). We would begin with A = B = C = 1, for which we immedi-

† Although mechanical (rotary) calculators have not been manufactured for some time, many of them are still around and, for purposes of transition, are better than the modern electronic versions.

**7**

ately have trouble, since the denominator goes to 0, and division by 0 is impossible, in mathematics, on desk calculators, and in computers. We could, of course, try it blindly, but the desk calculator will simply run away and have to be stopped by manual intervention. The cases we want to run through are shown in Figure 2.1. We are ready to try the case where A = 1, B = 1, and C = 2. The steps we will have to follow are:

1. Calculate A/B and write down the result.
2. Subtract the result of Step 1 from C and write down the new result.
3. Calculate B/C and write down the result.
4. Add the result of Step 3 to A.
5. Divide the result of Step 4 by the result obtained at Step 2. Do not perform this step if the result at Step 2 was 0. Record A, B, C, and Q after Step 5.
6. Proceed to the next case. Stop after A, B, and C all equal 10.

For the first permissible case, and perhaps several after that, some care is required to perform the steps properly and in order. Very quickly, this task would become dull, and hence error-prone. We would soon be painfully aware that:

1. All the brainwork has gone into our scheme of calculation, and from then on we would like to have the same sequence of operations performed 1000 times.
2. The **data** of the problem (that is, the successive values of A, B, and C) is itself systematic, and it is tedious to keep track of that.

In other words, we would like to have at least a **sequenced** desk calculator, for which we could spell out what to do. Given such a machine, we could dictate the entire course of our problem and then walk away and let the results grind out.

This was the transition phase in computation that took place in 1944. Desk calculators (in varying degrees of sophistication) had existed since 1885. Machines that could be controlled, or sequenced, had also existed since 1890; namely, punched card equipment. The two technologies came together in 1944 with the start of sequenced calculators. But the computer is far more than simply a high-speed sequenced calculator.

In order to be able to calculate at all, it is necessary to be able to **store** numbers. In our simple problem, Steps 1, 2, and 3 call for writing down intermediate results; that is, for storing by recording on paper. But within each operation of the desk calculator, numbers must be stored also. When we divide 70 by 4, the 70 must be held in the machine while successive 4s are subtracted from it (the 4 being stored in the keyboard). The intellectual breakthrough achieved by von Neumann in 1946 was the observation that the operations to be performed (such as add, divide, store, retrieve, etc.)

| A | B | C |
|---|---|---|
| 1 | 1 | 1 |
| 1 | 1 | 2 |
| 1 | 1 | 3 |
| 1 | 1 | 4 |
| 1 | 1 | 5 |
| 1 | 1 | 6 |
| 1 | 1 | 7 |
| 1 | 1 | 8 |
| 1 | 1 | 9 |
| 1 | 1 | 10 |
| 1 | 2 | 1 |
| 1 | 2 | 2 |
| 1 | 2 | 3 |
| 1 | 2 | 4 |
| . | . | . |
| . | . | . |
| . | . | . |
| 1 | 2 | 10 |
| 1 | 3 | 1 |
| 1 | 3 | 2 |
| 1 | 3 | 3 |
| 1 | 3 | 4 |
| . | . | . |
| . | . | . |
| . | . | . |
| 1 | 3 | 10 |
| 1 | 4 | 1 |
| 1 | 4 | 2 |
| . | . | . |
| . | . | . |
| . | . | . |
| 5 | 6 | 7 |
| 5 | 6 | 8 |
| . | . | . |
| . | . | . |
| . | . | . |
| 9 | 9 | 8 |
| 9 | 9 | 9 |
| 9 | 9 | 10 |
| . | . | . |
| . | . | . |
| . | . | . |
| 10 | 10 | 8 |
| 10 | 10 | 9 |
| 10 | 10 | 10 |

FIGURE 2.1 The thousand cases for the desk calculator problem.

could be expressed as numbers, so that the instructions for a machine could be stored in the same place and in the same form as the data. What we now call the stored-program computer had been born.

## 2.2   The Concept of the Computer

Before proceeding further, let us see what our simple problem looks like in a computer. Figure 2.2 shows a program for it, exactly as it would appear in the storage area of our mini computer. Everything is in numbers, and odd-looking numbers at that—all 1s and 0s. There have been valiant attempts to make decimal computers (and at one time there were thousands of them) but in today's world nearly every machine is internally **binary;** that is, they use numbers expressed in base 2 rather than our familiar base 10. Some of these numbers (five of them in this example) are **data** numbers. The rest are **instructions.** Every number, whether data or instruction, is contained in a computer **word** (in some cases, an instruction or a data number may occupy several words). In the case of our specific machine, each word contains 16 bit positions, where a bit position is a place to hold a 1 or a 0. The 1s and 0s themselves are bits (short for binary digit); a bit is defined as the smallest unit of information. There are 16,384 such words of storage, and each word has an **address** where it can be located, in much the same way as postal addresses locate homes, or geographic coordinates locate points on a map. These addresses in the computer range from zero to 16,383, but that is expressing the fact in decimal notation; to the machine, the addresses range from 00000000000000 to 11111111111111.

The short program looks like an incomprehensible hodgepodge of information, and to a certain extent it is. But it is a representation of what goes on inside the machine; that is, the collection of 1s and 0s is just what a working program looks like in storage.

Each word of storage is a number which can represent data (that is, numbers to be manipulated by the program) or it is an instruction. Both entities look the same, and are stored in the same medium.

The medium of storage in nearly all machines is the magnetic core. Cores are little doughnuts of ferric material that can be magnetized in one of two stable states. We can consider these two states as "on" or "off"; "present" or "absent"; or "one" or "zero." For convenience (and since we use the information as numbers), the two states are usually labeled 1 and 0.

Figure 2.3 shows the general scheme of the computer. The heart is storage: 16,384 places called words, in each of which we can store a 16 bit number (that makes 262,144 total bit positions of storage).

Shown below the storage words is another storage device called the **accumulator;** it is 16 bit positions wide and can hold the contents of one

| ØCTAL | | BINARY | |
| --- | --- | --- | --- |
| ADDR. | CØNT. | ADDRESS | CØNTENTS |
| 000000 | 005101 | 0000000000000000 | 0000101001000001 |
| 000001 | 050056 | 0000000000000001 | 0101000000101110 |
| 000002 | 050057 | 0000000000000010 | 0101000000101111 |
| 000003 | 050060 | 0000000000000011 | 0101000000110000 |
| 000004 | 005001 | 0000000000000100 | 0000101000000001 |
| 000005 | 020056 | 0000000000000101 | 0010000000101110 |
| 000006 | 170057 | 0000000000000110 | 1111000000101111 |
| 000007 | 010060 | 0000000000000111 | 0001000000110000 |
| 000010 | 060012 | 0000000000001000 | 0110000000001010 |
| 000011 | 006140 | 0000000000001001 | 0000110001100000 |
| 000012 | 000000 | 0000000000001010 | 0000000000000000 |
| 000013 | 050063 | 0000000000001011 | 0101000000110011 |
| 000014 | 001010 | 0000000000001100 | 0000001000001000 |
| 000015 | 000030 | 0000000000001101 | 0000000000011000 |
| 000016 | 005001 | 0000000000001110 | 0000101000000001 |
| 000017 | 020057 | 0000000000001111 | 0010000000101111 |
| 000020 | 170060 | 0000000000010000 | 1111000000110000 |
| 000021 | 005021 | 0000000000010001 | 0000101000010001 |
| 000022 | 120056 | 0000000000010010 | 1010000000101110 |
| 000023 | 004517 | 0000000000010011 | 0000100101001111 |
| 000024 | 170063 | 0000000000010100 | 1111000000110011 |
| 000025 | 060061 | 0000000000010101 | 0110000000110001 |
| 000026 | 002000 | 0000000000010110 | 0000010000000000 |
| 000027 | 000064 | 0000000000010111 | 0000000000110100 |
| 000030 | 040060 | 0000000000011000 | 0100000000110000 |
| 000031 | 010060 | 0000000000011001 | 0001000000110000 |
| 000032 | 140062 | 0000000000011010 | 1100000000110010 |
| 000033 | 001004 | 0000000000011011 | 0000001000000100 |
| 000034 | 000004 | 0000000000011100 | 0000000000000100 |
| 000035 | 005101 | 0000000000011101 | 0000101001000001 |
| 000036 | 050060 | 0000000000011110 | 0101000000110000 |
| 000037 | 040057 | 0000000000011111 | 0100000000101111 |
| 000040 | 010057 | 0000000000100000 | 0001000000101111 |
| 000041 | 140062 | 0000000000100001 | 1100000000110010 |
| 000042 | 001004 | 0000000000100010 | 0000001000000100 |
| 000043 | 000004 | 0000000000100011 | 0000000000000100 |
| 000044 | 005101 | 0000000000100100 | 0000101001000001 |
| 000045 | 050057 | 0000000000100101 | 0101000000101111 |
| 000046 | 040056 | 0000000000100110 | 0100000000101110 |
| 000047 | 010056 | 0000000000100111 | 0001000000101110 |
| 000050 | 140062 | 0000000000101000 | 1100000000110010 |
| 000051 | 001004 | 0000000000101001 | 0000001000000100 |
| 000052 | 000004 | 0000000000101010 | 0000000000000100 |
| 000053 | 000000 | 0000000000101011 | 0000000000000000 |
| 000054 | 001000 | 0000000000101100 | 0000001000000000 |
| 000055 | 000000 | 0000000000101101 | 0000000000000000 |
| 000056 | 000000 | 0000000000101110 | 0000000000000000 |
| 000057 | 000000 | 0000000000101111 | 0000000000000000 |
| 000060 | 000000 | 0000000000110000 | 0000000000000000 |
| 000061 | 000000 | 0000000000110001 | 0000000000000000 |
| 000062 | 000013 | 0000000000110010 | 0000000000001011 |
| 000063 | 000000 | 0000000000110011 | 0000000000000000 |
| 000064 | 000000 | 0000000000110100 | 0000000000000000 |
| 000065 | 001000 | 0000000000110101 | 0000001000000000 |
| 000066 | 100064 | 0000000000110110 | 1000000000110100 |

FIGURE 2.2 Machine code for the problem of Figure 2.1.

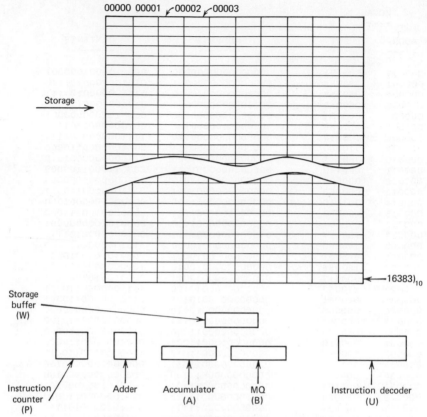

FIGURE 2.3  **The logical parts of a computer.**

word of storage. The name, accumulator, is traditional, but it is only a storage device. Most of the work done with the computer is done in the accumulator.

To the right of the accumulator is another 16 bit storage device generically called MQ, standing for Multiplier/Quotient register. If we need to multiply together the contents of any two computer words (each of 16 bits), we must provide a 32 bit place for the product; this is done by coupling together the accumulator and MQ. Similarly, to effect a division, we must start with a 32 bit dividend, and the coupled storage devices provide the place we need. This coupling of accumulator and MQ is done for us at the right time by the machine's control circuits.

Note that we are describing the machine in general and generic terms. The notation used for these units in each specific machine is different. In the Varian 620, the MQ unit is called the B register, for example.

To the left of the accumulator is the **adder,** a device that can perform binary addition. Simple addition is all the arithmetic capability that a computer needs. In all machines, addition is algebraic; that is, it follows the rules of signed numbers in algebra. Hence, subtraction is effected by the old rule of algebra; namely "change the sign of the subtrahend and add." Multiplication is performed essentially by repeated additions and shifts, and division by repeated subtractions and shifts. These actions parallel somewhat those of a rotary desk calculator.

At the far left in Figure 2.3 is the **instruction counter,** which is a device to keep track of where we are at any given moment. The contents of the instruction counter is a number (ranging from zero to 16383, decimal) that points to a specific word in storage. When the computer is executing instructions, the instruction counter continuously points to the next instruction word to be executed.

At the far right in Figure 2.3 is the **decoder,** a 16 bit device that can accept one instruction word from storage, decode it, and indicate to the control circuits what is to be done.

There are some other devices that make up the total machine and we will explore them later.

## 2.3   The Cycle of Operation of the Computer

When we approach the computer to use it, the machine contains a great deal of information, since it is in the nature of magnetic core storage that every bit position always contains a 1 or a 0 (that is, there is no neutral state). So all 16,384 words of storage contain numbers, as do the **registers** (accumulator, MQ, adder, instruction counter, and decoder). **None of this information concerns you;** it is left over from the last use of the machine; it can neither help you nor hurt you. It would not be wrong to **think of it** as all 0s (but it would be wrong ever to assume that it **is** all 0s in your use of the machine).

We begin any use of the computer by **loading** all the instruction and data words of the problem into storage.† The instruction counter is also loaded with the location of the first instruction word that is to be executed. [NOTE: A **location** is the address of an instruction. The distinction between these apparent synonyms is useful.]

After loading is completed, the action of the machine is initiated; that is, we figuratively push the START key. The following cycle then occurs:

---

† Later we shall examine the situation in which the program, while being executed, calls for data to be read in. For the moment, consider that data numbers are loaded into storage along with the instruction numbers before any execution takes place.

> 1. The control circuits examine the contents of the instruction counter. The number there points to an instruction word, whose contents is moved to the decoder.

This is a copying process. The information is read into the decoder, and read-in is always destructive; that is, the previous contents of the decoder is destroyed. The information is read out of the storage word, and read-out is always nondestructive; that is, the number is still there. Thus, in any movement of information, a copy is created, and the information exists in two places. We can read out of a storage device as many times as we please without altering the information.

We have moved one instruction word from storage to the decoder. An instruction has three main parts: a location (that is, its address in storage†); an **operation code**, or op-code for short, that indicates what is to be done; and an address portion that indicates what it is to be done with. For example, the instruction word located at the sixteenth position in storage might be

000000000001111        1010000000000001

Location             Contents

which would indicate "add the contents of word 1 to the accumulator."

> 2. The instruction word is decoded and whatever procedure is indicated is carried out. During this process, the contents of the instruction counter is automatically increased by **1**.

Thus, the computer does its **sequencing**. Since the instruction counter points to the word that is to be executed next, the process of adding **1** has enabled us to advance to the next instruction in sequence. If the instructions for our program are loaded into consecutive words of storage, the machine will advance through the instructions one at a time.

> 3. The normal cycle is now completed and we return to Step 1.

---

† Since an instruction normally occupies one word in storage, the location is not physically part of the instruction. The admonition that an instruction has three parts serves to remind you that an instruction can never exist without being at some address in storage.

## 2.4 Changes to the Normal Cycle

The cycle of operation just described would provide us with an electronic sequenced calculator programmed with instructions stored within the machine. Several additional ideas will take us to the full concept of a computer.

Go back to Step 2 in the normal cycle. A more exact statement would be "whatever procedure is indicated will be carried out if it can be." When could it not be? It might be that the instruction word contains an illegal op-code; the machine will then quite sensibly refuse to carry it out. Or, the indicated operation may lead to trouble, such as an attempt to divide by 0. The most common trouble is **overflow:** an attempt to add into the accumulator a number for which the sum is larger than 16 bits. Since the accumulator is only 16 bits wide, this would result in an overflow condition. Thus, it is not always true that the command specified by an instruction word will be carried out.†

But even if all our instructions were correct, we would still have a very weak machine. Whatever it is we wish to have done would require a set of instructions that would each be executed once and in **straight-line** fashion, after which, presumably, we would program a HALT. Little useful work could be performed this way. We must have a means of breaking the normal mode of sequencing.

For this purpose, op-codes are provided whose purpose is to operate **on** the instruction counter by changing its contents. The simplest of these op-codes is the unconditional jump, which allows us to proceed arbitrarily to any word in storage, rather than the next consecutive word. We can, for example, set up a group of instructions that are to be executed over and over by arranging an unconditional jump from the last of them back to the first of them.

There are also many conditional jump instructions that cause a jump in sequence depending on certain conditions that are met during execution. (Is the accumulator now negative? Is the MQ register now 0? Is a manual switch on the console turned on? And so on.)

In all cases of jump instructions, the action called for by the jump consists of replacing the contents of the instruction counter by some number other than the one generated by the normal addition of 1 called for in Step 2 of the cycle of operations.

The way a computer operates is basically very simple, but the simple notions are obscured by the new notation and by the words we use to describe

---

† In the specific case of overflow on most minis, the command **would** be executed (and the computer would continue to operate), but the result in the accumulator would simply be incorrect.

them. Return to this section from time to time; each time, it will appear to be written in clearer language.

In the process of learning computing, there are some two dozen basic concepts, each of which must be at least partially understood before anything begins to make sense. We will eventually get around to making them all clear by exploring some simple problems.

At this stage of your learning, it would be wise to begin exploring the reference manual of the computer you will be using. In particular, find its list of op-codes and study it.

Machine reference manuals are not honored in the field as being masterpieces of literature. As you browse through the reference manual, make notes about statements you find that seem obscure.

## 2.5   The Nature of Computing

The computer is a device for processing information. It is a logical device, which means that it can carry out long sequences of instructions that involve logical decisions that are made dynamically during execution. This means that the choice of paths through the instructions is made while the instructions are being executed on the basis of numerical conditions that are met as the problem solution unfolds.

Broadly speaking, the problems that lend themselves to computer solution are of two types: scientific and commercial. Scientific problems are those that arise in mathematics, science, and engineering. Following is a list of some typical scientific problems.

1.   Find the roots of a polynomial equation. For example, given the equation $X^3 - 2X - 5 = 0$, the value of the real root can be calculated (this is Wallis's equation, and the root is known to some 2000 decimal places).

2.   Find the roots of a system of simultaneous equations.

3.   Solve problems in maxima and minima. For example, find the dimensions of a cylindrical can that holds 1 quart, such that the surface area of the can is the least possible.

4.   Find the inverse of a 50 × 50 matrix.

5.   Integrate a system of differential equations.

And here are some typical commercial problems.

6.   Payroll.

7.   Inventory control.

8.   Production control.

9.   Accounts receivable and payable.

10.   Reservations systems (airline, hotel, car rentals, etc.)

Most interesting computing problems cannot be so neatly categorized. How about computing the optimum daily routes for a fleet of delivery trucks? The problem comes from a business environment, but its solution requires high-powered mathematical techniques which may be classified as scientific. Again, problems that involve severe time constraints (such as the control of a continuous physical process) tend to intermix the areas that are called "business" and "scientific."

## 2.6   The Flow of a Problem Solution

Seven stages in the development of a problem solution on a computer are:

1. *Analysis of the problem.* The most important question here is: Is the problem a good computer problem? Are there better (cheaper, faster, easier) ways to solve it? Can we find a method of solution? Is it even possible for there to be a solution? Has the problem, or one like it, been tackled by computer previously?

The most important part of analysis is problem definition—just what **is** the problem? If the inputs and outputs can be stated, and a method of solution is known, then much of the analysis has been done.

2. *Flowcharting.* After we have analyzed the problem thoroughly (and decided to forge ahead with a computer solution), we then display our intended solution in the form of a flowchart. Flowcharting will be taken up in detail in Chapter 4.

The first two stages call for our best brainwork. It is in these stages that our abilities are needed. This is not to imply that in subsequent stages we will not be challenged, or that we can afford to let down and become careless, but that the bulk of the thinking that needs to be done on any computer problem solution is done in analysis and flowcharting.

3. *Coding.* This is the stage in which the logic of the solution is expressed in instructions for the machine. It is the stage that most people think of as "programming."

The stages are being described as though they were separate and distinct. Actually, it is quite common during the coding stage to discover that the flowcharts are illogical, or incomplete, or obscure. Similarly, in the flowcharting state, it is not uncommon to discover that the analysis was weak or incorrect. The various stages are intertwined, but can be described as though they were isolated.

4. *Debugging.* The coded instructions are submitted to the computer for trial runs. These runs usually include an assembly or compilation pass (hang on—these terms are yet to be explained) and attempts to execute the program. This stage is more or less mechanical, simply to determine that the program **will** execute and do something. At the end of debugging, the program can be said to solve some problem.

5. *Testing.* This is the stage in which we verify that the program solves the problem that we set out to solve; that it solves it correctly; and that it will continue to function properly when its data changes. Testing is the most important (and most neglected) of these seven stages; Chapter 16 is devoted entirely to this topic. Try to keep this thought in mind: Every program should be thoroughly tested before committing it to production.

6. *Documentation.* This is the backup that is vital to every program's success. Without careful documentation, the program is worthless to others, and may become worthless to its author. Documentation includes an English statement of the program's purpose; its inputs and outputs; the flowcharts; a listing of the code; the test procedure; test cases; and indications as to the range of the solution, critical cases, and so on. Documentation is one of the sore points of computing; everyone is for it (and no one has ever overdone it), but most programmers tend to neglect it.

7. *Production.* When the first six phases are completed, the program can be put into production to calculate the required results.

## 2.7  The Criteria for Intelligent Use of a Computer

The computer is probably the most powerful tool devised by man for solving problems. It can be misused and misapplied, however. Not every problem whose solution involves numbers is suitable for computer application. The presence of the computer has not made other splendid ways of solving problems obsolete. Some problems can be solved analytically (e.g., mathematically); slide rules and desk calculators are still in use; punched card equipment is ideally suited to certain types of work; there are excellent graphic methods of problem solution.

The distinction between the use of a computer and the application of some other tool can be stated in the form of six criteria, **all of which** must be met to certify intelligent use of a computer.

1. *Usefulness.* The problem solution must be useful. The real question here is, useful to whom and for what? In the context of a beginning class in computing, any problem is useful if it drives home some point about the computing art. In the industrial world, usefulness frequently reduces to someone's arbitrary decision, plus his ability to pay the bill. Although computing power is relatively cheap, it is not free—ever—and the criterion of usefulness is settled when the person who wants a solution is willing to pay for it. Some of the problems we will consider in this book can be clearly labeled useless in the real world; that is, no one would pay to have them solved. They are included to aid in the learning of computational procedures and as such have value that someone pays for.

2. *Definition.* We must always have our problem clearly defined (which is

true also when we do not use the computer). In the computing world, we must have our problem precisely defined; that is, we must know all the inputs and outputs.

We might, for example, want to solve a system of equations. How big a system? What kind of system? To what precision do we want the solution?

Or, we might want to control the inventory in a warehouse. What is our data? How good is it? What kind of results do we seek? Is it enough to be able to print "we are running out of $1/4$ horsepower motors" or would we want more detail?

As a more mundane example, students are fond of asking "Do you grade on a curve?" A problem exists in the student's mind, but it is not well-defined. Tell me precisely what "grading on a curve" means, and then perhaps I can answer the question.

3. *Algorithm.* Algorithm means "a method." We must have a method of solution (and again, that's true with or without the computer). All we need is a method; this criterion doesn't require the best method and, indeed, we may never know the best method. But we must have a method, and have it before we plunge into a computer solution. There is a wistful hope on the part of neophytes that somehow the computer will come up with a method of solution for any problem. Dismiss that thought; you, the user, supply the method. All that the computer can do is carry it out for you.

Sometimes, algorithms are handed to us. You may be familiar with an algorithm for extracting square roots. There are standard algorithms for finding roots of equations. The Internal Revenue Service furnishes an algorithm for the calculation of withholding tax. But most often, for most problems, an algorithm must be devised.

4. *Machine fit.* The proposed solution must fit the available computer in two ways. It must fit spacewise; that is, the instructions and data must be containable in the available storage of the machine. There must also be a fit in time. A solution that requires 100 hours of use of a machine for which your access is three 5 minute passes a week is doomed from the start; in all likelihood, by the time you might have your results, the machine will have been replaced by a better one, not to mention the fact that the solution will have lost its charm.

In theory, anything that can be done with one computer can be done with any other computer (which means that all computers process information in much the same way), but in practice there must be a match between the problem solution and the available machine.

5. *Repetition in the solution.* Anything that a computer can be programmed to do, it can be made to do again. Part of the great power of the computer lies in this ability to repeat calculations over and over. The more we capitalize on this capability, the better use we make of the machine. The

criterion states "in the solution." The **problem** may not involve repetition, but the solution should; the more, the better. This is the least stringent of the criteria. We can, and do, use computers to solve problems for which the solution lacks repetition (so-called "one shot" problems).

6. *Cost-effectiveness.* The use of the computer must somehow have a payoff; in some sense, the use of the machine must be more efficient (in dollars, elapsed time, human effort) than any alternative method of solution.

For example, we would not write a computer program to solve a system of two equations in two unknowns. In order to verify that the program worked, we would have to solve the set algebraically. Moreover, the work we would expend to write the program, enter it into the machine, and debug it, would far exceed the work involved in simply doing the whole thing by hand. Even if we had five such sets of equations (and their coefficients were large numbers), it would be doubtful whether a computer solution would be cost-effective. On the other hand, if we had 5000 sets of equations, it would clearly pay to write and test a program. Somewhere between five and 5000 there is a crossover point at which the payoff begins. The choice of that point is a matter of judgment, to be made by the programmer. The point is, he should anticipate that decision before plunging into a computer solution.

## EXERCISES

**20.** See Figure 2.1. Select a dozen sets of values that span the range of 1000 possible sets, and calculate the values of Q by hand.

**25.** Take a 2 digit number. Reverse the digits and add to that new number the sum of the digits. If the sum exceeds 100, subtract 100 from it. Continue this process indefinitely. Some 2 digit numbers will reach 00 and some will not. We wish to find those that do. Is this a computer problem?

To make the procedure clear, the first few stages of the process, using 23 as the starting number, are listed:

```
23 ──→32 ──→37 ┐
└→37 ──→73 ──→83
       83     38     49
       49     94     07
       07     70     77
       77     77     91
       91     19     29
       29     92     03
       03     30     33
        .      .      .
        .      .      .
        .      .      .
```

**30.**   The number 4624 is a perfect square (of 68) and all its digits are even. How many other 4 digit numbers have this property? Would a computer be useful to find the answers?

**35.**   Suppose that you were responsible for maintaining the proper levels of inventory in a warehouse for 10,000 items. For every item, there are two opposing forces acting on the quantity that is held in stock. The quantity should be high enough to ensure not running out. But it should be kept low, to avoid tying up capital. The "correct" quantity is different for every one of the 10,000 items.

   (a)   What information would you want to have on each item in order to maintain some sensible quantity on hand?

   (b)   Should the inventory be controlled by a computer program, or could it be done as well (and as cost-effectively) by other means? (Inventory control is an area of business activity that predates computers.)

**40.**   Given two dates, we need to calculate the number of elapsed days between them. For example, with input data 07231971-04181975, the result should be 1365 days (take time now to check that calculation). Is there an application of computers here? For one or two pairs of dates, it is obviously easier and quicker to make the calculation by hand. If we have 10,000 pairs of dates (and especially if they are already in machine-readable form), it would be wise to write a computer program for the task. So the real question is this: For how many pairs of dates would this become a good computer problem?

**45.**   There are exactly 100,000 5 digit decimal numbers. We wish to find out how many of them have 2 digits alike. That is, we want to count how many 5 digit numbers are like those in column A, and how many are like the ones given in column B. Is this a computer problem?

| A | B |
| --- | --- |
| 11234 | 12345 |
| 37389 | 63638 |
| 41234 | 52225 |
| 63800 | 80808 |
| 00987 | 00056 |
| 85687 | 50300 |

**50.**   A prime number is an integer that cannot be factored; that is, a number that is not divisible by any other integer except itself and **1**. There must be a prime number having exactly 500 digits. If we had to find one, would the computer be the tool to use?

**51.** Your computer center receives a request from the astronomy depart-ment to calculate the fifth root of 100 to fifty decimal places. **They** have thus defined the problem as useful (to them). The result must be calcu-lated. We have a computer at our disposal. Is it the proper tool to use? After giving this problem some thought, read the discussion of it in Appendix 3.

**55.** Magazines must maintain mailing lists in order to mail out the copies and also to maintain their subscription fulfillment; that is, to keep track of expirations and renewals. At mailing time, the list should be in order by postal zones. At other times, it should be in order by name of the sub-scriber.

For magazines of small circulation (e.g., a few thousand), the bookkeeping can be done with a card index, or on Addressograph† plates. For mass circulation magazines (e.g., 10,000,000), the list must be maintained by computer. Where is the crossover point? That is, for what size of circulation does it become necessary to convert to computer handling of the lists?

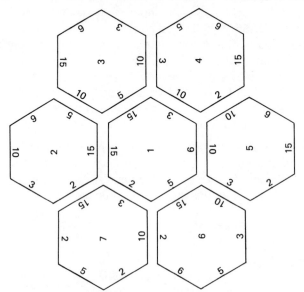

**FIGURE 2.4   The hexagon puzzle.**

**60.** Figure 2.4 shows a set of seven hexagons with numbers along the edges. The hexagons are to be rearranged so that none of the twelve pairs

† Trademark of Addressograph-Multigraph Corp.

of numbers at adjacent edges have a factor in common other than 1. The individual hexagons may be moved, but the numbers on any hexagon may not be altered.

In the pattern as shown, the edges between hexagons 4 and 5, for example, have a factor of 2 in common; the edges between hexagons 1 and 6 have a factor of 5 in common. There is a unique solution to this problem.

Is this a computer problem? Apply the criteria listed in Section 2.7. The criterion of usefulness should be waived for this exercise.

**65.** A lattice is a graph that exists only at the integer values of the coordinates. Ordinary squared graph paper illustrates a lattice, on the assumption that points exist on the lattice only where the lines cross.

Suppose we have a 32 × 32 lattice. It can be shown mathematically that it is possible to place no more than 62 points on the lattice such that no 3 of them form a right triangle. Suppose we wish to find such a set of points in other than a trivial way (that is, having all the 62 points lie along two perpendicular lines). Would this be a computer problem?

**70.** Figure 2.5 shows a typical pattern used in the daily crossword puzzle. The grid used for the puzzle is 15 × 15 cells, with some of them blacked out. The number of black squares varies from 27 to 42.

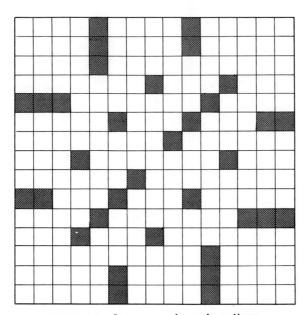

FIGURE 2.5 **A crossword puzzle pattern.**

Within the last 1000 such puzzles, the pattern of black squares has never been repeated. We wish to prove or disprove that statement. If it is not true, then we will have established that fact as soon as we can discover two patterns that are alike. On the other hand, if it is true, then we will have to check every pattern against every other pattern. Is this a computer problem?

# 3

# THE SIZES OF COMPUTERS

## 3.1 The Range of Computing Power

The characteristics that make for "large" or "small" computers are subjective and change with time. In its day (1953) the IBM 701 was a giant computer, costing close to a million dollars. Physically, it was huge; it took a very large room to house it, and an equal-sized room to hold its air conditioning equipment. In terms of computing capability, one of today's mini computers can do as much work, and the mini sits on a desk top, costs under $10,000, and plugs into a wall outlet.

There are many parameters used to classify computers, of which physical size is the least important. Perhaps the three leading variables of computing size are the storage capacity, the top speed (that is, the maximum number of additions that can be executed in 1 second), and the operation-code repertoire.

We are speaking here only of central processors; that is, the so-called main frames, or CPUs (central processing units). In a computer, the CPU includes storage, registers, arithmetic and logical circuits, and the operation console. It does not include peripheral devices (card readers, card punches, paper tape readers and punches, typewriters, line printers, magnetic drums, disk drives, magnetic tape drives, display devices, plotters, or inquiry stations).

25

Storage capacity refers to the number of bits in main (central) storage. In early machines, a storage capacity of 150,000 bits was fairly large. Today, central core storage of 16,000,000 bits is not unusual.

Consider processing speeds. In the mid-1950s, computer speeds of from 1 million to 2 million operations per **minute** were considered "high-speed." The typical high-speed machine of 1973 operates at speeds in excess of 1 million operations per **second,** and the fastest machines exceed 30 million operations per second.

## 3.2 The Minis

Just what is a mini computer? The type of machine called the mini appeared on the computing scene around 1967. They are machines that have certain common characteristics, among brands made by over forty manufacturers. Physically, their main frames measure about $19 \times 22 \times 8$ inches. Most of them have word lengths of 16 bits. They can support a complete range of peripherals. They are all fast, having operating speeds from 250,000 to over 2 million executed operations per second. All of them offer a fair range of software, including assembly language, Fortran, and packaged programs like RPG (Report Program Generator). Many of them offer complete operating systems, to the point where a mini can be the heart of a full-fledged computing installation.

It is estimated that, of the 85,000 computers in operation in the United States in 1973, some 40,000 are minis. This proportion is going up rapidly, with the minis being produced at a rate now exceeding 2000 per month. The prices of the minis have been coming down steadily (a complete mini, with a small amount of storage, can be obtained for under $3000 today) and will continue to decline.

## 3.3 The Mode of Operation with a Mini

In general, minis are operated in a fashion that was necessary with large machines two decades ago; that is, they are dedicated to a single problem at a time, and are probably operated hands-on by the user. This is in contrast to the present-day mode of operation of large machines, which process a continuous flow of problems through a monitor system, with the central processor working on bits and pieces of many problems at one time. The details of modern operating systems do not concern us here. The point is that, because of their size, the minis are used in a style that went out for the big machines many years ago. It is an intimate (and perhaps inefficient) way to live with a computer and, when properly done, can cut down the **elapsed time** for a problem solution.

## 3.4  Future Trends

Peeking into the future is always a risky business, but certain trends are clear. By 1977, over half the installed computers in the U.S. should be minis. Large-scale tasks will still head toward the giant machines, but the bulk of all computing in this country will be done on the minis, in the following categories:

1.  Routine calculations (e.g., payroll, inventory control, accounts receivable, production control). Many of these tasks will be done with packaged programs that will be furnished by the machine vendors or sold or leased by private software companies.

2.  Small scientific calculations (e.g., 200 statement Fortran problems). Many of these will also be done by library programs.

3.  Training, that is, computing done in order to learn computing. Here the minis will be particularly strong, since we can once again foster intimate contact between the student and the machine.

---

*The way to learn computing is to compute.*

Much of what has been said in this chapter must be obscure to anyone who has not yet used a computer. It will become remarkably clear after you have run one or two problems.

---

The fun—or work, depending on your point of view—begins in Chapter 6.

# FLOWCHARTING

## 4.1 Introduction

The second stage in the flow of a problem solution is flowcharting. A flow-chart is a pictorial device used to lay out the logic of a problem solution. Although the subject can be made quite complex (there are already five whole texts devoted to flowcharting), most of what a beginner needs can be expressed with a few symbols and some simple rules.

The notion of expressing system flow in pictures has been used in engineering for over a century. The idea of adapting it to the flow of a computer solution is due to von Neumann himself, who sketched the first problem solution in flowchart form some months before publication of the paper for which he is credited with the invention of the computer.

## 4.2 Some Flowchart Notation

Let us reconsider the problem discussed in Section 2.1 and develop the ideas of flowcharting as we go along. The problem was to calculate nearly 1000 values of Q, where

$$Q = \frac{A + \dfrac{B}{C}}{C - \dfrac{A}{B}}$$

**28**

and each of A, B, and C is to take on the values 1,2,3,4, . . . ,10 independently.

A rectangle is used on a flowchart to indicate some positive action that is to be taken. In the Q problem, we might have a rectangle like this:

$$\text{Set } Q = \frac{A + \dfrac{B}{C}}{C - \dfrac{A}{B}}$$

The verb "set" means "assign a value to."

Perhaps the level of sophistication used in that rectangle was too high. Perhaps a lower level would please the user more, like this:

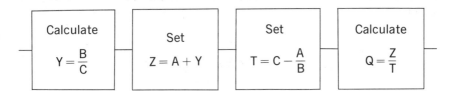

| Calculate $Y = \dfrac{B}{C}$ | Set $Z = A + Y$ | Set $T = C - \dfrac{A}{B}$ | Calculate $Q = \dfrac{Z}{T}$ |

It's a matter of taste. One should keep in mind two things:

1. The step following flowcharting is coding, so the flowchart should be at the level that the user finds convenient to use in coding.

2. The purpose of flowcharting, besides getting the logic of the solution arranged properly, is to provide a tool of communication. This communication may be from the author of the flowchart to someone else. For example, in this book flowcharts will be a vital avenue of communication from us to you. Most frequently, however, the communication is from the author of the flowchart to himself, when he begins to debug and test his programs. This aspect of flowcharting will become vivid only when the reader begins to use the computer actively.

Notice that everything contained in flowchart boxes is in the form of English sentences, even though they may be abbreviated and terse. They should also be clear and unambiguous sentences. For example, the rectangle

$$A = B$$

is an English sentence, but its meaning is not clear. Is A to be made equal to B, or is B to be made equal to A, or does it simply mean that A and B **are** equal? The latter case would be improper in any event, since the contents of flowchart rectangles is to indicate some action **to be taken.** In this case, we can make the intended meaning clear by the use of arrows, which mean "replaces." The following two rectangles express the same meaning:

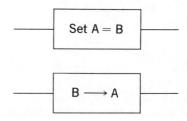

If it's the other meaning we intend, then we should use one of these two boxes:

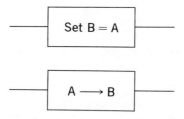

Note that the right-pointing arrow, which means "replaces," is not at all the same as "is replaced by." The latter meaning would be a **left**-pointing arrow. Notice that the two sets are distinctly different. If the arrow notation is confusing to you, use the English sentence form. The goal is to express clearly what you intend to have done.

While we're at it, let's look at a few more cases of flowchart notation that are common to beginners but which make little or no sense:

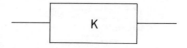

It might have been clear to the writer of the flowchart at the time he drew it what it meant to state "K," but it won't be to anyone else, and, more importantly, it won't be to **him** either some weeks later. Or this one:

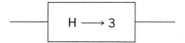

which might possibly make sense ("the contents of the word addressed at H is to replace the contents of word 3 in storage"), but it is more likely that what was intended was

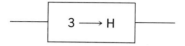

which says "the number 3 is to replace the contents of the word addressed at H."

Notice that a flowchart rectangle has only one entrance and one exit. There may be several actions called for within one rectangle, such as

$$\frac{B}{C} \longrightarrow Y$$
$$A + Y \longrightarrow Z$$
$$C - \frac{A}{B} \longrightarrow T$$

and it is understood that these actions are to be performed in the order in which they appear in the rectangle.

If it is necessary to arrive at a given rectangle from two other places, the proper notation is as follows:

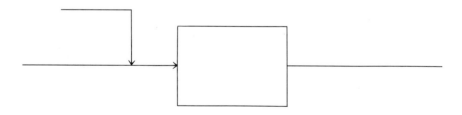

(rather than having two entrances to the rectangle).

A diamond is used on a flowchart to indicate a decision. The most common such decision is a comparison:

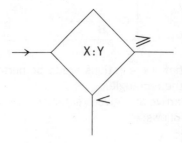

And, in computing as in everyday life, the result of a comparison is always a three-way outcome; namely, greater than, equal to, and less than. In the drawing, greater than is the branch going up, labeled with the mathematical symbol ($>$) for greater than. Similarly, the symbol $<$, meaning less than, labels the branch going down. Notice that the labels are drawn close to the diamond vertices, to ensure clarity.

Since comparisons are very frequently used, there is a shorthand notation that is handy. The colon means "compare," and we can write

which says "compare X to Y." We will proceed to the right if the value of X is greater than or equal to the value of Y; if the value of X is less than the value of Y, we will proceed down. As a general rule, flowcharts are read from left-to-right and top-to-bottom, like the printed page. If some other direction is needed, or if the traffic pattern is not clear, arrowheads may be added, as was done in the last diamond.

Again, notice that although we may use shorthand symbols, there is still an English sentence in every flowchart box. In the case of diamonds, there can be only one sentence. The following makes little sense:

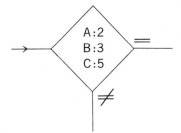

however clear it might have been to its author. Consider the analogous case in everyday work: Is George taller than Bill?; is John under 18?; does Henry own a Ford? How can you answer such a compound question? So it is in computing: One thing at a time is the rule.

We need, for the moment, only one more flowchart symbol. Small circles are used as connectors to guide us around the flowchart without having to draw long, and possibly confusing, connecting lines.

One more word, in general. Flowcharts are used to display the **logic** of a problem solution. They should not relate to any specific machine or any programming language.

## 4.3   A Complete Flowchart

We now have the tools we need to draw a complete flowchart for the Q problem. If you have explored the problem at all (as in Exercise 20, Chapter 2), it should have become apparent that the calculation itself is the trivial part of the problem. The sticky part is the generation of the A, B, and C values, and the avoidance of values that could lead to division by 0.

Figure 4.1 shows a flowchart for this problem. It is drawn neatly, with a template and lettering kit. Your flowcharts need not, and usually will not, have this air of finality and precision. It is not intended to represent **the** flowchart for the problem, but only **a** possible solution. The flowchart should be carefully studied, with certain points to be observed.

The circle connectors guide us around. Thus, we find ourselves at the right-hand end of the top line with directions to proceed to another circle labeled "4," which is at the left-hand end of the second line. The numbers in these circles are arbitrary, but they should be small integers. At two places we will proceed back to reference 3; notice that the first circle 3 is drawn off-stream so that it can be readily found.

The start of the flowchart is labeled reference 1, which is one standard way to indicate the start.

The logic at reference 2 is to bypass any attempt to divide by 0.

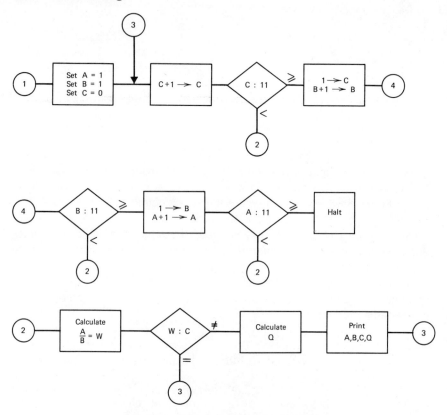

**FIGURE 4.1   A flowchart for the Q problem.**

All the logic of the actual calculation is suppressed; it could be expanded in the manner shown earlier. Another device for this purpose would be a **flag box** that could be added to the flowchart as shown in Figure 4.2. A flag box is off-stream (that is, it is not in the line of flow like normal rectangles) to explain some action on the flowchart. It serves to annotate the flowchart, in much the same way that comments are made on coding sheets, to tell us at a later date what it is we think we are doing at that point. In Figure 4.2, the action called for is "calculate Q," and the flag box in this case indicates how that calculation is to be made.

Figure 4.1 is a complete flowchart. It crowds a considerable amount of information onto one page. Saving paper is not a goal of flowcharting; we are free to use more than one page. As we shall see later, there are techniques for breaking up a flowchart into independent pieces and making it clear how

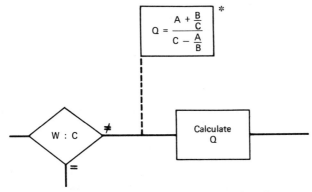

**FIGURE 4.2 The use of a flag box on a flowchart.**

these pieces are tied together. Notice that although most of the flowcharts in this book are laid out horizontally, there is no reason why your flowcharts cannot be drawn vertically, if you prefer.

There are a few more useful flowchart symbols; they will be discussed when the need for them arises.

## 4.4 Levels of Flowcharting

Most frequently flowcharts are used by the computer programmer to arrange **his** thinking on a problem solution and to remind **him** of what he did. Thus, flowchart notation tends to become personalized. There are plenty of suggestions on how to draw the symbols (see the Bibliography at the end of this chapter), but there is little standardization of what to put in the boxes.

The user of flowcharts can work at any level he pleases and, since a flowchart is a tool, he should pick the level that best suits him. There are extremes to avoid. Figure 4.3 illustrates some of these. Part A shows the highest possible level of flowcharting; it is the level that says essentially "Do my problem," and it is singularly useless.

Level B goes to the other extreme, in which there is such detail that the user is, in fact, already coding his problem for the machine. There is a rule: Don't code on flowcharts. Stick to the logic of the problem solution.

As an example of what we are talking about, consider a problem situation in which it is necessary at some point to take one of two paths, depending on whether two variables, X and Y, have the same or opposite parity (parity refers to the odd and even nature of an integer). Example C shows a high-

---

*The box shows the desired calculation, but this would be changed to $\dfrac{ABC + B^2}{BC^2 - AC}$ in the coding process, to cut down the number of divisions.

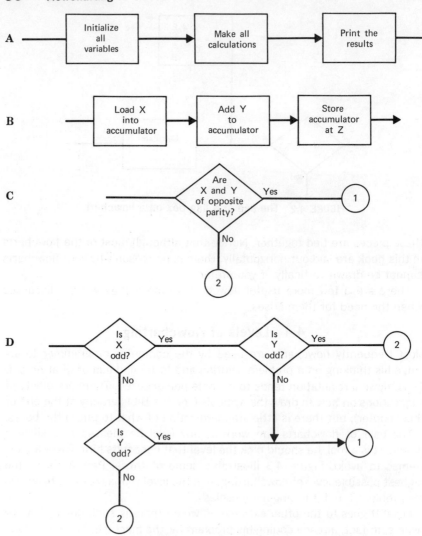

**FIGURE 4.3 Flowchart examples.**

level approach, which is certainly logically correct. Example D shows a more detailed approach of the same logic. The choice of level is up to the user.

[An alert programmer might notice that the implementation shown in D is not the only way that the logical action could be carried out. We could, for example, ask the question "Is X + Y odd?" which might save computer time. Can you see that (X + Y) is odd if and only if X and Y have opposite parity?]

## 4.5   Notes on Flowcharting

1.   In general, there should be only two dangling ends on a flowchart: the "start" point, where the flowchart begins, and the "halt" end, where the solution is concluded. Other dangling ends are possible (such as when an error condition calls for terminating the problem), but watch out for those that simply mean carelessness in accounting for every possible action.

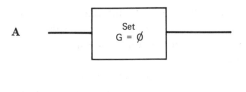

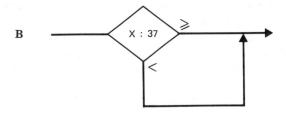

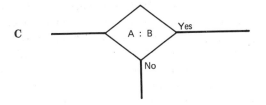

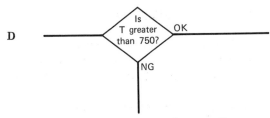

FIGURE 4.4   Poor flowcharting practices.

2.   See Figure 4.4, example A. What the rectangle calls for is "set the value of variable G to the value of variable O (capital letter 'oh'),'' which may be what the user wanted. The choice of the letter Oh for a variable would be poor. If what the user meant was "set the value of variable G to zero," then he is confused in his notation. In computing (and particularly on flowcharts), capital letters are used consistently, and the letters I, ∅, and Z are crossed whenever there can be any confusion with the digits 1, 0, and 2. If there is no chance for confusion, then there is little point in making the distinction, except as a matter of habit. (Although it is standard in computing to put the extra lines on the letters I, ∅, and Z, we should note that exactly the reverse notation is used, particularly by the military, and that many machines like the Teletype cross the zeros.)

3.   See Figure 4.4, example B. This flowchart notation looks neat, but it makes no logical sense. On a large and complex flowchart, the fact that both sides of a decision can lead to the same path can be cleverly disguised. In this case, the decision should be omitted completely.

4.   See Figure 4.4, examples C and D. The notation used in these examples is simply not English. It may be crystal clear to the person who draws the flowchart, but it will be confusing to anyone else.

In example C, the exits could be labeled "equal" and "not equal" or "greater than and equal" and "less than," or similar combinations. In example D, the proper English answers to the question in the diamond are "yes" and "no."

5.   "A flowchart that requires a personal lecture to go with it is a mighty poor flowchart." The meaning and logic of the solution that the flowchart displays should be clear to anyone. Paper is cheap; use a lot of it. Identify every variable. Add flag boxes when there is any doubt as to what is meant.

As with almost every aspect of computing, the only way to learn flowcharting is to plunge in. Plastic templates for drawing flowcharts are nice, but not at all necessary. Your first attempts at creating a good flowchart are likely to be messy. Be patient and keep at it; your first attempts at **anything** you've learned were probably laughable. We all find it amusing to watch an infant learn to walk.

## BIBLIOGRAPHY

American National Institute. *Standard Flowchart Symbols and Their Use in Information Process.* New York: ANSI, 1970.

Bohl, M. *Flowcharting Techniques.* Chicago: Science Research Associates, 1971.

Chapin, N. "Flowcharting with the ANSI Standard: A Tutorial," *Computing Surveys* **2**(2) (June 1970).

Chapin, N. *Flowcharts*. Philadelphia: Auerbach, 1971.
Farina, M. *Flowcharting*. Englewood Cliffs, N.J.: Prentice-Hall, 1970.
Gleim, G. *Program Flowcharting*. New York: Holt, Rinehart and Winston, 1970.
IBM Corporation. *Flowcharting Techniques*. C20-8152, White Plains, N.Y.: IBM Corporation, 1964.
IBM Corporation. *Flowcharting Template*. X20-8020, White Plains, N.Y.: IBM Corporation, 1969.
McGee, R. C. "Flowcharting," *Computing News* (76) (May 1, 1956).
Schriber, T. J. *Fundamentals of Flowcharting*. New York: Wiley, 1969.

### EXERCISES

**75.** Given three numbers, called A, B, and C, at a stage within a large problem, it is necessary to verify that the values of A, B, and C are as follows: either less than −100 and greater than −200 **or** greater than +500. Draw a flowchart for this logic. If all three numbers lie in the acceptable range, the problem solution can continue; if any of the three numbers does not lie in the acceptable range, the solution is to come to a halt.

This may be the first flowchart you have ever attempted. Give it a good deal of thought and several trials before you look up a possible answer in Appendix 3.

**80.** The suggested flowchart for Exercise 75 shows the same logic repeated three times. This won't do if there are 200 variables instead of three. The subject of **looping** will be taken up in Chapter 6, but for now, suggest ways in which the solution might be looped; that is, in which the same logic could be repeated for many variables.

**85.** Three numbers are stored in a machine; they are named X, Y, and Z. We want to rearrange the values so that the smallest number is at X, the largest is at Z, and the middle-sized number is at Y; that is, we want to **sort** the three numbers. Flowchart this logic. "Smallest" means algebraically less than, of course; −12 is less than +3. Our solution should work no matter what the values of the three numbers are. Think of the three addresses, X, Y, and Z, as three boxes that contain numbers, and imagine that you are giving directions to a robot that can do what you say, but what you say is restricted to elementary things like "compare the values of X and Y"; "move the value at X to a box called S"; and so on. Again, give this a good try before consulting a possible answer in Appendix 3.

**87.** Study the flowchart of Figure A3.2, which is a possible solution for Exercise 85. Extend the logic shown there for the case where we want to put four numbers (X, Y, Z, and W) in order.

**88.** We have 16 locations in storage that mark the start of 16 separate routines. The 16 locations are scattered and not at equal distances in storage from each other. We want to jump to one of the 16 routines depending on the condition of four storage words, A, B, C, and D, used as triggers; each of the four words contains a 1 or a 0 to indicate the presence or absence of some condition. We have, then, 16 possibilities, depending on the status of the four words:

| A | B | C | D | |
|---|---|---|---|---|
| 0 | 0 | 0 | 0 | Go to routine 1 |
| 0 | 0 | 0 | 1 | Go to routine 2 |
| 0 | 0 | 1 | 0 | Go to routine 3 |
| 0 | 0 | 1 | 1 | Go to routine 4 |
| . | . | . | . | |
| . | . | . | . | |
| . | . | . | . | |
| 1 | 1 | 1 | 1 | Go to routine 16 |

Draw a flowchart for this logic.

**90.** (This exercise is quite advanced, and should be worked on as a class project.) There are three integers addressed at P, Q, and R; they represent lengths of line segments. For any given set of values, we wish to determine whether the three integers could form a triangle and, if so, whether the triangle is equilateral (all three sides equal), isosceles (two sides equal), or scalene (no sides equal). Draw a flowchart for this logic.

# 5

# BINARY ARITHMETIC

## 5.1 The Need for Binary

It would be nice to have computers whose own makeup was decimal in nature. Many of the early machines **were** decimal, since the only model to go on was desk calculators, all of which have been decimal. There have been many decimal computers over the years (to name a few: the IBM 650, 1401, 1620, 702, 705, 7080, 7070, the RCA 301, and the Honeywell 200). At one time, over half the computers in the world were decimal.

The split between binary and decimal machines was once made on the basis of use; scientific users wanted internal speed above everything else, and speed is most easily obtained through binary organization. Commercial (that is, business) users wanted the convenience of internal decimal notation and were not concerned at the resulting loss of speed.

As it turns out, both groups can be made happy with binary equipment and, beginning around 1965, decimal machines were abandoned. There are still some IBM 1401s and 1620s around, but the majority of machines today are binary. All the minis operate in pure binary. We will have occasion to enter the machine with decimal numbers and we will certainly want to have our results printed out in decimal, but internally every part of the machine is built around base 2 notation. We must take the trouble to learn something about binary notation and arithmetic. We'll try to keep it down to the essentials.

## 5.2 Binary Counting

How do we count in decimal? There are just ten symbols and we use them in order, from 0 to 9. At that point we have run out of symbols, so we start over with 0, but advance from 0 to 1 in the position to the left. Thus, we advance from 09 to 10, and from 099 to 100. You can observe this action with the familiar mileage counter in an automobile. The whole process is familiar and "obvious," but by putting it into words, we can understand the similar process when the base is 2 rather than 10.

Looking at it another way, our decimal notation is positional, in which the positions have weights that are powers of 10. Thus, a number like 53,837 is really a compact way of expressing the following:

$$
\begin{array}{rcr}
5 \text{ times } 10^4 &=& 50000 \\
3 \text{ times } 10^3 &=& 3000 \\
8 \text{ times } 10^2 &=& 800 \\
3 \text{ times } 10^1 &=& 30 \\
7 \text{ times } 10^0 &=& 7
\end{array}
$$

Similarly, a number expressed in base 2 notation is a polynomial in powers of 2. Thus, the binary number 1101001001001101 represents

$$
\begin{array}{rcr}
1 \text{ times } 2^{15} &=& 32768 \\
1 \text{ times } 2^{14} &=& 16384 \\
0 \text{ times } 2^{13} &=& 0 \\
1 \text{ times } 2^{12} &=& 4096 \\
1 \text{ times } 2^{9} &=& 512 \\
1 \text{ times } 2^{6} &=& 64 \\
1 \text{ times } 2^{3} &=& 8 \\
1 \text{ times } 2^{2} &=& 4 \\
1 \text{ times } 2^{0} &=& 1
\end{array}
$$

(which adds up to 53,837).

Figure 5.1 shows some of the first 66 integers in the decimal and binary numbering systems. Both columns display the same pattern, except that there are ten symbols to use in the decimal column and only two in the binary column. Still, the binary numbering is neat and orderly; examine successive bit positions from top to bottom and notice the patterns. You will find it expedient to memorize the first eight binary numbers.

We will need to be able to convert from decimal to binary and from binary to decimal. Solely as a means of helping this conversion process, we operate through octal (i.e., base 8). There are many possible cases to consider, but we will need only a few.

| Decimal | Binary |
|---|---|
| 0 | 000 |
| 1 | 001 |
| 2 | 010 |
| 3 | 011 |
| 4 | 0100 |
| 5 | 0101 |
| 6 | 0110 |
| 7 | 0111 |
| 8 | 01000 |
| 9 | 01001 |
| 10 | 01010 |
| 11 | 01011 |
| 12 | 01100 |
| 13 | 01101 |
| 14 | 01110 |
| 15 | 01111 |
| 16 | 010000 |
| 17 | 010001 |
| 18 | 010010 |
| 19 | 010011 |
| 20 | 010100 |
| . | . |
| . | . |
| . | . |
| 31 | 011111 |
| 32 | 0100000 |
| 33 | 0100001 |
| . | . |
| . | . |
| . | . |
| 62 | 0111110 |
| 63 | 0111111 |
| 64 | 01000000 |
| 65 | 01000001 |

FIGURE 5.1 Decimal and binary numbering.

## 5.3 Number Base Conversion

**Decimal to Octal, Integers.** Divide the decimal number by 8 and write down both the quotient and the remainder. Divide the quotient again by 8, and record the new quotient and the new remainder. Continue this process until a quotient of 0 is reached, as shown in this example:

```
8 | 5349
  8 | 668    First quotient      5   First remainder
    8 | 83                       4
      8 | 10                     3
        8 | 1                    2
          0                      1
```

and read the result in the remainders, from the bottom up. Thus,

$$5349)_{10} = 12345)_8$$

Notice that with the smaller base, the number has a larger appearance.

**Octal to Binary, Integers.**   The conversion from octal to binary is done by using the table of binary numbers that you have memorized:

| | |
|---|---|
| 0 | 000 |
| 1 | 001 |
| 2 | 010 |
| 3 | 011 |
| 4 | 100 |
| 5 | 101 |
| 6 | 110 |
| 7 | 111 |

It is done on a digit-by-digit basis:

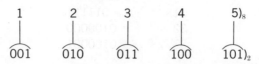

**Octal to Decimal, Integers.**   Just as a number in decimal notation is a compact way of expressing the sum of powers of 10 (actually, it is a polynomial in powers of 10), so a number in octal represents a group of powers of 8. Thus,

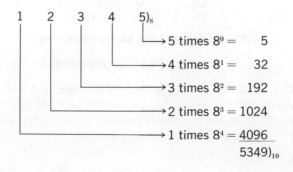

So we need to have at hand (or in our heads) a small table of powers of 8, as follows:

| Power | Value |
|-------|-------|
| 0 | 1 |
| 1 | 8 |
| 2 | 64 |
| 3 | 512 |
| 4 | 4096 |
| 5 | 32768 |

It is worth repeating: We go through base 8 to get to base 2 solely as a matter of convenience. Computers operate in base 2; we function in base 10. We could go directly from base 10 to base 2 and back, but the process is lengthy and tedious. [You may want to try it. To convert decimal integers to binary, divide by 2 successively and record the remainders. Try it out on $5349)_{10} = 1010011100101)_2$. To convert from base 2 to base 10, add powers of 2, starting with the 0 power on the right-hand, or low-order, end.]

If we go through the process of decimal-to-octal-to-binary and convert either the binary result or the octal result back to decimal, the whole procedure is self-checking. You can thus invent your own practice problems. For convenience, here are a few results:

$$12345)_{10} = \quad 30071)_8 = 011000000111001)_2$$
$$1000)_{10} = \quad 1750)_8 = 1111101000)_2$$
$$4096)_{10} = \quad 10000)_8 = 1000000000000)_2$$
$$55555)_{10} = 154403)_8 = 1101100100000011)_2$$

Notice also that all our arithmetic was **performed** in the familiar decimal system. The arithmetic itself could be performed in any number system, and particularly in base 2 arithmetic, which is how a computer would have to do it.

That leaves yet the conversion of fractions from decimal to octal and octal to binary and back. We need not worry about these cases, for the simple reason that **computers operate only in integers.**† You may find this a comforting thought, since it greatly simplifies the world of numbers. However, we will eventually have to devise schemes for handling fractions, since most of the problems in the world involve fractions. For now, think of the computer as a device to manipulate positive and negative integers.

† There have been several attempts, over the years, to construct computers that would operate on fractions. All these machines were dismal failures.

We are ready now to do some arithmetic in the unfamiliar number system. Consider an addition in decimal:

$$3685$$
$$\underline{5737}$$
$$9422$$

In your head (or perhaps marked on paper) you would have noted the "carries" as you proceeded from right to left. The most that has to be carried is a 1. You do the addition by using a table of sums that you memorized in the fourth grade:

|   | 0 | 1 | 2 | 3 | 4 | 5 | 6 | 7 | 8 | 9 |
|---|---|---|---|---|---|---|---|---|---|---|
| 0 | 0 |   |   |   |   |   |   |   |   |   |
| 1 | 1 | 2 |   |   |   |   |   |   |   |   |
| 2 | 2 | 3 | 4 |   |   |   |   |   |   |   |
| 3 | 3 | 4 | 5 | 6 |   |   |   |   |   |   |
| 4 | 4 | 5 | 6 | 7 | 8 |   |   |   |   |   |
| 5 | 5 | 6 | 7 | 8 | 9 | 10 |   |   |   |   |
| 6 | 6 | 7 | 8 | 9 | 10 | 11 | 12 |   |   |   |
| 7 | 7 | 8 | 9 | 10 | 11 | 12 | 13 | 14 |   |   |
| 8 | 8 | 9 | 10 | 11 | 12 | 13 | 14 | 15 | 16 |   |
| 9 | 9 | 10 | 11 | 12 | 13 | 14 | 15 | 16 | 17 | 18 |

which you may have learned in the form "6 plus 7 is 3 carry 1." In any event, you learned at least 55 sums. The corresponding add table for binary is much shorter:

|   | 0 | 1 |
|---|---|---|
| 0 | 0 |   |
| 1 | 1 | 10 |

which is one of the many reasons why computers are built to operate in binary; namely, the arithmetic is simpler. So a complete addition in binary is rather trivial:

$$1011100101$$
$$\underline{1100101110}$$
$$11000010011$$

We will consider binary multiplication and division later, when we have learned more about the machine. The important items at this point are counting in binary and number base conversion.

## 5.4   Data Numbers

Each word in our computer is 16 bit positions long. For data words, each word can be considered as a binary counter that has 16 positions, in the same way that an automobile odometer is a five-place decimal counter. Consider the latter case first. If we see an odometer that reads

> 23456

we might conclude that its car has traveled 23,456 miles forward. We could also conclude that the car has traveled 123,456 miles, or 223,456 miles, or 76,543 miles backward. The counter functions in a range of 100,000 (that is, $10^5$ for a five-place decimal counter). Beyond that range, the counter "rolls over" and restarts from 00000 without any indication that it has done so. If we were to examine a car that looks new, with an odometer reading of 999998, it would be proper for us to reason that the car had traveled 2 miles backward since it was manufactured.

Similarly, the long counter in a desk calculator, having twenty decimal wheels, functions in a range of $10^{20}$. If the counter reads 99999 . . . 9998, that figure could have been reached by counting forward, or it could have been reached by counting down **2** from 0. In sequenced operations, the machine is programmed to sense the leftmost (or high-order) 9 as representing negative numbers.

Now go back to our sixteen-place binary counters. Starting from 0, we can count (add, multiply, or whatever) forward as far as

$$0111111111111111$$

which is equal to decimal 32,767, or $2^{15} - 1$. If we now add **1,** the counter will roll to

$$1000000000000000$$

but the machine is built to sense the high-order 1 bit as representing a negative number. Thus, 16 bit words can contain data numbers in the range $\pm(2^{15} - 1)$. The $-1$ comes from the fact that we start counting from 0.

### EXERCISES

**95.**   One thousand numbers are stored. They are all 3 digit numbers; that is, no number is greater than 999. We wish to find the sum of the 1000 numbers. How much room should we allow for this sum?

# 48　Binary Arithmetic

This type of problem occurs over and over in computing. We must antici-pate the size of the results in order to provide space for them. In this case, suppose that each of the 1000 numbers had the greatest possible value, 999. Then the result is equivalent to multiplying 1000 by 999, which yields 999,000. The answer to the above question is then six decimal digits. How much room should be allowed in binary bit positions?

**100.** Using the same data as in Exercise 95, suppose we want to calculate the sum of the squares of the 1000 numbers? Now how much room should be reserved for the result?

**105.** The product of the decimal numbers 1048576 and 57210473 is one of the following:

　(a)　6384927066
　(b)　59989528936448
　(c)　59989151218193644872
　(d)　63840009395278463106 1406527

If you know that one of the four choices is correct, can you find it without doing the long multiplication? By all means, look up the answer in Appen-dix 3.

**110.** Numbers are stored in binary words in our computer. We have a set of such data words, each of them known to have values less than or equal to $111111111)_2$. How many such numbers can be added together before the sum would exceed the capacity of one word to hold it as a positive number? Putting it another way, how many 9 bit numbers can be added together before the sum exceeds 15 bit length?

**115.** A mini computer has 16,384 words of storage. If each word is given a unique address, starting with 0, how many bit positions must there be in the largest address? The number 16,384 is a power of 2; computer stores usually come in sizes that are powers of 2.

**120.** The Control Data 3170 has a word size of 24 bits. Assuming that its number representation is the same as we have described for a mini, what is the largest positive number that can be stored in a data word? (The word "positive" implies that one bit is utilized to denote the sign.)

[NOTE: The problems posed in Exercises 115 and 120 are met frequently. You will find it convenient to memorize a few powers of 2, such as:

| N | $2^N$ | |
|---|---|---|
| 2 | $2^2 =$ | 4 |
| 3 | $2^3 =$ | 8 |
| 4 | $2^4 =$ | 16 |
| 5 | | 32 |
| 6 | | 64 |
| 7 | | 128 |
| 10 | | 1024 |
| 12 | | 4096 |
| 14 | | 16384 |
| 16 | | 65536 |
| 20 | | (1048576) |

It is only necessary to remember that the last number in parentheses is about 1 million.]

# 6

# GETTING STARTED

## 6.1 A Simple Program

Let us begin with an extremely simple problem. We have three numbers in storage—call them A, B, and C. We wish to do the following:

$$A + B - C = R$$

that is, add A to B; subtract C from that result; and store the final result in a new word called R. We will have the following situation:

The value of A is 13, stored at address 151.
The value of B is 28, stored at address 152.
The value of C is 15, stored at address 153.
The address of R is 154; initially it will have the value 0.

The addresses given are expressed in octal, which you will recall is a convenient way to compress binary notation. The values of A, B, and C are expressed in decimal. When they appear in computer storage, they will be 15, 34, and 17 (octal).

To perform the required calculations, we must write a program. The program must exist in storage, and we will have to choose specific addresses of words to contain the instructions and data.

Instruction words, at the moment, have the following format:

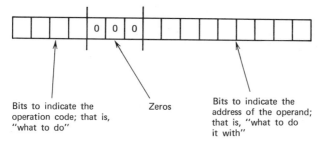

The operation codes are listed in the reference manual of the machine; for the Varian 620, the manual is titled *Varian 620 Computer Handbook.*

A complete program is shown in Figure 6.1. You should study it, and then watch while it is loaded into the machine and executed. The result in word 154 should be octal 32 (binary 011010) and can be displayed on the console. The program should be executed in single-cycle mode in order to see what takes place. "Single cycle" on the Varian 620 means "single instruction cycle" — each depression of the STEP switch on the console causes execution of one complete instruction (regardless of how many machine cycles that instruction may require). (If executed at full speed, the entire program would take about 18 microseconds.) Directions for loading and operating the machine are found in Appendix 4.

| LOCATION | OP | | ADDRESS | REMARKS |
|---|---|---|---|---|
| 000144 | 01 | 0 | 151 | Load accumulator with A |
| 000145 | 12 | 0 | 152 | Add B to accumulator |
| 000146 | 14 | 0 | 153 | Subtract C from accumulator |
| 000147 | 05 | 0 | 154 | Store accumulator at R |
| 000150 | 00 | 0 | 000 | Halt |

| ADDRESS | VALUE | REMARKS |
|---|---|---|
| 000151 | 000015 | This is A |
| 000152 | 000034 | This is B |
| 000153 | 000017 | This is C |
| 000154 | 000000 | This is R |

FIGURE 6.1  Our first program. This is the appearance of numbers in storage before the program is executed.

## 6.2  Observations on the First Program

With a program of five instruction words and four data words, we can observe a few things:

1.  The program is useless. It would make little sense to use a computer

to make the calculation shown; the proper tool would be pencil and paper, or, if the numbers were larger, an adding machine. The program utilizes virtually none of the power of the computer. Moreover, the effort of loading the instructions and data far overshadows the executed work.

2.  The program does show how the machine is normally sequenced. The information in the machine is that between the two vertical lines in Figure 6.1. The numbers labeled LOCATION and ADDRESS indicate **where** the information is. LOCATION refers to instruction words; ADDRESS refers to data words.

3.  The intelligence of the problem is in the column headed REMARKS. As humans, we would much prefer to operate at that level, rather than with the coded numbers.

4.  The operation codes are purely arbitrary. They are fixed (that is, code 14 is always "subtract from the accumulator") but intrinsically meaningless.

5.  The word ADDRESS has been used in two senses. In the left-hand column, it means "the place where this word is stored." As part of an instruction word, it means "the place to go to obtain the operand for this instruction." The proper term for the latter case is "address **portion** of an instruction word," but we say "address" for short.

6.  The addresses in the instructions refer to specific words of data; namely, those stored at 000151–000154. If the data words were to be moved anywhere else in storage, the program segment would not function properly at all. Thus, this sort of coding is dependent on where things are in storage. In technical terms, the data in this code is not **relocatable.**

7.  The bits in each instruction word between the op-code and the address are 000. Keep in mind that all the numbers shown in Figure 6.1 are in octal notation, and that each octal digit represents three binary bits. Those 3 bits will be nonzero in more complicated instructions that we will see later.

8.  (Most important of all.) The address portion of the instructions in our program is effectively 9 bits long. With 9 bits, we can address 512 words directly. Thus, our simple program must reside within the first 512 words of storage. Our computer will be of little use unless we can arrange to address all of storage, so we will next consider the various ways in which that can be accomplished.

### 6.3   Modes of Addressing

The bit positions in an instruction word are identified as follows:

| 15 | 14 | 13 | 12 | 11 | 10 | 9 | 8 | 7 | 6 | 5 | 4 | 3 | 2 | 1 | 0 |
|----|----|----|----|----|----|---|---|---|---|---|---|---|---|---|---|
|    |    |    |    |    |    |   |   |   |   |   |   |   |   |   |   |

For the instructions we have considered so far, the makeup of the instruction is that shown in Section 6.1; namely, with bit positions 15–12 for the op-code; positions 11–9 as 0s; and positions 8–0 for the address portion. As we have seen, this format restricts the addressing capability to the first 512 words of storage.

Provided that position 11 is 0, the address portion can be extended to use positions 10–0. Now the range of addresses, using 11 bits, extends to the first $2^{11} = 2048$ words of storage.

For example, the instruction

$$1010 \quad 010 \quad 000000000$$

indicates "add to the accumulator the contents of word 10000000000," which refers to word $1024)_{10}$ in storage. Our first type of addressing, then, is direct; that is, the address stated within the instruction word points directly to the word containing the desired operand.

If positions 11–9 are 1, 0, and 0, then the address in positions 8–0 is taken to be **relative** to the current location of the instruction, which is our second mode of addressing. For example, the instruction

$$1010 \quad 100 \quad 000000111$$

indicates "add to the accumulator the contents of the word that is 8 words farther along in storage than where this instruction is located." The address portion is added to the current value of the instruction counter. Since, in the Varian 620, the instruction counter points to the next location after the instruction currently under execution, the effective address will thus be the stated address (which is 7 in the example shown) plus the value of the location, plus 1. Relative addressing allows us to address any word within a range of 512 words forward from where we are at the moment. (Relative forward addressing is useful. The details of creating such addresses are usually cared for by a programming language, such as an assembler.)

A third type of addressing calls for 2 words to be used for one instruction, in which the second word is devoted entirely to the address portion of the instruction. Fourteen bits of this second word can be the address. In this mode of addressing, all 16,384 words of storage can be directly addressed.

A fourth type of addressing, also using 2 words per instruction, calls for the second word to **be** the operand (rather than the address of the operand). This constitutes **zero-level addressing.** In normal **first-level addressing,** the number we want is **one** step away, so to speak. In zero-level addressing, the number we want is **no** steps away; it is built into the instruction.

A fifth type of addressing is **second-level addressing,** in which the address portion of the instruction gives the address of a word in storage whose contents is the address of the number we want. In other words, the number we seek is **two** steps away from where we are. This notion can be extended to third-level addressing (or higher levels).

The details of these modes of addressing will become apparent later. In any event, the short word length of the mini is not a real restriction to our ability to get at any word in storage when we need to. We need now to examine more examples of how a computer may be used for more complex work.

## 6.4  Useful Work

Here is our second programming problem: Two hundred numbers are stored in consecutive words; we wish to add them and place the result in the 201st consecutive word.

There are significant differences between this problem and the first problem we programmed:

1.  The task is now highly repetitive. Where we could spell out the individual steps in performing $A + B - C = R$, we now have 200 things to do, and they are all alike.

2.  The task is now highly systematic. Where the numbers A, B, and C could have been scattered anywhere in storage, the 200 values in this problem are in consecutive words. This is not a coincidence. The machine is ours to use and control; we naturally arrange the numbers that we wish to manipulate in neat blocks of storage.

3.  Besides the repetition within the task, the task itself is to be considered repetitive; that is, we should think of it as part of a much larger problem. We will want to arrange to repeat the task over and over with many sets of 200 numbers.

Logically, we could perform this new task the same way as we did the first. Figure 6.2 shows the outline of a **straight-line code** that is basically like our first program. After you have studied the code carefully, consider the following observations:

1.  As before, and as a matter of convenience to us, everything is expressed in octal, though within the machine everything is in binary. For example, the first instruction is actually at location 0000001000000000 and the contents of that word is 0001010000000000.

2.  The values of the 200 words of data are now left blank in writing the code, since the program is intended to operate properly on **any** 200 values. It should be clear that since the sum must be less than 32,767 (why?), the 200 numbers must be small, or the program would produce an **overflow** in the accumulator.

3.  The entire program is as big as the block of data. In other words, for

```
001000                       ,ORG     ,01000
001000   012000    STRT      ,LDA     ,B1       LOAD ACCUMULATOR WITH FIRST VALUE
001001   122001              ,ADD     ,B2       ADD SECOND VALUE TO ACCUMULATOR
001002   122002              ,ADD     ,B3       ADD THIRD VALUE TO ACCUMULATOR
001003   122003              ,ADD     ,B4       ADD FORTH VALUE TO ACCUMULATOR
001004   122004              ,ADD     ,B5       ADD FIFTH VALUE TO ACCUMULATOR
001005   122005              ,ADD     ,B6       ADD SIXTH VALUE TO ACCUMULATOR
001006   122006              ,ADD     ,B7       ADD SEVENTH VALUE TO ACCUMULATOR
001007   122007              ,ADD     ,B8       ADD EIGHTH VALUE TO ACCUMULATOR
001010   122010              ,ADD     ,B9       ADD NINTH VALUE TO ACCUMULATOR
                                .
                                .
001307   122307              ,ADD     ,B200     ADD TWO HUNDREDTH VALUE
001310   052310              ,STA     ,SUM      STORE RESULT
001311   000000              ,HLT     ,         HALT
002000                       ,ORG     ,02000
002000   000000    B1        ,DATA    ,0        FIRST VALUE
002001   000000    B2        ,DATA    ,0        SECOND VALUE
002002   000000    B3        ,DATA    ,0        THIRD VALUE
002003   000000    B4        ,DATA    ,0        FORTH VALUE
002004   000000    B5        ,DATA    ,0        FIFTH VALUE
002005   000000    B6        ,DATA    ,0        SIXTH VALUE
002006   000000    B7        ,DATA    ,0        SEVENTH VALUE
002007   000000    B8        ,DATA    ,0        EIGHTH VALUE
002010   000000    B9        ,DATA    ,0        NINTH VALUE
                                .
                                .
002307   000000    B200      ,DATA    ,0        TWO HUNDREDTH VALUE
002310   000000    SUM       ,DATA    ,0        THE SUM IS TO GO HERE
         001000 R            ,END     ,STRT
```

LITERALS

POINTERS

SYMBOLS

```
1   002310  R   SUM
1   002307  R   B200
        .
        .
1   002010  R   B9
1   002007  R   B8
1   002006  R   B7
1   002005  R   B6
1   002004  R   B5
1   002003  R   B4
1   002002  R   B3
1   002001  R   B2
1   002000  R   B1
1   001000  R   STRT
```

**FIGURE 6.2   A straight-line machine code for summing two numbers.**

the amount of work it does, the program occupies an inordinate amount of storage space.

4. The program would execute at maximum possible speed. If each ADD instruction takes 3.6 microseconds, the entire program would be executed in 7236 microseconds.

5. It would be difficult to alter the range of the program; that is, to make it handle more or less than 200 words. Moreover, if we wished to extend it to the point of adding together more than 8200 words, it would be physically impossible to hold the program and the data in storage.

6. If any errors are made in writing the program, it will be difficult to find them. Indeed, it may be difficult to detect that there **are** errors.

7. This is not the way to get any work done. Humans simply cannot write straight-line code; it is monotonous and boring, and monotony and boredom are not conducive to clear thinking.

## 6.5  Programmed Loops

In every computer ever built, all the instructions that can be contained in central storage can be executed—in straight-line fashion—in a second or less. But it takes more than a second—and perhaps several minutes—to load those instructions into storage. Thus, unless we have ways of using the same instructions over and over, we will not obtain useful work from the machine. One such way is the programmed loop. *A loop is a set of instructions that perform a repetitive task by using the same set for each part of the task.* Our task of adding 200 numbers is typical of the tasks that should be looped.

There are five parts of a programmed loop, illustrated in general in Figure 6.3. The specific loop for our addition problem is shown in Figure 6.4. A code for the loop is given in Figure 6.5. Notice that all addresses and instructions are in octal.

The heart of the loop—the DO block—consists of three instructions:

Load the accumulator with the contents of 2310.
Add the contents of X to the accumulator.
Store the accumulator at 2310.

The address X, written as 0000 in the code, is a **supplied address.** It is a variable address; it will change in value 200 times during the execution of the loop.

The instructions beginning at location 1000 initialize the loop by providing the address X with the value 2000, so that the DO block is set up for the first case. Notice that we have here some instructions that operate on other instructions. This is the number one reason why computers are dif-

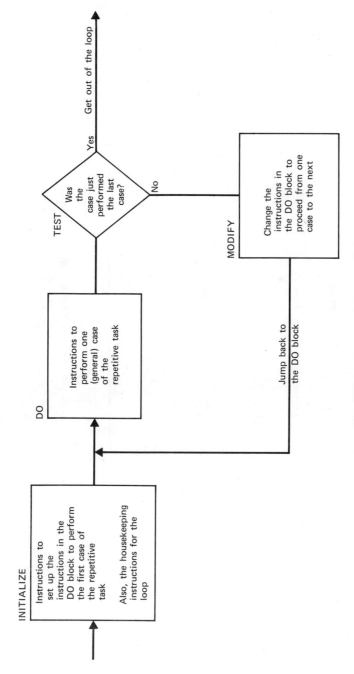

**FIGURE 6.3  The general pattern of a programmed loop.**

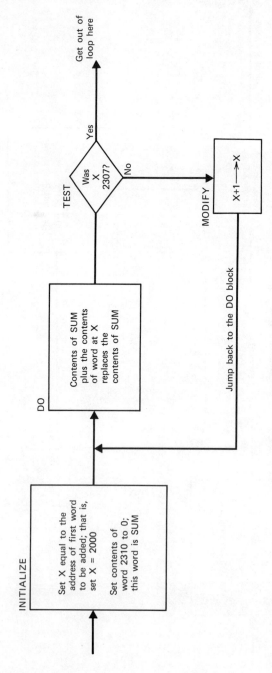

FIGURE 6.4   The looping pattern for the addition problem.

PAGE      000001

```
001000                          ,ORG     ,01000
001000    011022    BEGN   ,LDA     ,CON1
001001    051026           ,STA     ,X
001002    011024           ,LDA     ,ZERO
001003    052310           ,STA     ,SUM
001004    012310    REF1   ,LDA     ,SUM
001005    006127           ,ADDE*   ,X
001006    101026 R
001007    052310           ,STA     ,SUM
001010    011026           ,LDA     ,X
001011    141023           ,SUB     ,CON2
001012    001002           ,JAP     ,REF2
001013    001021 R
001014    011026           ,LDA     ,X
001015    121025           ,ADD     ,ONE
001016    051026           ,STA     ,X
001017    001000           ,JMP     ,REF1
001020    001004 R
001021    000000    REF2   ,HLT     ,
001022    002000 R  CON1   ,DATA    ,(B)
001023    002307 R  CON2   ,DATA    ,(B+199)
001024    000000    ZERO   ,DATA    ,0
001025    000001    ONE    ,DATA    ,1
001026              X      ,BSS     ,1
002000                     ,ORG     ,02000
002000              B      ,BSS     ,200
002310              SUM    ,BSS     ,1
          001000 R         ,END     ,BEGN
```

LITERALS

POINTERS


SYMBOLS

```
1    002310 R   SUM
1    002000 R   B
1    001026 R   X
1    001025 R   ONE
1    001024 R   ZERO
1    001023 R   CON2
1    001022 R   CON1
1    001021 R   REF2
1    001004 R   REF1
1    001000 R   BEGN
```

**FIGURE 6.5** Assembly language code for the loop of Figure 6.4.


ferent from other calculating devices. Not only are instructions and data stored in the same medium with the same appearance, but instructions can treat other instructions **as** data.

The instructions at 1002 perform the **housekeeping** of the loop; in this case, to set the contents of the sum word to 0.

The instructions beginning at 1010 are the TEST portion of the loop. In flowchart terms, we want to implement the decision:

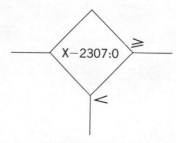

which is logically equivalent to

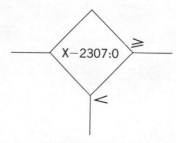

We express it on flowcharts the former way, but we implement it in code the latter way, since a comparison to 0 in the accumulator is one of the things that computers are built to do. We load the accumulator with the word containing X, subtract 2307 from it, and execute a JUMP out of the loop if the result is positive.

The instructions at 1014 perform the MODIFY phase of the loop. The value of X is increased by 1.

Refer again to Figure 6.4. The term X is used on the flowchart with two meanings. In the INITIALIZE and MODIFY boxes, X refers to an address. In the DO box, we want to refer to the "contents of word X," and we took pains to say so. When we draw flowcharts more compactly, with less English verbiage, we will frequently have to distinguish between the two uses of the same symbol. The standard notation uses parentheses around a symbol to denote "contents of." Thus, the DO block might be expressed as

$$(2310) + (X) \longrightarrow (2310)$$

but the MODIFY block is still

$$X + 1 \longrightarrow X.$$

## 6.6   Observations on the Loop

Compare the codes of Figures 6.2 and 6.5. Clearly, the code with the loop is shorter (which will be generally true), and hence we see the first advantage of looping; namely, that it conserves storage space.

As a matter of fact, there is only one advantage to the straight-line code—it executes faster. The loop to perform the same task will take perhaps ten times as long to execute, since only one of its instructions does the work we want done; namely, the instruction to ADD X.

Much greater care goes into the writing of a loop, and this is its second advantage. If any single character in the loop's instructions is wrong, the whole loop tends to go awry. It is only when the coder's attention remains keen that useful and correct code can result. The looping technique avoids the monotony and boredom that make straight-line coding error-prone. In general, we will find it easy to debug our loops, whereas we might never be able to debug a straight-line code.

The range of a loop is readily expanded or contracted. To make our loop add 20 numbers, or 2000 numbers, or every word in storage, we must change only the test constant.†

Looping is one of our two basic building blocks in programming (the other is subroutining). The beginner tends to cling to straight-line codes too long. The proper situation in which one should write a loop is a repetitive task that is to be done **two** or more times. Looping cannot be avoided; get used to it as quickly as possible.

The chief reason for using programmed loops is that we must; without loops, we would get little useful work out of our machine. Loops are somewhat costly in terms of execution time, but they are a powerful tool and tend to greatly shorten the **elapsed time** of a problem; that is, the calendar time between problem origination and final results.

## 6.7  A Third Program

We don't want to go too far with the notion of writing programs in machine language. It is instructive, but only up to the point at which you are convinced that it is extremely awkward and tedious. You may be at that point already.

Nevertheless, let us carry through one more example of a simple repetitive problem: A block of $250)_{10}$ words of storage is located at addresses 1000, 1001, . . . , 1371 (check that octal arithmetic). A second block of $250)_{10}$ words is located at addresses 2000, 2001, . . . , 2371. Call these two blocks A and B. The numbers in block A are to be moved to block B with their order reversed; that is, the number at 1000 is to be moved to 2371; the number at 1003 is to be moved to 2366; the number at 1371 is to be moved to address 2000; and so on. The flowchart of Figure 6.6 expresses the logic; Figure 6.7 shows a possible code.

---

† Actually, it's a little more complicated than that. In order to address every word in storage, we must resort to one of the schemes described in Section 6.3.

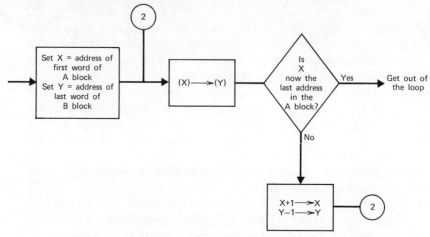

**FIGURE 6.6  A loop to move and reverse a block of words.**

| LOC'N | OP | ADDRESS |
|-------|------|---------|
|  | ORG | 0200 |
| STRT | LDAI | A |
|  | STA | X |
|  | LDAI | B+249 |
|  | STA | Y |
| REF2 | LDAE | 00000 |
|  | STAE | 00000 |
|  | LDA | X |
|  | SUBI | A+249 |
|  | JAZ | OUT |
|  | LDA | X |
|  | IAR |  |
|  | STA | X |
|  | LDA | Y |
|  | DAR |  |
|  | STA | Y |
|  | JMP | REF2 |
| OUT | HLT |  |
| X | EQU | REF2+1 |
| Y | EQU | REF2+3 |
|  | ORG | 01000 |
| A | BSS | 250 |
|  | ORG | 02000 |
| B | BSS | 250 |
|  | END | STRT |

**FIGURE 6.7  Assembly language code for the loop of Figure 6.6**

This third program is just a little bit more complicated than the second. There are two supplied addresses to be initialized and modified (although we tested out of the loop on only one of them). Our **address modification** called for subtraction in one instance. Although the problem is simple and straightforward, the chore of producing a machine language code is becoming excessive.

## 6.8   Indexing

Refer to Figure 6.5 and in particular to the MODIFY instructions at locations 001014. They form a triplet of the form:

> Load accumulator.
> Add 1.
> Store accumulator.

which is common to most programs. In fact, during the running of meaningful programs, it is striking how much of the machine's time seems to be devoted to adding 1. This was first noticed around 1954, when all computers cost over a million dollars, and it struck someone as inefficient that the giant machine seemed to be spending a large portion of its time on this trivial task.

This thinking led to the device that we now call an **index register.** Index registers provide yet another mode of addressing. If an instruction is indexed, its **effective address** is the stated address plus the contents of the index register. The index register is a hardware device (there are two of them as standard equipment on the Varian machine). The address modification is performed as the instruction is moved from storage to the decoder. An example will help to clarify these notions. Figure 6.8 shows the coding for our second problem (the sum of 200 numbers) redone making use of one of the X registers.

The codes that are photoreproduced in this book are intended to be studied carefully. In the loop of Figure 6.8, the instruction at 1000 initializes the index register to the address of B. The next two instructions are the same as in the previous loop; they initialize the word SUM to 0. At REFI, the DO block of the loop begins. We LOAD, ADD, and STORE, but the ADD is now an indexed instruction. The stated address is 0, but the effective address is formed by having the instruction word pass through the index register. On the first traverse of the loop, the effective address will be B; on the second traverse it will be B+1, and so on. The instructions at 1006–1010 test the index register, and get us out of the loop, to REF2, when the contents of the index register is B+99. Notice that the JAP instruction occupies two computer words. The instructions at 1012–1014 increment the index register contents by 1.

```
PAGE        000001

001000                        ,ORG    ,01000
001000    031020    BEGN      ,LDX    ,CON1
001001    011022              ,LDA    ,ZERO
001002    052310              ,STA    ,SUM
001003    012310    REF1      ,LDA    ,SUM
001004    125000              ,ADD    ,0,1
001005    052310              ,STA    ,SUM
001006    005041              ,TXA    ,
001007    141021              ,SUB    ,CON2
001010    001002              ,JAP    ,REF2
001011    001017 R
001012    005041              ,TXA    ,
001013    121023              ,ADD    ,ONE
001014    005014              ,TAX    ,
001015    001000              ,JMP    ,REF1
001016    001003 R
001017    000000    REF2      ,HLT    ,
001020    002000 R  CON1      ,DATA   ,(B)
001021    002307 R  CON2      ,DATA   ,(B+199)
001022    000000    ZERO      ,DATA   ,0
001023    000001    ONE       ,DATA   ,1
002000                        ,ORG    ,02000
002000              B         ,BSS    ,200
002310              SUM       ,BSS    ,1
          001000 R            ,END    ,BEGN

LITERALS

POINTERS

SYMBOLS

1    002310  R   SUM
1    002000  R   B
1    001023  R   ONE
1    001022  R   ZERO
1    001021  R   CON2
1    001020  R   CON1
1    001017  R   REF2
1    001003  R   REF1
1    001000  R   BEGN
```

**FIGURE 6.8**  Summing a block of 200 words using an index register.

## 6.9  Advantages of Indexing

A comparison of the two loops (Figures 6.5 and 6.8) reveals some of the advantages of using index registers:

1.   The code is shorter when the index register is used. The longer and more complicated the loop, the greater the saving in instructions will be over normal address modification.

2.   Instructions that are not there will waste no time in execution. The indexed code will run considerably faster.

3.   As far as address modification is concerned (and the chief use of index registers is for address modification), all of the initialization of most

loops can be performed in one instruction, and the test and modify parts of the loop can be performed with two or three instructions each (depending on how the logic is arranged). Once the details of these few instructions are mastered, the writing of loops becomes mechanical and simple. In computing, the simple and straightforward techniques get us to our results much faster than coy and clever tricks.

4.   But by far the greatest advantage of indexing lies in the fact that instruction words in storage do not change during execution. Addresses are modified in the index register (and on the fly, as the instruction words move from storage to the decoder), rather than in storage. Thus, with normal address modification, the appearance of words in storage before and after execution will be radically different. When the address modification is done by indexing, instruction words in storage are the same before and after execution. Provided that our programs work properly, this distinction is of no consequence. But experience tells us that most of the time new programs do **not** work the way we intended, and the processes of debugging and testing are facilitated when our loops are written to use index registers.

5.   There is one small bonus. If the index registers are not being used for address modification, they can be used for counters. Normally, words of storage are used for counters, and the common operations of incrementing a counter and testing a counter for a limit are done as follows:

> Load accumulator with contents of counter.
> Add to accumulator.
> Store accumulator.
>
> Load accumulator with contents of counter.
> Subtract the amount of the limit.
> Jump (on 0, or negative, etc.).

When an index register is used as a counter, the first of these operations can be performed with one instruction, and the second with two instructions. This use of index registers is of marginal benefit.

## 6.10   Subroutining

We must arrange to use sets of instructions over and over in order to get useful work done with a computer. Looping is one such technique. Another is the writing of **subroutines.** A subroutine is a self-contained program that may be invoked from any place in another (main) routine. We speak of one routine **calling** a subroutine; when the task of the subroutine is completed, control returns to the main routine at or near the instruction that did the calling.

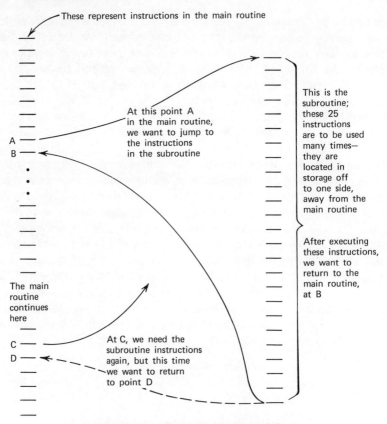

FIGURE 6.9   The logic of subroutining.

The classic case is that of extracting square roots. There are many ingenious ways to calculate square roots. Let us assume that we can write the code for one of them. Now, suppose that in the course of a large problem there are many places on the flowchart where a square root must be calculated. We could, of course, rewrite the code for square root at each place in the program where it is needed. There are several things wrong with that idea:

1.   It is wasteful of storage space. If the set of square rooting instructions is 25 instructions long and is to be repeated 20 times within the larger program, we will consume 500 words of storage, of which 475 are redundant. No computer will ever have enough central storage so that we can waste it in this fashion.

2.   No matter how those instructions are written and loaded into storage, the mere fact that they are repeated 20 times is conducive to creating errors.

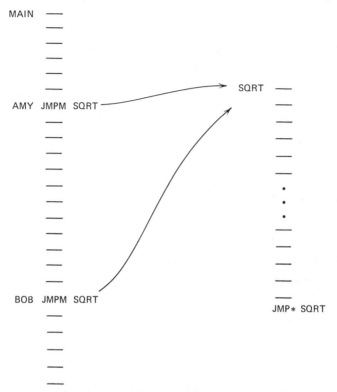

**FIGURE 6.10** The mechanics of linking to a subroutine. (The *
denotes indirect addressing.)

3.   If there is an error in the coding, the error will be repeated 20 times
and will have to be corrected in 20 places—another procedure that tends to
inhibit correct results.

4.   Above all, the notion of having a human repeat an action 20 times is
in contradiction to good computing practice. **Computers** should do repetitive
work, not humans.

For all these reasons, the code for square root should be put in the form
of a subroutine. The basic logic is shown in Figure 6.9.

Getting from the main routine is logically trivial; an unconditional jump
would do it. The trick is in getting back again, since we want to return from
the subroutine to a different place in the main routine each time we go to
the subroutine. Figure 6.10 shows the mechanics of this procedure for the
Varian 620 (and the procedure is typical of the action on any mini). The
subroutine entry point is at some location, called SQRT in the example. At
the place in the main routine marked AMY, it is desired to go to the subrou-

tine; this process is called **linking**. The operation code is JUMP AND MARK; it is an unconditional jump, and it puts the value of AMY+1 at the location SQRT itself. For example, if we are at location 1234 in the main routine and we want to link to the subroutine SQRT, which is located at 2345, we write a JUMP AND MARK instruction at 1234, with the address SQRT. The location 1235 is then put at 2345 and the jump is made to location 2346. All of this is automatic. After the instructions of the subroutine are executed, we JUMP INDIRECT to SQRT. That is, we jump to the location indicated by the contents of SQRT, which will take us to 1235, which is where we want to be. Similarly, the linkage at BOB will take us to the same subroutine, but return us to BOB+1. The JUMP INDIRECT is second-level addressing, and here we see one of its more common applications.

## 6.11   The Advantages of Subroutining

The use of subroutines should clearly refute all objections (listed in Section 6.10) to repeating a given code many times in storage. Storage space is conserved, and human effort is exerted only once on a repetitive problem. The likelihood of errors is cut down.

The chief advantage to the technique of subroutining, however, lies in the facility it gives us to **segment** our problem solutions. We can break up a large problem into a set of smaller problems, each of which can be thoroughly debugged and tested in isolation. The main routine, then, is frequently just a collection of linkages (plus perhaps some housekeeping to get started on the problem). If the principle of segmenting problem solutions is applied intelligently, we need never write large programs; we write only many small programs. The question then is, how small is "small"? As a general rule, the largest routine you should write as a unit should be 100 instructions or less.

## 6.12   Calling Sequences

When a subroutine is used, there is a communication problem in the programming. The main routine must communicate to the subroutine the necessary information about how to get back. As we have seen, the mechanics of doing this takes place in the JUMP AND MARK facility (or its equivalent on other machines). Most subroutines require additional information; namely, what to work **on**. For the square root subroutine, this would be the number whose square root is needed. At the end of the subroutine, the result must be communicated back to the main routine. The proper notation here is **function** and **argument**. The subroutine is fed the argument (e.g.,

169) and returns the function value (e.g., 13). A subroutine might demand several arguments, and could return several function values. We will defer for the moment the mechanics of this second communication problem. Suffice it to say that the values of the arguments can be included in the code with the linking instructions; the combination constitutes a **calling sequence,** and we normally speak of calling a subroutine.

The flowchart notation is as follows:

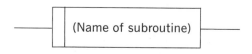

The bar at the left end of the rectangle signifies that, at this point, the routine should link to the subroutine named in the rectangle, and return.

To summarize, here is what is needed to call a subroutine from a main routine:

1.   Arrange to get back to the main routine, which usually means storing the location of the first calling instruction.

2.   Arrange to transmit to the subroutine the values of the arguments it will need, or the addresses of the arguments.

3.   Jump to the subroutine.

## 6.13   Another Subroutine Example

The fraction $^{15}/_{21}$ is not in lowest terms; we can see that the factor 3 can be canceled. The fraction $^{3213}/_{4488}$ is also not in lowest terms, but it is not so easy to see what should be canceled. The amount to be canceled is the largest number that divides both 3213 and 4488; in other words, their greatest common divisor (GCD). An **algorithm** for finding the GCD of two numbers was devised by Euclid and is a classic of elegance. It can be best explained in terms of the above example.

1.   One of the numbers must be greater than the other.

2.   This being so, the two numbers can always be arranged in the division transformation, like this:

$$4488 = 3213(\quad) + 1275$$

(4488 is the dividend; 3213 is the divisor; the quantity in parentheses, which is not needed, is the quotient; and 1275 is the remainder).

3.   The number we are seeking divides both 4488 and 3213, since that's the problem. Look at it this way:

$$4488 = 3213(\quad) + 1275$$

So the number we seek divides the left side of the equation. But since the two sides of the equation are equal, the number we seek divides the entire right side of the equation also. But the number we seek divides the first term of the right side, as indicated by the arrows. Therefore, the number we seek divides the other term also. We now have this situation:

$$4488 = 3213(\quad) + 1275$$

4.   The remainder in a division is always less than the divisor. So we have reduced the problem to a new one involving smaller numbers. The process now begins over:

$$3213 = 1275(\quad) + 663$$

and continues as follows:

$$1275 = 663(\quad) + 612$$
$$663 = 612(\quad) + 51$$
$$612 = 51(\quad) + 0$$

5.   The series of remainders must eventually reach 0. When it does, we have expressed the problem as the GCD of 612 and 51, and the result must be 51.

Euclid's algorithm calls for division, for maximum efficiency. When the numbers are small, we can operate more simply, as shown in Figure 6.11. We have arranged to have the algorithm expressed as a subroutine. Notice that the action of the algorithm will destroy the numbers involved. This is a common situation, so we follow a standard rule: Make a copy of the numbers and destroy the copy. Notice the notation on the flowchart for a subroutine. We enter the subroutine and later return to the main routine from which it was called.

## EXERCISES

**125.**   Rewrite the program of Figure 6.1 starting at location 000271.

**130.**   Write a new program like the one in Figure 6.1 to evaluate

$$A - B + 2C = R$$

(Add C twice.)

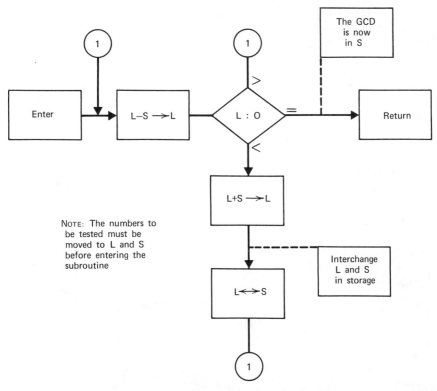

NOTE: The numbers to be tested must be moved to L and S before entering the subroutine

**FIGURE 6.11  A subroutine for Euclid's algorithm.**

**135.**  Mr. X and Mr. Y shake hands. For each of them, the required object is directly at hand, quite literally; they are zero-level addressed from each other. Mr. X is now first-level addressed with everyone that Mr. Y has ever shaken hands with, and Mr. Y is similarly first-level addressed with everyone that Mr. X has ever shaken hands with. Through second-level addressing, each of them is linked with a significant fraction of the whole population. With the exception of those who do not shake hands, and some isolated tribes, everyone on earth can be connected. To what level of addressing would it be necessary to go to connect you to, say, all of the fifty national senators? What level of addressing might it take to connect you, through such handshakes, to Abraham Lincoln, or George Washington?

**140.**  Three words in storage are labeled Y, M, and D. They contain the numbers 72, 6, and 8, respectively, representing June 8, 1972. We want the three words to act as counters, to advance on demand as a calendar. Thus,

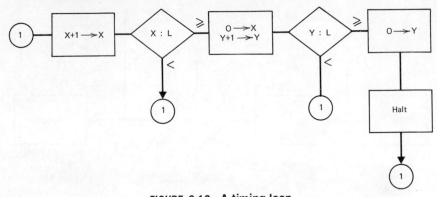

FIGURE 6.12 A timing loop.

we want a subroutine that will advance our calendar counter by one day each time that it is called. Draw a flowchart for the logic of this subroutine. (This is a moderately difficult piece of logic. A possible flowchart is shown in Appendix 3.)

**145.** Figure 6.12 shows the logic of a pair of counting loops. Two counters, X and Y, each count up to some limit, L. If L = 1000, then from start to halt the machine will make $L^2$ counts, which is 1,000,000. Write a code in machine language for this task. Count carefully the number of machine instructions that will be executed, and take into account the fact that some of them will be one-cycle instructions and some will take two machine cycles (consult your machine reference manual for these statistics about each op-code). Run the program, observing the time between successive HALTs, and calculate the actual operating speed of your machine.

**150.** Using Euclid's algorithm, find the GCD of the three numbers 1638, 10,920, and 29,744.

**155.** In Exercise 75 (Chapter 4), there were three numbers in storage at addresses A, B, and C. Each number was to be tested to verify that it was either in the range from −100 to −200 or was greater than 500. Figure A3.1 shows a possible solution.

Suppose there are 200 numbers stored at addresses A, A+1, A+2, . . . , A+199 and each of them is to be tested for the same range as in Exercise 75. Draw a flowchart for a loop to perform that logic.

# 7

# BARRIERS

## 7.1   What Are the Barriers?

We have had a glimpse of how our computer operates at its own level, in binary. All the work done by the machine will be at that level, but it is awkward to live with. The sheer complexity of binary notation is baffling to humans. It is possible to devise small programs at that level, and it is well to gain some understanding of how the machine actually works, but we need some tools to enable us to control the machine effectively.

The awkwardness of the machine's mode of operation is one barrier to extensive use, but there are others.

1.  *Word size.* A 16 bit word allows for direct manipulation of integers in the range $\pm 32,767$. There are precious few real problems that can be contained in that range. We must find ways to extend the arithmetic range of the machine.

2.  *Integers.* Even if we can handle numbers larger than 32,767, we must also arrange to handle fractions.

3.  *Language.* Above all, we must seek methods of writing instructions for the machine that are more comfortable and convenient than the strings of 1s and 0s of pure binary.

4.  *Storage size.* Our machine has 16,384 words (each of 16 bits) of core storage. Although a great deal of good computing can be done with that amount of storage, sooner or later problems will be encountered that require much greater storage capacity.

## 7.2 Can the Barriers Be Surmounted?

The four barriers just listed are common to all computers. Medium-sized machines today may have 65,000 words of 32 bits each. With a 32 bit word size, the range of numbers that can be handled directly is ±2,000,000,000, which is nice, but still not large enough. 65,000 words is more convenient than 16,000, but there is always a need for more. The barriers of integer capability and language are just as acute. With any binary computer, we must find ways—usually by writing programs—to extend the built-in capabilities of the machine.

We will remove the four barriers one by one. The language barrier is the one that bothers us the most at this point, and in Chapter 8 we will explore a tool to make it tractable; in Chapters 12, 13, and 14 we will see even more sophisticated tools for this purpose.

The word size barrier will be disposed of in Chapter 9, and the fraction barrier in Chapter 10. The storage size barrier is removed (as of today) only on larger machines; a discussion of the method used is in Chapter 17.

There are still other barriers. The size of the instruction set can be a barrier, particularly on a mini. Good programming (for example, by means of subroutines) can readily surmount this barrier. Another barrier is the intrinsic one-operation–one-operand nature of the von Neumann computer—but that barrier has long since been removed, as we shall see in Chapter 10.

The point is this: The purpose of a computer is to process information. Given a machine that exceeds a certain minimum size (and our mini does), there are standard techniques for processing any information and powerful tools to make the job relatively easy. In this book, we are starting at the lowest possible level and working our way to efficient and intelligent use of a computer.

Computers are built to manipulate only numeric information. At the level at which computer programs are executed, the logical capability can be summarized as follows:

1.   Numbers of a fixed size (16 bits in our machine) can be added, subtracted, multiplied, and divided.
2.   Any single number can be tested for being positive or negative, odd or even, or zero.
3.   The logical operations of AND and OR can be performed on two numbers.
4.   Any part of a number, down to a single bit position, can be isolated and tests can be performed on the character of any such group of bits.

That's about it, and it seems somewhat primitive. Nevertheless, out of these primitive operations we can build up logical structures of great complexity. The fact that the machines are constructed to manipulate numbers doesn't restrict us to problems that are numeric. Consider, for example, the serious attempts since 1957 to produce a computer program that will translate one natural language into another (e.g., Russian to English). There are no numbers in that problem, but most of the research on the subject centers around the computer. Russian or English words can be transliterated into number equivalents by any of many schemes, and then those numbers can be manipulated in any way we please. To date, this line of research has been rather fruitless, since it appears that the problem is significantly more complex than was first imagined. And that, of course, constitutes the ultimate barrier; namely, our inability to solve some problems, even given the truly awesome power of computers to do whatever we choose to have done.

# 8

# ASSEMBLERS

## 8.1 Removal of the First Barrier

In Chapter 6, we dealt with the computer at its own level; that is, in terms of machine language. This language is awkward, to say the least. It is possible to live with it, but most people prefer to function at a higher level. **Assembly language** is the next higher level.

Refer again to Figure 6.1. The machine code is the part between the vertical lines. The Remarks indicate what it is we are doing with each instruction. We would much prefer to write code that resembles those remarks. That is, we would prefer to use symbols for locations, op-codes, and addresses. In order to be able to do this, it will be necessary to use the computer to translate from symbols to actual machine language, and for this purpose we will need a program, called an **assembler**. Every computer has such a program, furnished by the vendor. To implement a computer solution, then, we will have to make two computer runs: one to translate our symbolic notation into machine language, and the second to run the resulting program. Most assemblers automatically combine these into one smooth pass that appears to the user as a single computer run.

The code for $A + B - C = R$ has been rewritten in assembly language in Figure 8.1. Each of the op-codes is expressed in mnemonics (LDA for "load accumulator"; SUB for "subtract"; and so on). Your machine reference manual lists for you all the available op-codes and their mnemonics.†

---

† Usually, these mnemonics are three letters long, but some, such as JMPM for JUMP AND MARK, go to four letters.

76

| LOCATION | OP-CODE | ADDRESS | REMARKS |
|----------|---------|---------|---------|
| HERE | LDA | A | Get value of A |
|  | ADD | B | Add value of B |
|  | SUB | C | Subtract value of C |
|  | STA | R | Store result at R |
|  | HLT |  | Halt |
| A | DATA | 13 |  |
| B | DATA | 28 |  |
| C | DATA | 15 |  |
| R | DATA | 0 |  |

FIGURE 8.1   Figure 6.1 redone in assembly language.

The locations are identified, as needed, with symbolic names that are completely arbitrary. They are restricted to, say, four characters, of which the first must be alphabetic. Constants and variables follow all the instructions. Notice that we can now enter our values in decimal; the assembler will translate them into binary for us. We will still find it expedient to include the REMARKS column to make the meaning of each line clear.

## 8.2   A Second Problem

Let's try to make all these ideas clearer by exploring a more complex problem: We have a number, N, in storage. Set $X = N$. Then follow this algorithm:

If X is odd, replace X by $3X+1$.
If X is even, replace X by $X/2$.
Stop when $X=1$.

For example, when $N = 9$, we will generate the following sequence: 9, 28, 14, 7, 22, 11, 34, 17, 52, 26, 13, 40, 20, 10, 5, 16, 8, 4, 2, 1. Counting the original number, we get 20 values. Call this (the number of terms) A. We wish to explore the range of A as N proceeds from 5 to 500.

You might try your hand at flowcharting this logic. A possible flowchart is shown in Figure 8.2, and an assembly language code is given in Figure 8.3. It will pay to study the code carefully, noting certain features:

1.   Our choice of symbols is arbitrary, but we are free to pick them meaningfully. Thus, we can use REF2 as the symbolic location for the instruction that corresponds to reference 2 on the flowchart. Similarly, our variables and constants are named to correspond to the problem, for example, the constant 500 is named LIM for "limit."

2.   At REF2, the instructions for "$N+1 \rightarrow N$" are implemented by use of a constant, ONE. Later, for "$A+1 \rightarrow A$," the same logic is performed with a

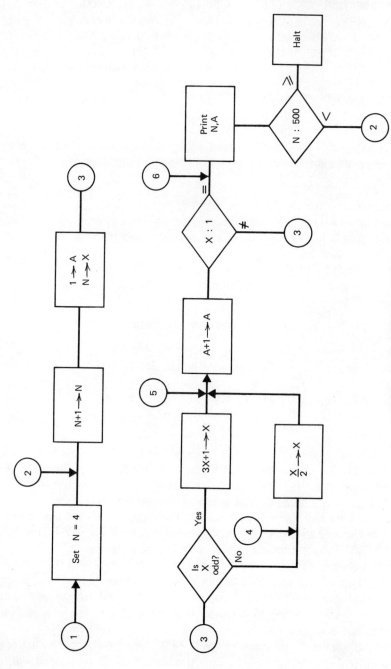

FIGURE 8.2 The 3X+1 problem.

zero-level address command which creates the **one** within the instruction. This simply illustrates that there are usually several ways to do things.

3. The operation "3X+1 → X" has been done in the simplest way. We could achieve the same result by loading X into the accumulator, shifting the accumulator left two places (which gives the effect of multiplying by 4), and then subtracting X. Or, we could have actually multiplied X by 3.

4. The requirement to "print N and A" would normally require a fairly lengthy program of its own. The numbers to be printed are in storage in binary form, and must be converted to decimal for us to read. That's fairly easy. What is hard is to explore the nature of the printing device (e.g., a Teletype) and program its operation to fire the decimal digits out to paper. Now, this task (binary to decimal conversion, and printer control) is common to every program we will write. We leave it to the experts; the whole task has been packaged as a subroutine in the assembly program, and we need only call that subroutine when needed.

5. We notify the assembler, with an ORG (for "origin") pseudo-operation, that we want the code assembled starting at location 00100. Later, with another ORG, we force the constant LIM to be placed at address 05000. This has been done only to demonstrate the freedom we have, and to show the addressing schemes needed to access our data. Other than the word LIM, all our instructions and data will fall into consecutive words of storage, starting at 00100. To access LIM, we have used a 2 word instruction (at location 150 octal).

The numbers 00100 and 05000, used in the code, follow a convention of the Varian DAS† assembler that numbers furnished to the assembler beginning with 0s are taken to be octal. If those numbers had been given as 100 and 5000, the assembler would have taken them to be decimal and converted them to octal for use in the assembly process.

6. Recall that there are many ways in which instruction addresses can be expressed (normal first-level addressing; zero-level addressing; indirect addressing; relative addressing; indexing).

In assembly language coding, we can force the type of addressing, as we must if we want indirect addressing or indexed addressing. The assembler will choose the proper form of addressing if we want to address words over a wide range. Notice, in particular, the addressing needed to get to LIM, which we deliberately put at 05000. What we can observe here is that a good assembler should help us with the bookkeeping of our instructions, and does.

---

† Large packaged programs are usually given names by their authors; DAS stands for Data Assembly System.

```
                              *
                              *        3X+1  PROBLEM
                              *
       000100                           ,ORG    ,0100
       000100    010161     REF1        ,LDA    ,FOUR
       000101    050155                 ,STA    ,N
       000102    010155     REF2        ,LDA    ,N
       000103    120160                 ,ADD    ,ONE
       000104    050155                 ,STA    ,N
       000105    010160                 ,LDA    ,ONE
       000106    050157                 ,STA    ,A
       000107    010155                 ,LDA    ,N
       000110    050156                 ,STA    ,X
       000111    010156     REF3        ,LDA    ,X
       000112    150162                 ,ANA    ,MASK
       000113    001010                 ,JAZ    ,REF4
       000114    000124 R
       000115    010156                 ,LDA    ,X
       000116    120156                 ,ADD    ,X
       000117    120156                 ,ADD    ,X
       000120    120160                 ,ADD    ,ONE
       000121    050156                 ,STA    ,X
       000122    001000                 ,JMP    ,REF5
       000123    000127 R
       000124    010156     REF4        ,LDA    ,X
       000125    004301                 ,ASRA   ,1
       000126    050156                 ,STA    ,X
       000127    010157     REF5        ,LDA    ,A
       000130    006120                 ,ADDI   ,1
       000131    000001
       000132    050157                 ,STA    ,A
       000133    010156                 ,LDA    ,X
       000134    140160                 ,SUB    ,ONE
       000135    001010                 ,JAZ    ,REF6
       000136    000141 R
       000137    001000                 ,JMP    ,REF3
       000140    000111 R
       000141    010155     REF6        ,LDA    ,N
       000142    002000                 ,JMPM   ,PRT
       000143    010000 R
       000144    010157                 ,LDA    ,A
       000145    002000                 ,JMPM   ,PRT
       000146    010000 R
       000147    010155                 ,LDA    ,N
       000150    006147                 ,SUBE   ,LIM
       000151    005000 R
       000152    001004                 ,JAN    ,REF2
       000153    000102 R
       000154    000000                 ,HLT    ,
       000155    000000     N           ,DATA   ,0
       000156    000000     X           ,DATA   ,0
       000157    000000     A           ,DATA   ,0
       000160    000001     ONE         ,DATA   ,1
       000161    000004     FOUR        ,DATA   ,4
```

**FIGURE 8.3   Assembly language code for Figure 8.2**

```
PAGE      000002

      000162   000001    MASK   ,DATA  ,1
      005000                    ,ORG   ,05000
      005000   000764    LIM    ,DATA  ,500
      010000                    ,ORG   ,010000
      010000   005000    PRT    ,NOP   ,
               000100  R        ,END   ,REF1

LITERALS

POINTERS


SYMBOLS

1    010000  R    PRT
1    005000  R    LIM
1    000162  R    MASK
1    000161  R    FOUR
1    000160  R    ONE
1    000157  R    A
1    000156  R    X
1    000155  R    N
1    000141  R    REF6
1    000127  R    REF5
1    000124  R    REF4
1    000111  R    REF3
1    000102  R    REF2
1    000100  R    REF1
```

FIGURE 8.3   (Continued)

7.   Besides allowing us to use symbols (rather than absolute addresses and binary op-codes), the assembly process primarily does bookkeeping for us. The assembler first assigns consecutive addresses to each instruction and data word, in exactly the order in which you write them. Then, having created lists of the symbols and their numerical equivalents, the assembler can go back over the code and complete the translation.

8.   Figure 8.3 is the symbolic listing from the DAS 8A assembler for the Varian 620. The right half of the listing shows what the programmer wrote in the symbolic language of the assembly system. The left half (the first two columns of numbers) shows the result of the translation. The first column is the absolute location, in octal; the second column is the instruction word, in octal. All symbols used in the program are listed, together with the location or address at which they are defined. It will pay rich dividends if you will explore the listing for some time with the flowchart of Figure 8.2 at hand.

9.   On the flowchart, at reference 3, the logical question is "Is X odd?" Of all possible ways to implement that decision, we chose to do it with a mask. We set up a constant named MASK, with the value 1. This gives us a word in storage that has a 1 bit in the low-order position, and 0s in the other 15 bit positions. In the code, at location 000112, we use one of the logical opera-

tions that is built into the machine. These operations provide the capability of applying to the accumulator (together with a selected word in storage) the actions of "inclusive OR," "exclusive OR," and "AND," as they are used in symbolic logic. For the moment, it is only the AND operation that concerns us. When the accumulator is ANDed with a word in storage, the result in the accumulator will be 1 bits for those bit positions that are 1 in both words. So when we AND the accumulator with our mask, which has only the low-order position 1 bit, the result will be 0 in the accumulator for an even number and 1 in the accumulator for an odd number.

10.  The flowchart of Figure 8.2 shows reference numbers 4, 5, and 6 simply to tie the code to the flowchart; those numbers are not needed for the logic of the flowchart itself.

## 8.3   Sorting

A subproblem that is common to many large problems is that of **sorting**. Exercises 85 and 87 (Chapter 4) were an approach to direct internal sorting schemes to apply to 3 or 4 words. Such schemes could perhaps be extended to more than 4 words, but generally we seek repetitive solutions to the sorting problem when there are 5–30 words to be sorted.

Let's take the simplest case first. We have a block of 21 words, addressed at B, B+1, B+2, . . . , B+20. These words contain numbers, and we want to rearrange the numbers to be in ascending order within the block.

One commonly used algorithm for this purpose is the interchange, or bubble, sort. Its logic is shown in the flowchart of Figure 8.4, and a program following that logic is given in Figure 8.5. We will want to explore the logic of the sorting procedure; new features of the assembly system that can be observed in the program; and the logic of the assembly process itself. First, the sorting scheme.

Since we are ordering 21 numbers, the process is a loop. The heart of the loop is at reference 2, where two adjacent numbers are compared. If they are in descending order, then they are interchanged. The process is initialized to the first 2 words of block B, and a word, T, is set to 0. If, at any time during the sort, two numbers need to be interchanged, T is set to 1. The second diamond tests for the end of a sweep over the entire block. If we have not compared all pairs of consecutive words, we modify the addresses X and Y to move to the next pair, and we return to the comparison block. When we have compared all pairs of consecutive words, we go on to test the word T. If it is still 0, then all numbers in the block have been certified as being in ascending order, and the sort is completed. If T is not 0, then the entire process is repeated. We can observe some points:

1.  During the sorting process, large numbers will move to the right, and

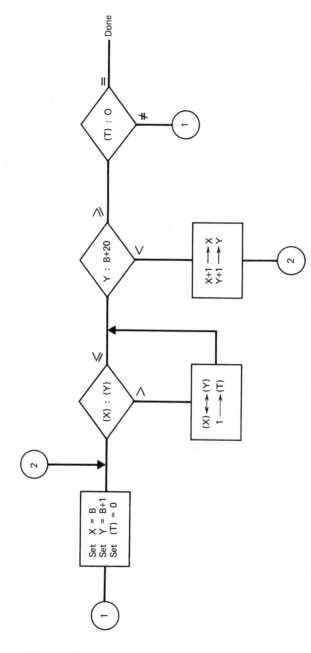

FIGURE 8.4  Interchange sorting. The block of words addressed at B through B+20 is to be sorted in ascending order.

```
                                  *
                                  *    BUBBLE  SORTING
                                  *
   004000    006010     REF1   ,LDAI    ,(B)
   004001    004057  R
   004002    054046           ,STA     ,X
   004003    006010           ,LDAI    ,(B+1)
   004004    004060  R
   004005    054044           ,STA     ,Y
   004006    014046           ,LDA     ,ZERO
   004007    054043           ,STA     ,T
   004010    017200  I  REF2   ,LDA*    ,X
   004011    147201  I         ,SUB*    ,Y
   004012    001004           ,JAN     ,REF3
   004013    004026  R
   004014    001010           ,JAZ     ,REF3
   004015    004026  R
   004016    017200  I         ,LDA*    ,X
   004017    054034           ,STA     ,TEMP
   004020    017201  I         ,LDA*    ,Y
   004021    057200  I         ,STA*    ,X
   004022    014031           ,LDA     ,TEMP
   004023    057201  I         ,STA*    ,Y
   004024    014031           ,LDA     ,ONE
   004025    054025           ,STA     ,T
   004026    014023     REF3   ,LDA     ,Y
   004027    006140           ,SUBI    ,(B+20)
   004030    004103  R
   004031    001002           ,JAP     ,REF4
   004032    004043  R
   004033    014015           ,LDA     ,X
   004034    124021           ,ADD     ,ONE
   004035    054013           ,STA     ,X
   004036    014013           ,LDA     ,Y
   004037    124016           ,ADD     ,ONE
   004040    054011           ,STA     ,Y
   004041    001000           ,JMP     ,REF2
   004042    004010  R
   004043    014007     REF4   ,LDA     ,T
   004044    001010           ,JAZ     ,REF5
   004045    004050  R
   004046    001000           ,JMP     ,REF1
   004047    004000  R
   004050    000000     REF5   ,HLT     ,
   004051    000000     X      ,DATA    ,0
   004052    000000     Y      ,DATA    ,0
   004053    000000     T      ,DATA    ,0
   004054    000000     TEMP   ,DATA    ,0
   004055    000000     ZERO   ,DATA    ,0
   004056    000001     ONE    ,DATA    ,1
   004057               B      ,BSS     ,21
             004000  R         ,END     ,REF1
```

LITERALS

POINTERS
   000200    104051

FIGURE 8.5   Code for the interchange sort.

```
PAGE        000002
       000201   104052

SYMBOLS

1   004057  R   B
1   004056  R   ONE
1   004055  R   ZERO
1   004054  R   TEMP
1   004053  R   T
1   004052  R   Y
1   004051  R   X
1   004050  R   REF5
1   004043  R   REF4
1   004026  R   REF3
1   004010  R   REF2
1   004000  R   REF1
```

**FIGURE 8.5** (Continued)

small numbers will move to the left; hence the process is frequently referred to as bubble sorting.

2. As with other loops, the variables X and Y are dummy variables, used on the flowchart mainly as a matter of notation. The words have addresses in block B, but these addresses vary. The pair being worked on at any given moment is called X and Y.

3. The word T is a trigger. It takes on only the values 0 and 1. Its function could be performed by 1 bit position in storage.

4. If the numbers in block B are already in ascending order when the process begins, then there will be only one sweep over the data, and the entire procedure amounts to a sequence check. On the other hand, if the data is in descending order to begin with, then there will be (in our example) a large number of comparisons and interchanges, $21 \times 20/2 = 210$, to be exact. Thus, the interchange scheme for sorting will be very inefficient as the number of things to be sorted gets large and/or the starting order of the things to be sorted approaches the exact reverse of the order we seek.

5. The example used a block of 21 words, and sorted the contents of those words. In theory, the procedure will work on a block of any size. Moreover, we could use it to sort whole **records** (that is, groups of related words), for which the sort is performed on some **key** in each record, but the entire records are moved in storage. For example, suppose we have 3 word records in which the 3 words show year, month, and day for a set of dates. If we wish to sort these records into ascending order by months, then the key for the sort would be the middle word of each record, but if an interchange is called for, the entire record must be moved.

6. The scheme in Figure 8.4 is shown for ascending order. To sort in descending order, the exits from the comparison diamond must be interchanged.

7. Bubble sorting is an inefficient, upsophisticated, crude algorithm. Its virtue is that it is the easiest algorithm to program. Thus, its use is justified when the number of things to sort is small, or when the programmer feels that the waste of machine time compensates for possible waste of **his** time in programming some more efficient scheme.

## 8.4 Comments on the Code

See Figure 8.5. It is worthwhile to study a completed assembly to gain insight into how the process works.

The heart of the loop is at REF2, where two successive words are compared. The two instructions at locations 4010 and 4011 have addresses X and Y, but these are referred to with second-level addressing (indicated by the asterisks). The address modification for the loop is done **on** the values of X and Y (see locations 04033–04040). The value of X must be initialized to the first address in block B, which is B itself. This is done by the first two instructions of the routine, which are quite tricky to follow. Stick with it. The first instruction has the op-code LOAD ACCUMULATOR, which should be clear by now. Its address portion specifies the **address** of B, indicated by the parentheses around B. Moreover, the op-code specifies "immediate." The directions to the assembler, then, are: "create an instruction, using zero-level addressing, whose address portion will be the address of word B."

When that instruction is executed, the accumulator will hold the address of B, which is to be put into word X. The second instruction does this. Its op-code is 05 (for STORE A) and its address portion specifies word X by using relative addressing; that is, word X is 46 (octal, of course) words downstream from this instruction.

Let us repeat: Any time you spend studying such a listing will be worth it. Be sure you can follow the logic of the second instruction at REF3, for example. It is SUBTRACT IMMEDIATE, for which the op-code is 006140, and the address (contained in word 004030) is 004103, which is correct for the address of B+20.

Your reaction to such study could properly be "I can just barely follow what is going on here, but I will never be able to learn how to do such things." That reaction is quite normal. You had the same reaction to learning how to tie your shoelaces, or to learning how to ride a bicycle, or any other skill that you now do with ease. You learn by doing, and eventually such things become easy. The person who wrote the code you are examining wasn't born with that skill; he learned it, and so can you. It **is** tricky, and requires great care (and later we will explore ways of making such things easier), but for now we want to provide insight into how things work at a level close to the machine itself. There is no substitute for acquiring this insight.

## 8.5  What the Assembler Does

Let us reiterate that the purpose of all computer languages is to get to machine language. Assembly language is one way to get to machine language, and perhaps the simplest way. The language of an assembler has these two characteristics:

1.  The format of an instruction will be the same as that of the machine language. Thus, an instruction in our computer has a location, op-code, indexing designation, and address portion. Each instruction written in assembly language has these same parts.

2.  As a result, assembly language tends to be 1:1 with machine language; that is, every instruction written in assembly language will translate into one machine instruction. There are exceptions to this, as noted below, but the 1:1 ratio is a good general description.

As we have noted, the use of assembly language costs us some machine time in order to effect the translation to machine language. Most people regard this as an excellent bargain, since it buys us many benefits:

1.  *Symbolic notation.* The freedom to name words in storage, either as addresses of data words or locations of instruction words, and to keep all the resulting cross-references straight is of vital help to humans in getting a program created and running.

2.  *Error analysis.* While performing all the cross-referencing and translating of our symbols, the assembly program cannot avoid catching all our mechanical errors. Thus, if we use a nonexistent op-code (which isn't in the list of legal codes that is built into the assembler), we will be informed of that fact, and execution of our program will be inhibited, as it should be. Similarly, if we refer to a symbol that we have not properly defined (i.e., an undefined symbol) or if we attempt to define a symbol more than once (i.e., an ambiguous symbol), the assembler will promptly pinpoint the errors. Figure 8.6 shows examples of such bugs caught by the assembler. Notice that all such errors are mechanical in nature, not logical. If we write SUB when we mean ADD, the assembler cannot know that we are logically wrong — and errors of this type will **not** be caught by any language.

3.  *Storage overflow.* If our instructions and data exceed the capacity of storage, the assembler will report this fact.

4.  *Pseudo-ops.* The assembler can offer more op-codes than exist in the machine language. Some of these are directions to the assembler itself, as in the use of ORG, for example. The pseudo-op OPSY lets us create our own mnemonics if we wish, as in these two instructions:

```
CLA     OPSY    LDA
RA      OPSY    LDA
```

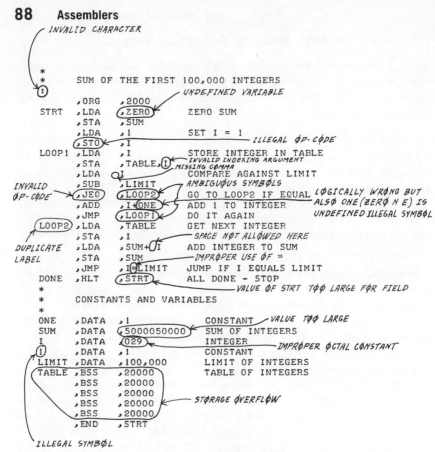

**FIGURE 8.6** A bugged code.

which would let us use three mnemonic op-codes, LDA (load accumulator), CLA (clear and add), and RA (reset add), synonymously.

Pseudo-ops can also be created in the assembly system for new op-codes. For example, we have available JAP (Jump if A register Positive), JAN (Jump if A register Negative), and JAZ (Jump if A register Zero). It might be handy in our work to have also JANZ (Jump if A register NonZero) and JAG (Jump if A register Greater than zero). It would be simple to add those op-codes to the assembler's repertoire (note that the DAS 8A assembler doesn't do this), so that when they are met during the assembly process, a string of legal machine operations could be inserted in our program to yield the desired effect.

5. *Number base conversion.* The short routines for decimal-to-binary and binary-to-decimal conversion are part of every assembler.

6. *Relative addressing.* There is a form of machine addressing (described in Chapter 6) that is relative to the value of the location of its own instruction. In an assembly system, we have another form of relative addressing:

$$
\begin{array}{ll}
\text{LDA} & \text{T+8} \\
\text{ADD} & \text{BOB}-3 \\
\text{STA} & \text{AMY+JIM}
\end{array}
$$

All symbols used in the addresses of these instructions have numeric values, and hence the assembler can perform the simple arithmetic shown.

7. *Symbolic listing.* The output of the translation phase of an assembly pass is a machine language code ready for execution. If the computer is geared to Teletype and paper tape input/output, then the output will be a paper tape of **object code,** ready for reloading prior to execution. A by-product of this process is a printed listing (as in Figure 8.5), showing the **source code** (that is, the symbolic code as written by the programmer) side-by-side with the translated object code. This listing, together with the flowcharts of the solution, constitutes an essential part of the **documentation** of the solution.

An assembler should report back to the programmer all the mechanical bugs that it can detect while it attempts to translate his symbolic code into machine language. Figure 8.6 shows a code that is full of such bugs and Figure 8.7 shows the resulting symbolic listing, with coded error messages along the left margin. These are results obtained from the Varian DAS 8A assembler. They will be different for other mini computers; indeed, they will be different for other versions of DAS.

The way to learn computing is to compute. In the exercises at the end of this chapter are some problems that lend themselves to solution in assembly language. Before going on to more advanced concepts and languages, you should select and run at least one of these problems.

See Figure 8.6. The bugs that have been inserted in the (meaningless) program were chosen to represent typical mistakes that people make in writing assembly language code. The DAS 8A assembly program for the Varian 620, like all assemblers, requires certain conventions, such as the comma before each instruction address (but it should be noted that later versions of this assembler relaxed that particular convention). In the assembly language shown in Figure 8.6, all symbols are restricted to four characters; thus, although the programmer may use LOOP1 and LOOP2 as location names if he chooses, they would be taken as the same symbol by the assembler, and hence be ambiguous. As with almost everything else in computing, the way to become familiar with such local rules is to use them.

```
                        *
                        *      SUM OF THE FIRST 100,000 INTEGERS
                        :
*OP
  003720                        ,ORG    ,2000
  003720   010000      STRT    ,LDA    ,ZERO         ZERO SUM
*SY
  003721   053746              ,STA    ,SUM
  003722   010001              ,LDA    ,1            SET I = 1
                              ,STO    ,I
*OP
  003725   013747      LOOP1   ,LDA    ,I            STORE INTEGER IN TABLE
*DD
  003726   003753              ,STA    ,TABLE,I
*AD
  003727   010000 R            ,LDA    I             COMPARE AGAINST LIMIT
*VF
  003730   143751              ,SUB    ,LIMIT
                              ,JEQ    ,LOOP2        GO TO LOOP2 IF EQUAL
*OP
  003733   123747              ,ADD    ,I+ONE        ADD 1 TO INTEGER
*AD
  003734   001000              ,JMP    ,LOOP1        DO IT AGAIN
  003735   003725 R
  003736   013753      LOOP2   ,LDA    ,TABLE        GET NEXT INTEGER
*DD
  003737   053747              ,STA    ,I
  003740   013746              ,LDA    ,SUM+ I       ADD INTEGER TO SUM
  003741   053746              ,STA    ,SUM
  003742   001000              ,JMP    ,I=LIMIT      JUMP IF I EQUALS LIMIT
*EX
  003743   001077
  003744   003720      DONE    ,HLT    ,STRT         ALL DONE - STOP
*SZ
                        *
                        *      CONSTANTS AND VARIABLES
                        *
  003745   000001      ONE     ,DATA   ,1            CONSTANT
  003746   132520      SUM     ,DATA   ,5000050000   SUM OF INTEGERS
*SZ
  003747   000035      I       ,DATA   ,029          INTEGER
*DC
  003750   000001      1       ,DATA   ,1            CONSTANT
  003751   000144      LIMIT   ,DATA   ,100,000      LIMIT OF INTEGERS
  003752   000000
  003753               TABLE   ,BSS    ,20000        TABLE OF INTEGERS
  053013                       ,BSS    ,20000
  122053                       ,BSS    ,20000
  171113                       ,BSS    ,20000
  040153                       ,BSS    ,20000
            003720 R           ,END    ,STRT

LITERALS

POINTERS
```

**FIGURE 8.7   DAS 8A listing of Figure 8.6.**

```
SYMBOLS

1   003753  R   TABL



PAGE      000002

1   003751  R   LIMI
1   003747  R   I
1   003746  R   SUM
0   003745  R   ONE
0   003744  R   DONE
1   003725  R   LOOP
1   003720  R   STRT
0   004000  R   :
```

**FIGURE 8.7** (Continued)

# EXERCISES

**160.** A block of 1000 words in storage is addressed at G, G+1, G+2, . . . , G+999. We want to tally, in five counters, how many of these 1000 numbers are (a) zero; (b) positive and nonzero; (c) even; (d) greater than +100; (e) negative and odd. Draw a flowchart for this logic.

**165.** If the solution logic of the flowchart for Exercise 160 is correct and a program is written, assembled, and debugged to follow that logic, how will we go about testing the program to ensure that it works correctly and will continue to do so regardless of the data? For this purpose, we can create our own test data to fill the G block, and we can (and must) predict what those five counters will contain when the program operates on that data. This may be your first try at program testing, which will concern us more in Chapter 16. Suppose, for this problem, we generated the numbers from −500 to +499 in the G block, which is easily done with a loop−could you predict the contents of the five counters? Would that procedure constitute a complete and valid test of the program?

**170.** A block of storage of 500 words is to have its contents cleared to 0. The block is addressed at M, M+1, M+2, . . . , M+499. Draw a flowchart.

**171.** The flowchart of Exercise 170 can be expanded to call for clearing **all** of core storage. Would it be possible to write a program to do that?

**175.** Write a routine in assembly language for the problem of Exercise 170.

**180.** In Section 8.3 we saw the use of a trigger, and it was noted that a trigger need be only a single bit position in storage. We could thus have 16 triggers in one computer word, or in 20 words we could have 320 triggers. In a given problem solution, suppose that we have assigned 320 consecutive bits as triggers and during the course of the solution each of them is set to either 0 or 1. We now want to count how many of the triggers are "on"; that is, how many 1 bits there are in 20 consecutive words.

We will need two loops—an inner loop to count the 1 bits within a single word, and an outer loop (for which the entire inner loop is the DO block) to cycle through the 20 words.

Recognition of single bits in the computer is limited to these cases:

(a) The leftmost bit in the accumulator can be tested by a JUMP A NEG-ATIVE command.

(b) The rightmost bit in the accumulator can be tested by any scheme that will determine the odd–even nature of the contents. We could, for example, divide by 2 and test the remainder for 0 or 1.

(c) All bit positions in the accumulator can be tested for 0 by a JUMP A ZERO command.†

One possibility for the inner loop, then, is an odd–even test on the accumulator, followed by shift commands to move the other bit positions to the right successively so that the odd–even tests can be repeated. On the Varian 620, the LSRA command will do nicely.

Your task, however, is to flowchart the logic of the bit counting problem. You need not (and should not) concern yourself about coding details while you are drawing the flowchart.

This exercise may be difficult. Make an attempt at a good flowchart before examining one possible solution in Appendix 3. Assume that the 20 words are addressed at A, A+1, . . . , A+19.

**185.** The thirteenth of the month falls on Friday more often than on any other day of the week. Exercise 140 (Chapter 6) suggested the construction of a counting device to simulate a calendar. Write a program to construct the simulated calendar, and arrange to run it for 400 years (our current calendar repeats precisely every 400 years), counting the number of times the thirteenth of the month falls on Sunday, Monday, . . . , Saturday, and thus demonstrate that the first sentence in this exercise is true.

**190.** The integer 153 has the curious property that the sum of the cubes of its digits (that is, $1 + 125 + 27$) equals the number itself. There are three other nonzero integers with this property. Draw a flowchart for the logic of finding them (the four numbers are all less than 1000).

If you wish to code and run this problem, you must recognize that the

---

† Of course, as we saw earlier, any bit position in a word can be isolated by an appropriate mask combined with an AND operation, after which the value of that position can be tested by a JUMP A ZERO command.

problem is intrinsically decimal and we are using a binary machine. We must either (a) program our machine to function in decimal mode or (b) devise a method for extracting decimal digits from a binary number.

For alternative a, we might arrange a decimal counting scheme, using three words in storage called H, T, and U (for hundreds, tens, and units). Each word can operate like a decimal counting wheel; when the counter increases from 9 to 0, the counter to its left increases by 1. The three numbers in H, T, and U are now the digits of numbers we wish to test for the desired property.

For alternative b, consider the number 153, which normally appears in storage as 10011001. If we divide it by $10)_{10} = 1010)_2$, the remainder will be the unit's digit of the original number; in this case, $011)_2 = 3)_{10}$. The quotient can again be divided by ten to extract the tens digit of the original number, and so on.

**195.**   A block of 960 words of storage is addressed at T, T+1, T+2, . . . , T+959. For each set of four consecutive words (and there are 240 such sets), we want to do the following:

(a)   Determine that each of four categories, A, B, C, and D, is present. These categories could be (for example) numbers between 0 and 9, numbers between 100 and 199, numbers between 1000 and 1999, and numbers greater than 5000. The exact nature is unimportant; it is only important that there be four types and that all four are present.

(b)   If the four types are present, they should be in the order A, B, C, and D. If they are present but not in that order, they should be put in that order.

(c)   If the four numbers in each set of four consecutive words are not the types A, B, C, and D, then the set number for those 4 words should be printed.

Draw a flowchart for this logic. This is a nontrivial problem.

**200.**   If we have in storage 4 words, M, K, C, and D, representing the month, day, century, and year for any date after 1752, then we can calculate the day of the week. For example, for June 25, 1972, we would have M = 6, K = 25, C = 19, and D = 72. We first alter M, C, and D as needed to make March the first month of the year, and January and February the eleventh and twelfth months of the preceding year. In our example, we need only change M to 4. Then the day of the week is given by

$$F = [2.6M - 0.2] + K + D + \left[\frac{D}{4}\right] + \left[\frac{C}{4}\right] - 2C$$

with F expressed modulo 7; that is, as the remainder on division by 7. In this equation (known as Zeller's congruence) Sunday is 0, Monday is 1, Tuesday is 2, . . . , Saturday is 6. In our example, we have

$$F = [2.6 \cdot 4 - 0.2] + 25 + 72 + \left[\frac{72}{4}\right] + \left[\frac{19}{4}\right] - 2 \cdot 19$$

where the square brackets denote "greatest integer in"; in other words, drop all fractions.

$$F = [10.4 - 0.2] + 25 + 72 + 18 + 4 - 38$$
$$F = 10 + 25 + 72 + 18 + 4 - 38 = 91$$

and 91 modulo 7 is 0, a Sunday.

Write a program in assembly language to calculate the day of the week for any valid values of M, K, C, and D. Here are some other test values:

| | |
|---|---|
| January 1, 1800 | Wednesday |
| December 7, 1941 | Sunday |
| November 11, 1991 | Monday |
| January 14, 1964 | Tuesday |

There is one more interesting test date. March 1, 1900 was a Thursday. If you insert 1, 1, 19, 0 (for M, K, C, and D, respectively) into Zeller's formula, you will wind up with a negative value for F. Add sufficient multiples of 7 (say, the number 70) before reducing F modulo 7.

**205.** The normal action of a computer for the instruction

                STA     Q

is to move the contents of the accumulator to word Q. We read-in to word Q, which destroys Q's previous contents (read-in is always destructive), and we read-out of the accumulator, which remains unchanged (readout is always nondestructive).

Suppose we want to alter this normal mode of operation, so that the act of storing a number will preserve the number previously stored. We want to store the contents of the accumulator at Q, but save what was in Q. As shown in part A of Figure 8.8, Q is now a small block of storage and contains at the moment the number 17. The accumulator contains 23. We want to produce the situation shown in part B; the 23 has been stored in block Q, but the whole block has been **pushed down** to preserve all previous numbers. Part C shows another application of the same idea, adding the number 5 to the push-down stack.

Draw a flowchart for the logic of pushing down the stack Q. All words in the block must be copied to the right one word. The contents of Q+9 will be lost. The process must proceed from right to left.

**210.** The logic of the push-down list (Exercise 205) has the rightmost element of the list moved off the list. Draw a flowchart for circular shifting of a list; that is, in which each word in the stack moves to the right, but the rightmost word moves to the first position on the list. We are not adding a new word to the list; we are only rotating the elements.

| A | 17 | 0 | 0 | 0 | 0 | 0 | 0 | 0 | 0 | 0 |
|---|----|---|---|---|---|---|---|---|---|---|
|   | Q | Q+1 | Q+2 | Q+3 | Q+4 | Q+5 | Q+6 | Q+7 | Q+8 | Q+9 |

| B | 23 | 17 | 0 | 0 | 0 | 0 | 0 | 0 | 0 | 0 |
|---|----|----|---|---|---|---|---|---|---|---|
|   | Q | Q+1 | Q+2 | Q+3 | Q+4 | Q+5 | Q+6 | Q+7 | Q+8 | Q+9 |

| C | 5 | 23 | 17 | 0 | 0 | 0 | 0 | 0 | 0 | 0 |
|---|---|----|----|---|---|---|---|---|---|---|
|   | Q | Q+1 | Q+2 | Q+3 | Q+4 | Q+5 | Q+6 | Q+7 | Q+8 | Q+9 |

FIGURE 8.8  A push-down stack.

**215.** The inverse operation to a push-down list (Exercise 205) is the operation "pop up," in which the leftmost word is removed from the stack and the remaining words all move to the left. Draw a flowchart for this logic.

**220.** Given as input to a computer a series of numbers, each of which can be contained in one computer word, we wish to print out this series of numbers, together with their first, second, and third differences. Figure 8.9 shows the sort of output to be created. Draw a flowchart for this logic. Devise a procedure for testing this logic, given a debugged program that follows your flowchart.

This is an important exercise. As a matter of fact, it was the first problem ever suggested for automatic computation. Even if you do not develop your own flowchart, be sure to study the one shown in Appendix 3.

**222.** One hundred words in storage represent a 10 × 10 array. We wish to process the numbers in the array, replacing each number by the average of the numbers surrounding it. For each of the 81 numbers in the center of the

| INPUT DATA | FIRST DIFFERENCE | SECOND DIFFERENCE | THIRD DIFFERENCE |
|---|---|---|---|
| 123 | | | |
| − 17 | −140 | | |
| − 58 | − 41 | + 99 | |
| 100 | +158 | + 199 | + 100 |
| 0 | −100 | − 258 | − 457 |
| 12 | + 12 | + 112 | + 370 |
| 563 | + 551 | + 539 | + 427 |
| 87 | − 476 | −1027 | −1566 |

FIGURE 8.9  Differencing.

array, there are 8 numbers surrounding it; the number in question is to be replaced by 1/8 of the sum of those 8. The corner numbers each have 3 numbers to be averaged. The remaining border numbers each have 5 numbers to be averaged.

Let the 100 numbers be addressed at B, B+1, B+2, . . . , B+99. The corner words are then B, B+9, B+90, and B+99. The border words are B+1 through B+8; B+91 through B+98; and B+10, B+20, B+30, . . . , B+80; B+19, B+29, B+39, . . . , B+89. For a typical central word, such as B+46, the surrounding words are B+35, B+36, B+37, B+45, B+47, B+55, B+56, and B+57.

Draw a flowchart for the logic of this problem.

Consider now how much easier this problem would be if the border words were not exceptional. Think of the $10 \times 10$ array as embedded inside a $12 \times 12$ array, with the new border words all 0 or some fixed value; only the center $10 \times 10$ words need have the averaging process applied to them. The results will be different, of course.

The process originally described may be repeated many times. If the numbers in the array represent temperatures across a metal plate, then after many applications of the averaging process we will achieve an approximation to the steady-state condition in a heat-transfer situation. The numbers in the dummy border can be fixed at some predicted steady-state (for example, room temperature, where the center of the plate is a source of heat); the final results will not then be in serious error.

# 9

# SUBROUTINE PACKAGES

## 9.1 Removing the Word Size Barrier

An assembly system (the assembly language and its associated translating program) is the simplest device to lower the language barrier that lies between humans and the binary codes of machine language.

The next barrier to consider is the word size of the machine. With a 16 bit word, we are restricted to the range ±32,767 in normal machine language, and that is hardly adequate for most problems. Figure 9.1 shows how we can relax that constraint. If we let two adjacent words in storage, $A_1$ and $A_2$, represent one number, then we can operate with numbers that are twice as large. "Twice as large" may be 30 or 31 bits, depending on how the logic of this **double-precision** arithmetic is implemented. By tying 2 words together, we have 32 bits to play with. One bit, as usual, is needed for the sign. The question is, "What should we do with the sign position of the low-order word of each pair?" In the logic shown on the flowchart, that bit position is sacrificed, so that our 2 word numbers are limited to 30 bits of precision. We can then function within the range ±1,073,741,823.

A tight code for this logic is shown in Figure 9.1 as an **open** subroutine; that is, a subroutine that can be inserted in-line into a program. It can, of course, be made into a closed subroutine; that is, one that is linked to.

The details of such coding are not important, since the subroutine library

**97**

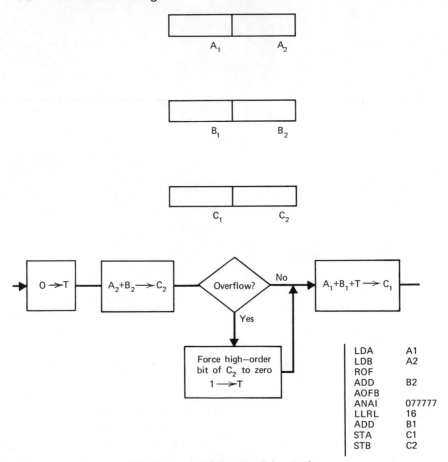

**FIGURE 9.1** Double-precision logic.

of the machine includes **packaged** subroutines for double-precision add, subtract, multiply, and divide. These subroutines can be extracted from the subroutine library, inserted into a program, and called on demand. For all practical purposes, the operation code list of the machine has been extended then to include double-precision arithmetic commands.

There is no reason why this procedure should be restricted to 2 word logic. We can similarly tie 3 words or more together to hold one number, and extend the capability of the machine to 45, 60, 75, or any number of bits of precision. If subroutines are not immediately available, they will have to be written. In theory, then, the word size barrier has been removed. Any machine can perform arithmetic to any degree of precision, subject only to the limitations due to storage capacity.

## 9.2   Using Multiple-Precision Arithmetic

Consider the problem given in Section 8.2 and Figure 8.2. For any even number, X, in storage, we can always form X/2. For an odd value of X, however, we rapidly reach a point at which 3X+1 will exceed the capacity of one word, at which point we will need double or triple precision. If the 3X+1 problem is to be run for values of N greater than about 5000, multiple-precision routines will be needed for X, at least.

Notice that we are still restricted to using only integers, albeit now integers of almost any size. Our programs will contain many linkages to subroutines, which makes for awkward coding, but we can remove that restriction, too (in Chapter 11).

## 9.3   Modular Arithmetic

Any physical counting device has an upper limit. Most devices, upon reaching this limit, then roll back to 0 and begin again. The mileage counter on a car is a fine example. In technical terms, the odometer counts miles modulo 100000. After reaching 99999 (its limit), it rolls to 00000 and repeats.

We are used to many such counting schemes. We count days of the week by sevens, for example, and then start over. The minute hand on a clock counts by 60s; we seldom refer to 137 minutes past the hour. We count months by 12s, and sheets of paper by 500s. So it goes. All such schemes use modular arithmetic; that is, arithmetic that has some modulus as a limit. In a 16 bit computer word, with 1 bit devoted to the sign, we are dealing with an arithmetic system with a modulus of 32768.

To illustrate modular arithmetic, let us develop tables of powers of 2 with various moduli, as shown in Figure 9.2. In the first column, the modulus is 19. In such a system of arithmetic, all integers are reduced to the range 0–18. The first four terms are normal (2,4,8,16). The next term is 13; that is 2 × 16 reduced modulo 19. In technical terms,

$$32 \equiv 13 \bmod 19$$

which can be read as "32 yields a remainder of 13 on division by 19." Be sure you see how all the figures in all three columns are derived. Try the same procedure for yourself, using moduli of 31, 41, and 59. In the latter case, you will develop 58 terms before the series repeats. The flowchart logic of what you are doing is simple, as shown in Figure 9.3. All the moduli used have been prime numbers, so the diamond on the flowchart has only the labels for "greater than" and "less than," since there can be no equals case.

You probably noticed that some moduli seem to yield much longer strings

| mod 19 | mod 23 | mod 29 |
|---|---|---|
| 2 | 2 | 2 |
| 4 | 4 | 4 |
| 8 | 8 | 8 |
| 16 | 16 | 16 |
| 13 | 9 | 3 |
| 7 | 18 | 6 |
| 14 | 13 | 12 |
| 9 | 3 | 24 |
| 18 | 6 | 19 |
| 17 | 12 | 9 |
| 15 | 1 | 18 |
| 11 | | 7 |
| 3 | | 14 |
| 6 | | 28 |
| 12 | | 27 |
| 5 | | 25 |
| 10 | | 21 |
| 1 | | 13 |
| | | 26 |
| | | 23 |
| | | 17 |
| | | 5 |
| | | 10 |
| | | 20 |
| | | 11 |
| | | 22 |
| | | 15 |
| | | 1 |

FIGURE 9.2 Powers of 2, with several moduli.

of numbers than others. One might expect that a larger modulus would always lead to a longer string of numbers, but this is not so. The modulus 29 produces a string of 28 numbers, which consists of every possibility. Try the same thing for the modulus 127—the string is quite short. Some prime moduli lead to full-size strings, and some do not.

When the string is full-sized, as with 59, the logic of Figure 9.3 provides a means of scrambling a series of integers. What we are doing can be expressed in the form of a **recursion**:

$$X_{n+1} = 2 X_n \bmod P \tag{1}$$

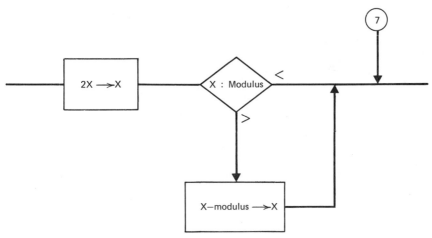

**FIGURE 9.3 Powers of 2 in modular arithmetic.**

which is a special case of

$$X_{n+1} = M X_n \bmod P \tag{2}$$

The latter is widely used as a scheme for generating what are known as pseudo-random numbers. We choose to use the multiplier 2 for its ease in coding.

## 9.4 Random Numbers

The scheme in (1) above, using a sufficiently large modulus, would serve as a crude generator of numbers that might be called random in the sense of being somewhat unpredictable. However, examination of the results for P = 29 in Figure 9.2 reveals that the scheme is weak. When the number generated is small, it is followed by a series of small numbers. Similarly, when the number generated is large (e.g., 28 for a modulus of 29), then subsequent numbers will also be close to the modulus. This effect gets worse as the modulus gets bigger.

The scheme shown in Figure 9.4 provides a workable random number generator (RNG). We use the idea of (1) to form three independent generators, using the moduli shown on the flowchart (they are primes that will give the maximum possible cycle length; for example, the modulus 16381 produces 16380 numbers before repeating). The results of the three independent generators are added into a word called S. This would normally cause overflow, so we arrange to force 0s into the leftmost positions of S just before returning from the subroutine.

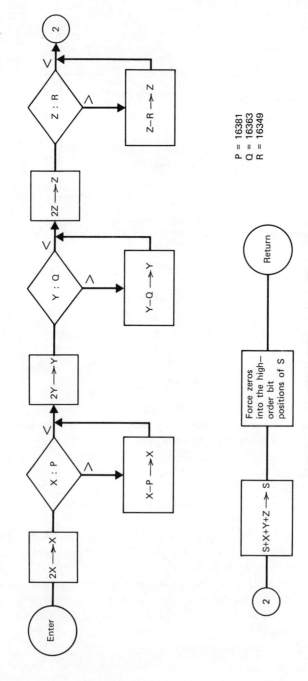

P = 16381
Q = 16363
R = 16349

**FIGURE 9.4  A workable random number generator.**

The starting values for X, Y, Z, and S can be any nonzero positive numbers. If the values of X, Y, Z, and S are the same as they were the last time the subroutine was used, then the subroutine will yield the same series of numbers again. If the values of those variables are changed, then the subroutine will furnish new numbers. The cycle length of the entire subroutine is long; it will furnish billions of numbers before the sequence repeats.

A code for this subroutine is given in Appendix 5. In that code, the two high-order positions of S have been made 0. You may wish to alter the subroutine to blank out more positions.

## 9.5  Validating the RNG

We have stressed several times that every computer program should be tested before it is committed to production. This admonition applies with particular force to packaged programs that are handed to you. *No matter how earnestly and sincerely the author of the package tells you how well it functions, it is always prudent to test it yourself.* The RNG described in Section 9.4 is just such a package. Before you use it in any important program, you should test it to verify, to your satisfaction, that it delivers numbers that meet your needs.

First, arrange to call the subroutine a few hundred times and print the output. As given in Appendix 5, the subroutine purports to generate numbers in the range 0–16383 at random. Every number in this range should have an equal chance of appearing, and the order in which they appear should seem unpredictable.

The generator generates random **numbers.** If we need random **digits,** we can obtain them from the numbers in various ways. We could, for example, divide an output number by 10 and use the remainder of the division; this would extract the unit's digit from each number. Generated digits should be evenly distributed; that is, each of the digits from 0 to 9 should appear about 10% of the time.

(The procedure just described will work nicely with the generator of Figure 9.4, but not with many other generators. A generator built to produce random numbers may be a poor source of random digits, and particularly for digits extracted at the low-order end of the numbers. But then, we just finished telling you never to use any packaged routine—or any part of any packaged routine—without testing it for yourself.)

There are eight standard tests that can be applied to the output of an RNG. They deal with the theoretical aspects of the subject. (See, for example, the article by Hull and Dobell listed in the Bibliography at the end of this chapter.) In day-to-day work, it is more fruitful to devise new tests that relate to the work at hand. Suppose, for example, that you wish to use random numbers to simulate the toss of two dice. A cubical die is itself an

RNG whose output is the numbers 1–6 at random. We can simulate a die by taking the output of our RNG, dividing by 6, and adding 1 to the remainder of the division. We can simulate a second die by repeating this process. Then the simulation of the toss of two dice is the sum of the two results (which is **not** the same as generating a random number in the range 2–12). Now, if dice tossing is what we want to do, then we should test **that** procedure; that is, we should make a computer run solely to verify that, say, 3600 dice tosses conform closely to the theoretical distribution, which is:

| Appearance of | This many times out of 3600 |
|:---:|:---:|
| 2 | 100 |
| 3 | 200 |
| 4 | 300 |
| 5 | 400 |
| 6 | 500 |
| 7 | 600 |
| 8 | 500 |
| 9 | 400 |
| 10 | 300 |
| 11 | 200 |
| 12 | 100 |

## 9.6   Using the RNG

Why do we want a source of unpredictable data? There are several broad areas in which a RNG subroutine is of interest.

1.   As a data generator. The RNG subroutine is a cheap source of data that can be used by other programs, particularly for test purposes. Suppose that you have written a program for interchange sorting (Section 8.3). To test the program, and to time it in order to compare it with other sorting techniques, we should run it on the following data:

(a)   Numbers already in sequence
(b)   Numbers that are completely out of sequence; that is, numbers in descending order
(c)   Random numbers

2.   For sampling. The RNG lets us select entries from a table at random. Suppose we have a table of numbers in storage, at addresses 12345–12450 (106 numbers). To select one of these numbers at random, we can do the following: Call the RNG. Reduce the output number modulo 106; that is, calculate the remainder on division by 106. This yields a number in the

range 0–105. Add that result to 12345. We now have an address between 12345 and 12450 taken at random.

Consider another example. For purposes of a research study, we wish to select two groups of 100 students each from the freshman class, which numbers 5438 students. There is a punched card for each student on file in the registrar's office. Using our RNG, we can generate random numbers that can be punched into the deck of cards, one number per card. Then the deck can be sorted on the random numbers, and our two random samples will consist of the first and second hundred cards of the sorted deck.

3.  For the Monte Carlo technique. A fairly large class of problems can be solved by a sampling procedure called Monte Carlo. Essentially, we turn the problem into a game, play the game, and count the results.

For example, picture 13 dice. If we toss them all at once, what is the chance that we will get all the numbers from 1 to 6 at least once? There are three ways we could solve that problem:

(a)  If we are adept at the rules and formulas of permutations, combinations, and probability, we could solve the problem analytically.

(b)  We could get 13 real dice and toss them a few thousand times and count the successes and failures.

(c)  We have seen how we can simulate a die, using random numbers. We can readily arrange to repeat that procedure 13 times. Then we can search the 13 dice to determine whether or not the numbers from 1 to 6 are each present, and tally in a counter if they are. Another counter can tally the number of tries. The ratio of those two counters, after, say, 10,000 tries, will give a fair approximation to the desired probability.

Procedure c is an example of a Monte Carlo solution to a problem. It is easier to perform than method b; it will proceed much faster; and it works better. The mathematical dice that we can create by programming function better than real dice, in the sense that they yield the numbers from 1 to 6 with equal probability and never wear out.

4.  As a subject of intrinsic interest. The two topics that have received the most attention in all the literature of computing are sorting and random number generators. The study of different ways of creating random numbers and testing the resulting output can be fascinating, and the computer is the only tool available for this research.

## 9.7  Other Packaged Programs

We have discussed two program packages. In Chapter 10 we will discuss what is probably the most widely used package; namely, subroutines for floating-point arithmetic.

Every machine type acquires a library of program packages that is made available to users. You may find packaged programs for analysis of variance, regression analysis, correlation, factor analysis, coordinate conversion, curve fitting, roots of equations, Bessel functions, Fourier analysis—the list goes on and on. By using programs written by someone else, you can save yourself endless work. But be sure to test any packaged program to assure yourself that it does what you want it to do.

It is worth repeating that the way to learn computing is to compute. Some of the exercises at the end of this chapter suggest modest projects that should now be within your capability.

## BIBLIOGRAPHY

Gruenberger, F. *Computing: An Introduction.* New York: Harcourt Brace Jovanovich, 1969, Chapter 18.

Hemmerle, W. J. "Generating Pseudorandom Numbers on a Two's Complement Machine such as the IBM 360," *Communications of the ACM* **12** (7) (July 1969). [The title is self-explanatory. This article has an extensive bibliography.]

Hull, T. E., and A. R. Dobell. "Random Number Generators," *SIAM Review* **4**, 230 (1962).

Juncosa, M. L. *Random Number Generation on the BRL High-Speed Computing Machines.* BRL Report 855, Aberdeen Proving Ground, Maryland.

Moshman, J. "Generation of Pseudo-Random Numbers on a Decimal Calculator," *Journal of the ACM* **1**, 88 (1954).

Payne, W. P., J. R. Rabung, and T. P. Bogyo. "Coding the Lehmer Pseudo-Random Number Generator," *Communications of the ACM* **12** (2) (February 1969). [This article includes a code for a workable Fortran subroutine. The authors claim that it will generate 2 million numbers per minute on a System 360/67 and that the low-order digits of the output will test properly for randomness. This article has an extensive bibliography.]

## EXERCISES

**225.** In double precision, we can deal directly with integers in the range 0 to $\pm 1,073,741,823$ (the latter figure being $2^{30} - 1$). The square root of any positive number in this range will be a number in the range from 0 to 32,767. The flowchart of Figure 9.5 shows an algorithm for finding the square root of a number stored at N. It is not an efficient algorithm, but it is easy to code and it does not involve division; the average called for can be effected by adding LOW and HIGH and shifting the sum one bit position to the right. The final result is stored at SR.

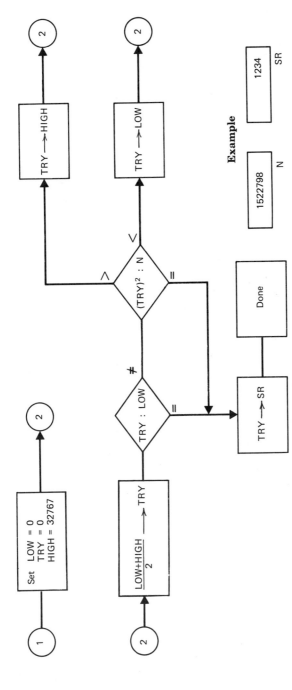

FIGURE 9.5  A scheme to find the square root of N. All numbers are in multiple-precision arithmetic.

Write a program for this square rooting scheme, using packaged (or self-written) double-precision subroutines. Devise a procedure to convince yourself that your program works properly.

**230.** The sequence of Fibonacci is the series of numbers 1,1,2,3, 5,8,13,21, . . . , in which each subsequent term is formed by adding the two previous terms. In ordinary machine language we could develop this sequence for 23 terms, at which point we would overflow the capacity of one 16 bit word. How many terms could we calculate using double precision? (The terms increase in size by one decimal digit about every 5 terms; they increase in size by 1 bit about every 1½ terms.) If we wished to calculate the first 100 terms of the sequence, how much precision would we need?

**235.** In the Fibonacci sequence (Exercise 230), the units digit of the terms repeats every 60 terms. The low-order 2 digits repeat every 300 terms. Problem: What is the cycle length for the low-order 3 digits? Is the computer the proper tool to use to solve this problem?

**240.** Factorial N is defined as

$$N! = N(N-1)(N-2) \cdots (3)(2)(1)$$

Thus, $1! = 1$; $2! = 2$; $3! = 6$, and so on. In single-precision arithmetic (that is, normal machine language), we can calculate this function up to $7! = 5040$. In double-precision arithmetic, how far can we calculate a table of factorials? [NOTE: Tables of exact factorials have been calculated up to factorial 1500, which has 4115 digits.]

**245.** Our packaged RNG delivers numbers in the range 0–16,383, uniformly distributed in this range. Indicate how you would operate on the output of the RNG to deliver random numbers with these characteristics:

   (a)   In the range 167–385.

   (b)   In the range 167–385 **and** 1280–1319 (with all 259 numbers having an equal chance of appearing).

   (c)   As 4 digit numbers which, with a decimal point assumed at the left end, are uniformly distributed in the range 0–1.

   (d)   The output from c will be a flat distribution in the range 0–1. If we wish a series of random numbers to be drawn from a population with a mean of M and a standard deviation of S, we can do the following:

$$X = M + (X_1 + X_2 + X_3 + \cdots + X_{12} - 6) \cdot S$$

where $X_1$, $X_2$, . . . , $X_{12}$ are twelve successive random numbers calculated as in c above. Flowchart and code this logic. Set $M = 17$ and $S = 3$, and arrange to select 1000 numbers of type X. Calculate the mean and standard deviation of these 1000 numbers, using the formulas

$$M = \frac{\Sigma X}{1000}$$

and

$$S = \sqrt{\frac{1000 \, \Sigma X^2 - (\Sigma X)^2}{1000^2}}$$

where $\Sigma X^2$ is the sum of the squares of the Xs and $\Sigma X$ is the sum of the Xs.

**250.** Flowchart, code, and run the 13 dice problem described in Section 9.6.

**255.** A man carries two books of 30 matches in his pocket. Whenever he uses a match, he picks a book from his pocket at random. When one book is exhausted, how many matches are left in the other book?

The answer to this problem is not a number; it is a **distribution.** Two numbers are initialized to 30 for each of many runs. One number is selected at random to be decremented (call RNG; let the odd–even nature of the called number dictate which of the two numbers to pick). When one number reaches 0, the value of the other number is the result for that run. Make 1000 such runs and enter the results in a table in storage. The table will be 30 words long. If the table is defined by

```
T     BSS     30
C     DATA    T−1
```

the constant C gives the address of the **dogear** of the table; that is, the address of the word that is just off the table. Then for a result of, say, 7, the word at dogear + 7 is to have its contents increased by 1.

Before you commit computer time to 1000 runs of this game, give some thought to what you expect to happen. During the debugging stages of the problem, have your program make 10 runs, rather than 1000. What do you expect the final distribution to look like?

**260.** Figure 9.6 shows a chess board. A knight is placed on square 33, marked X. The knight can move to any of the squares marked 1. From any of these 8 squares, the knight can make 8 moves, and 8 of these 64 will carry it off the board. Moving at random, starting at square 33, how many moves will the knight make before going off the board? Again, the answer to this question is not a number, but a distribution. The numbering scheme suggested for the board will be handy.

The chessboard situation resembles problems in nuclear physics, in which the so-called "random walk" of atomic particles is simulated in a computer.

**265.** Suppose that one decimal digit is extracted from a random number. One of the standard tests of randomness concerns random digits. Given a

|   | 0 | 1 | 2 | 3 | 4 | 5 | 6 | 7 |
|---|---|---|---|---|---|---|---|---|
| 0 |   |   |   |   |   |   |   |   |
| 1 |   |   | 1 |   | 1 |   |   |   |
| 2 |   | 1 |   |   | 1 |   |   |   |
| 3 |   |   | X |   |   |   |   |   |
| 4 |   | 1 |   |   | 1 |   |   |   |
| 5 |   |   | 1 | 1 |   |   |   |   |
| 6 |   |   |   |   |   |   |   |   |
| 7 |   |   |   |   |   |   |   |   |

FIGURE 9.6  The Knight's random walk.

long stream of such digits, how many must be generated to accumulate a complete set of the digits 0–9? Consider, for example, the digits in the number pi:

3141592653589793238462643383279502884197169399375 10 . . .

The first complete set occurs in 33 digits; starting at that point, the next complete set occurs in 18 digits, and so on. The smallest possible set would take 10 digits; the most probable number for a set is 24. The probabilities for every set size from 10 to 75 are known to 35 digit precision.†

Write a program to generate a stream of random digits and count the lengths of the successive sets that contain all digits; form a distribution of these results. Set up a table in storage for all set lengths from 10 to 75, plus one more word for the counts of sets of length 76 or greater. During debugging and testing of your program, count a dozen or so sets, and print out your stream of random digits so that you can validate your work. Your production run might count 10,000 sets.

**270.**  Figure 9.7 shows two triangles drawn on a lattice. If the sides of the triangle lie on the lattice lines, then the triangle is clearly a right triangle. If two sides of the triangle lie at 45° to the lattice lines, as in the second triangle shown, then again it is clear that the triangle is a right triangle. Here's the problem: Is it possible to have a right triangle on a lattice in an orientation

† This is just one of the sidelights in the fascinating history of the search for randomness. See R. E. Greenwood, "The Coupon Collector's Test for Random Digits," *Mathematical Tables and Other Aids to Computation* **IX** (49), 1–5 (January 1955).

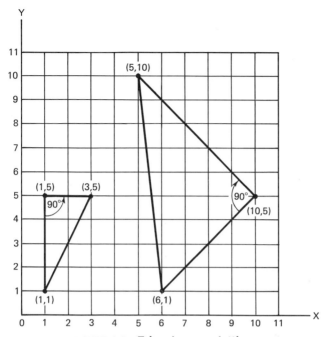

FIGURE 9.7  Triangles on a lattice.

other than these two obvious cases? Is this a computer problem? Would the following be a sensible attack?

(*a*)  Select three points at random (say, within the bounds of a 64 × 64 lattice).

(*b*)  Calculate the squares of the lengths of the three sides and determine whether or not the largest squared distance is the sum of the other two (that is, the converse of the Pythagorean relation).

(*c*)  If it is a right triangle, determine whether or not two sides lie along the lattice lines, or two lines lie at 45° with the lattice lines.

(*d*)  If we find such a triangle, the problem is solved. Suppose we don't?

**275.**  Random numbers are generated as in part *c* of Exercise 245. Two such numbers, considered as decimal fractions, can be considered as the coordinates of a point (X,Y) in the unit square, as in Figure 9.8. Any given point is in or on the circle of radius 1, depending on whether or not $X^2 + Y^2 \leq 1$. If a large number of points are selected (and counted in a counter $C_1$) and the numbers lying in or on the circle are tallied in a counter $C_2$, then the ratio of those two counters should approximate the ratio of the areas involved. The area of the square is 1; the circular sector has the area $\pi/4$.

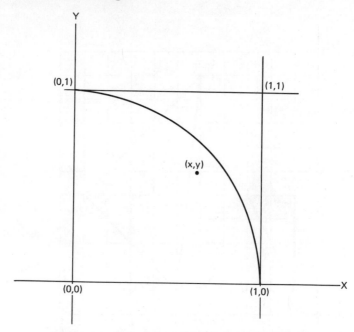

**FIGURE 9.8 Calculating pi with random numbers.**

Thus, using random numbers, we can calculate an approximation to pi. It would be a crude approximation. Our input data is good to only 4 digits of precision, so at best we could hope for pi to 4 digits. Even at that, you should not expect more than three correct digits after selecting 10,000 points.

In practice, the numbers we generate lie in the range 0–9999. We may think of them as decimal fractions, but actually we are operating in a square of side 10,000 and dealing with integers.

# 10

# FLOATING-POINT ARITHMETIC

## 10.1 The Integer Barrier

Multiple-precision subroutines take care of the word size barrier of a computer; they allow for arithmetic operations on integers of any size, at the cost of additional storage usage, extra time in execution, and some complexity in coding.

We now want to remove the integer barrier, to enable us to handle fractions. The solution to this problem will also provide a new way to handle large numbers.

We have already seen several examples of **scaling.** In calculating square roots, for example, the square root of 13 would come out to be 3, which is as close as you can come in integers. If we wanted the square root to more significant digits, we could calculate the root of 1300 and get 36 (again, the closest value in integers). If we choose to interpret that result as 3.6, that is our concern, but not the concern of the subroutine.

In similar fashion, we could program the machine to deal with fractions and mixed numbers by scaling each number as required in order to utilize the integer capability of the machine. Indeed, mechanical desk calculators are operated in just this way (although their makers did provide movable markers to help the user keep track of his imaginary decimal points).

Suppose we have in storage the numbers 56 and 1234 in two words. If we

**113**

write instructions to add the contents of the two words, the sum will be 1290. If, in our thinking, the numbers are really 5.6 and 12.34, then we must alter at least one of the numbers to achieve the sum we really want (17.94). Scaling numbers in order to perform fractional arithmetic on an integral device is always possible, but it is usually awkward and tedious.

## 10.2   Floating-Point

Scientific notation for numbers was devised a long time ago to facilitate handling of numbers that cover a wide range. Consider some examples:

$$
\begin{aligned}
3.1415927 &= 3.1415927 \times 10^0 \\
31415.927 &= 3.1415927 \times 10^4 \\
0.0000063897 &= 6.3897000 \times 10^{-6} \\
\text{negative one} &= -1.0000000 \times 10^0 \\
\text{feet per mile} &= 5.2800000 \times 10^3 \\
\text{national debt} &= 5.0000000 \times 10^{10} \text{ dollars} \\
\text{length of year} &= 3.1556925 \times 10^7 \text{ seconds} \\
\text{zero} &= 0.0000000 \times 10^0 \\
\text{voting age} &= 1.8000000 \times 10^1 \text{ years}
\end{aligned}
$$

We reduce all numbers to their first 8 significant digits; we put them in the range 1–10; and we append a power of 10 to indicate where the decimal point should be. The number 0 is exceptional, since it cannot be put into the proper range, and any power of 10 that would be appended to it would be logically correct.

This scheme of number notation was adapted to computer usage in the late 1940s under the name of floating-point. A floating-point number will have four parts:

1.   The first 8 significant digits of the number. By analogy with logarithms, this part is sometimes called the mantissa.
2.   The power of 10.
3.   The sign of the number.
4.   The sign of the power of 10.

The first two parts will be stored as separate integers; the last two parts require 1 bit each. Notice in our examples that the decimal point, the times sign, and the 10 are all redundant to this internal representation of floating-point numbers. The number 0 will be assigned the exponent 0, as a matter of definition.

When we use floating arithmetic, we will use it consistently; that is, we will not try to mix floating arithmetic with our normal (machine) fixed-point arithmetic.

## 10.3  Floating-Point Subroutines

Given numbers in storage that are in the standard notation described above, we then need subroutines to perform addition, subtraction, multiplication, and division on such numbers, with results in the same form. Programming for floating-point arithmetic will then consist of the writing of calling sequences to the subroutines. This is awkward, and we will explore ways (in Chapters 11 and 12) to make it easy.

Easy or awkward, the job can be done, and the use of the floating-point subroutines extends the arithmetic range of the machine. Let us suppose that the package of subroutines furnished with your computer is designed to handle numbers of 7 significant digits, with an allowable range on the exponent of $\pm(2^6 - 1)$. The 7 significant digits can be contained in 24 bits; the exponent will need 6 bits, and the sign of the number and the sign of the exponent take 1 bit each. One floating-point number can thus be contained in 32 bits, or two computer words. For 8 digit precision in the numbers, or a wider allowable range on the exponents, or both, the internal representation of a single floating-point number would need at least 3 words of storage.

But these decisions have been made for you; the vendor supplies you with a complete set of subroutines. The directions that come with the set specify how the subroutines are to be used. For example, the floating multiplication routine for the Varian 620 requires this calling sequence (for the operation A∗B → C):

```
LDA    A
LDB    A+1
CALL   $QM,B
STA    C
STB    C+1
```

## 10.4  Observations on Floating-Point

In fixed-point arithmetic, the operations of multiplication and division are fairly complex compared to addition and subtraction. In floating arithmetic, it is the other way around—addition is the complicated process. Let us express a floating-point number in this fashion:

$$12345678,03$$

to indicate the number 1234.5678. In the process of addition, we have these cases:

1.  If the exponents of two numbers are the same, as in

$$12345678,03$$
$$37684029,03$$

then the two numbers can be added, more or less directly, and the result has the same exponent:

50029707,03

2. Even in this situation, an adjustment to the exponent might be called for, as in

12345678,03
+88630297,03
100975975,03

which must be changed to

10097598,04

on return from the addition subroutine. All results must be put into standard form; in this case using the first 8 significant digits, rounded from 9 digits.

3. The adjustment may go the other way, as in this case:

12345678,03
−12344321,03
00001357,03

which must be changed to:

13570000,−01

(This is called normalizing the number.) Thus, although both numbers entering the (algebraic) addition have 8 significant digits, the result has only 4 significant digits. This is one of the built-in pitfalls of floating arithmetic; that is, that *a single addition may result in severe loss of significance with no warning.*

4. In the extreme case:

12345678,03
−12345678,03
00000000,03

the result must be changed to the standard zero of the system:

00000000,00

5. If the exponents differ by more than 8, as in this case:

12345678,03
72583171,−06

then the logic of addition is very simple — the answer is the larger number.

6. When the difference in the exponents is greater than 0 and less than 9, as in

$$12345678,03$$
$$44270317,05$$

then one number must be moved left or right to align the decimal points:

$$1234.5678$$
$$442703.17$$
$$443937.7378$$

with the sum rounded to 8 digits and the exponent adjusted accordingly.

The total logic for floating addition is thus quite complicated. The subroutine is written for algebraic addition (that is, either addend could be negative), and so floating subtraction involves nothing more than the old rule of algebra; namely, change the sign of the subtrahend and add.

7. The result of an operation in floating arithmetic can fall outside the allowable range on either end. Thus, the product of

$$12345678,29$$
$$27182818,37$$

where the exponent is limited to $\pm63$, would cause an **exponent overflow.** The action that is taken in this situation differs according to the philosophy of the writer of the subroutine:

(a)  Return with the product replaced by the largest admissable number.
(b)  Return with an error message.

Similarly, the product of the numbers

$$12345678,-29$$
$$27182818,-37$$

leads to **exponent underflow,** since the multiplication attempts to produce a number with an exponent of $-66$. In this case, it is quite common to replace the result with 0 and continue.

## 10.5  Summary

The complete battery of floating-point subroutines includes more than just subroutines for arithmetic. There are routines to **float** a fixed-point integer, and to **fix** a floating-point number; to separate the mantissa from the exponent; and to read and write floating-point numbers.

We have not discussed how any of the routines in the floating-point library are used, or what they are used for. The purpose of this chapter is to provide insight into ways of removing the integer barrier. The tool for this purpose exists, and it is instructive to dwell on how it works. Considered

# 118 Floating-Point Arithmetic

simply as a collection of subroutines, the tool is a dull one. We must explore how the tool can be made attractive and efficient for the user.

## EXERCISES

**280.** Given the following floating-point numbers:

A = 37862947E02
B = 12345678E00
C = 87654321E−03

(this is the notation used in Fortran, where the E stands for exponent; that is, the power of 10), calculate by hand the values of the following expressions and put the result into the same form:

(a) A + B + C
(b) A · C + B
(c) C³ + A
(d) (A + B)/C

# 11

# INTERPRETERS

## 11.1 The Problem

Suppose we have a battery of related subroutines, such as all the subroutines for floating arithmetic mentioned in Chapter 10. To use the subroutines, we would normally have to write long strings of calling sequences to trigger off the proper subroutines in order. This is tedious, and hence prone to error. It is also very dull work, and distracting to what we really want to do; namely, solve some problem.

*An interpreter is a subroutine whose function is to control the operation of a battery of other subroutines.*

Figure 11.1 shows what we are trying to do. The left-hand column shows the kind of instructions we might have to write, using normal linkages to subroutines to effect the floating arithmetic for

$$\frac{A + B}{C} \longrightarrow D$$

We have in storage the necessary subroutines for the arithmetic operations, as well as subroutines to load and store a pseudo-accumulator, which is simply a storage area reserved to act as an accumulator (since the machine's own registers will be needed by the subroutines). For each operation, we write a calling sequence to the pertinent subroutine and specify the address of the required floating-point number. What we really want to do is shown on the right. We want to write code that looks like normal machine code, but with the understanding that we mean floating-point arithmetic.

**119**

120 Interpreters

| JMPM | FLDA | LDA | A |
| DATA | A | ADD | B |
| JMPM | FADD | DVD | C |
| DATA | B | STA | D |
| JMPM | FDVD | | |
| DATA | C | | |
| JMPM | FSTA | | |
| DATA | D | | |

FIGURE 11.1 Subroutine linkages versus interpretive mode.

The interpreter is just one more subroutine, so that storage looks like Figure 11.2. At the top of storage, there is indicated a string of machine instructions (say, the housekeeping and initialization of our problem). The vertical lines indicate the place at which we wish to begin using floating arithmetic; we write a linkage to the interpreter.

The instructions in the interpreter now operate on successive instructions that follow the linkage and interpret them. This means that each instruction

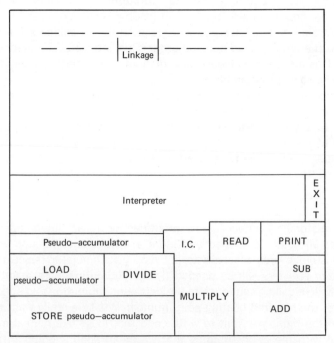

FIGURE 11.2 The pattern of an interpretive package.

is moved to a work area in the interpreter, dissected, and carried out. The interpreter builds up the necessary calling sequence and triggers it off. The interpreter must have its own pseudo-instruction counter (I.C.) to perform the same function with the pseudo-instructions that the machine's I.C. does with machine instructions.

Suppose that the linkage to the interpreter is at locations 3000 and 3001 in storage. Then the first pseudo-instruction (LDA A in the example of Figure 11.1) is at 3002. The interpreter's I.C. is set to 3002 upon entry to the interpreter. The interpreter moves the information at 3002 into a work area and breaks it up into its components:

What to do (load pseudo-accumulator)
What to do it with (number A)

And from this builds up the required calling sequence (that is, the structure on the left side of Figure 11.1). The calling sequence is then executed (by the interpreter), which effects the desired action. The interpreter then adds 1 to its I.C. and the cycle begins again. The interpretive package must have at least one more subroutine, to recognize the pseudo-op-code EXIT. This subroutine should add 1 to the interpreter's I.C.; move that number to the machine's I.C.; and then resume normal machine language processing.

## 11.2 A Complete Interpretive Package

We have sketched out the bare minimum of an interpretive package. Keep in mind that such packages are usually written by experts and handed to you to use. The hard work in such a package is in the writing of the arithmetic subroutines and the READ and PRINT routines. The interpreter itself is a rather simple subroutine.

If the experts have done their job right, you have at your disposal a new and powerful tool. It is still, however, somewhat awkward to use. Examine again the right side of Figure 11.1. We want to be able to write code that resembles normal machine code, but so far we have only nine op-codes (LDA, STA, ADD, SUB, MUL, DIV, READ, PRINT, and EXIT). If the logic of our problem calls for any kind of JUMP, we would have to exit from the interpretive system, make the jump (which might involve some awkward testing of the condition of floating-point numbers in storage), and then link back to the interpreter. So as long as the experts are creating the package for us, let's have them construct more subroutines for these operations:

JMP   Jump unconditionally
JAN   Jump if the contents of the pseudo-accumulator is negative
JAP   Jump if the contents of the pseudo-accumulator is positive
      (which includes 0)
JAZ   Jump if the contents of the pseudo-accumulator is 0.

> JAG   Jump if the contents of the pseudo-accumulator is greater than 0
>
> JNZ   Jump if the contents of the pseudo-accumulator is nonzero.

While we're at it, let's also throw in subroutines for the elementary functions: square root, logarithm, exponential, sine, cosine, and arctangent.

Now we have a workable and fairly efficient package. Besides the interpreter itself, we have 21 subroutines working for us, and a device to make that work easy. Such packages have been written for most large computers, and for some of the minis, including the Varian 620. Although the concept provides a powerful tool, we suggest that you hold off using it for a while. For the moment, let us stand back and contemplate what has been accomplished.

## 11.3   Observations on the Interpretive Package

1.   The floating-point interpretive system has extended the arithmetic range of the machine. In a very real sense, the package creates a new machine. The basic hardware, as delivered from the factory, is designed to handle integers, and small integers at that. Now we have a machine that can handle fractions, and numbers that can have a wide range. The package you may have access to probably is written for 7 digit precision, with a range on the exponent of $\pm 10^{38}$. There is no reason, conceptually, why one could not be written for any number of digits of precision, or any range on the exponent.

2.   We casually created some new op-codes that the machine itself lacks. The operations JAG and JNZ are missing from the machine's repertoire, and of course there are no machine op-codes for the six functions. Again, there is no theoretical limit to this type of thing; we can invent new op-codes freely if we can arrange to create subroutines to implement them. It would be nice, for example, to have an interpretive analog to the JUMP AND MARK op-codes.

3.   By the same token, we could postulate having the interpretive package alter the mode of operation of the machine. Our machine has single-address logic; that is, each instruction specifies one op-code and one operand. It might be convenient to be able to write instructions with triple-address logic, so that we could have instructions like

ADD   A,B,C

which says "add the numbers at A and B and put the result at C." As long as the instructions we write are pseudo-instructions (which are never directly executed), then we can have them in whatever form is most convenient to us.

4.   Although an interpretive package extends the capability of the machine, there is a price to pay. We pay a small price in storage, since the subroutines take up space. Figure 11.2 is greatly distorted; a complete floating-point system occupies only a few hundred words. The big price we pay is in time. Where machine instructions execute at speeds up to a quarter of a million per second, our interpretive instructions will be perhaps 20 times slower, or at about 15,000 per second. Each instruction requires the execution of at least two subroutines (the interpreter itself, plus the specified operation subroutine). Moreover, all the red tape of interpretation is repeated each time the pseudo-instruction is executed.

5.   The whole concept was illustrated in terms of floating-point arithmetic. The arithmetic range of the machine could be extended in other ways. Multiple-precision arithmetic could be made into an interpretive package, for example. Or we could make an interpretive system out of complex arithmetic, where the operations are performed on pairs of numbers:

$$(3 + 5i)(5 - 7i) = (50 + 4i)$$

in which $i^2 = -1$. Such arithmetic is of great use in electrical engineering calculations. We would need a battery of subroutines to add, subtract, multiply, and divide complex numbers (all the arithmetic is performed on the coefficients; the letter i does not need to appear), plus subroutines for reading and printing such numbers, plus more subroutines for jumps and elementary functions.

In matrix arithmetic, the elements we deal with are arrays of numbers called matrices. Again, with the appropriate battery of subroutines, we can handle matrix operations with ease. We turn our computer into a new machine that has matrix operations for its op-codes.

These various forms of extended arithmetic can be combined. We can have double-precision complex arithmetic; floating-point matrix arithmetic — any form of arithmetic that is useful to us can be implemented on any machine.

6.   If any such form of extended arithmetic is used extensively enough, it could be cast into machine hardware. This principle is illustrated by the basic machine operation of multiplication. For about half of the mini computers now on the market, fixed-point multiply is available in two forms: by subroutine, or as an optional hardware feature. A few of the minis offer the same choice for floating-point arithmetic; you can have it by subroutine, or you can pay more rent and have it as a hardware feature (and it will then execute at close to normal machine speeds).

On large computers, hardware floating-point and multiple-precision operations are standard items. No machine has ever offered complex arithmetic op-codes in hardware, but there is no reason why it couldn't be done, if enough users wanted it.

7. Since we can create new op-codes at will, we can write an interpretive package to create all the op-codes of machine B on machine A. Such a package is called a **simulator.** Within reasonable limits, a simulator can be written to make any computer function exactly like another. Machine simulation is usually limited to central processors; it is difficult to simulate peripheral devices such as a disk drive or a card reader. We can, however, simulate a Data General *Nova* on a Varian 620, or vice versa. Such simulators are quite useful. For one thing, they open up the subroutine library of one machine type to the users of a different machine type.

One significant use of simulators is in handling the problems of machine conversion. Suppose that an installation is using a Hewlett-Packard 2114 and (for any one of many good reasons) must exchange it for a Varian machine. During the time that the new machine is on order, the various working programs of the installation can be recoded. They must also be checked out, and the easiest way to do this is to have a simulation program on the Hewlett-Packard 2114 that makes it operate like the Varian computer. After the machine switch is made, the inverse simulator (i.e., a program to cause the Varian machine to operate like the Hewlett-Packard 2114) is useful, in order to run any programs that did not get converted in time.

8. If we can simulate another real machine, we can also simulate a nonexistent machine. In other words, we can "build" a new computer by simulating it on an existing machine. Every current computer was designed just that way.

## 11.4   The Next Natural Step

Consider again the floating-point interpretive package that we developed. It contains the op-code SQRT (for square root) so that the user of the package can write

SQRT   G

as one instruction. When that instruction is executed, the following action takes place:

1. The interpreter links to the SQRT subroutine.
2. In that subroutine, the square root will be calculated by iterating on the recursion

$$X_{i+1} = \frac{1}{2}\left(\frac{G}{X_i} + X_i\right)$$

A starting value, $X_0$, is set up.
3. The SQRT subroutine calls on the divide, add, and multiply subroutines in turn to effect one iteration.

4. The SQRT subroutine tests for convergence of the process.

5. Steps 3 and 4 are repeated as many times as are necessary; perhaps six times.

There is a lot of red tape in that procedure. All of it will be repeated for every SQRT instruction in the user's program. Our calculations could be greatly speeded up if all the red tape could be done just once, in advance. In broad terms, that is what a **compiler** does. We will discuss the most popular compiler, Fortran, in Chapter 12.

## 11.5   A High-Precision Package

To make the concept of an interpretive package clear, we will outline the construction of a package of subroutines to perform high-precision floating-decimal arithmetic.

Widely used floating-point systems offer 7 or 8 digit precision, or, in double-precision, 15 or 16 digit precision. This is adequate for most work. There are problem situations, however, for which it is vital to have 20 digit precision or higher.

A decimal digit can be stored conveniently in 4 bits. Four decimal digits can be packed into one 16 bit word. Our high-precision package will use 25 computer words for each number. The last 24 of these words will contain the first 96 significant digits of the number. The first word will contain the exponent in 14 bits (thus allowing for exponents as high as 16,383) and use 2 bits more for the sign of the number and the sign of the exponent. We will use existing machine op-codes for all our instruction codes, which will allow us to use the DAS 8A assembler for our interpretive instructions. We will need the following subroutines:

1. ADDE, SUBE, MULE, DIVE.

2. LDAE, STAE. This implies creating a pseudo-accumulator in storage. When we manipulate numbers, we will do so in unpacked form, one word per digit. Thus, our pseudo-accumulator (PAC) will be 98 words long (96 digits, plus exponent and signs).

3. Similarly, to parallel the normal action of the machine, we will construct a pseudo-MQ (PMQ), also 98 words long. (In the Varian machine, the MQ is called the B register.) We will want the operations of LDBE and STBE.

4. Operations corresponding to JMP, JAP, JAN, JAZ (respectively, unconditional jump, jump on positive accumulator, jump on negative accumulator, jump on zero accumulator).

5. Operations of READ and PRINT, to provide for input and output of our 96 digit numbers. There are no Varian op-codes that correspond, and we are free to use any otherwise idle op-codes for our purpose. Since the op-codes

in the interpretive system are purely arbitrary (they will never be executed as written), we can use IME for read, and OME for print.

6. We'll provide, for the moment, just two functions—square root and absolute value. Again, we need a dummy op-code, and we choose EXC. If we call our absolute value function EXC 1 and square root EXC 2, we can plan ahead to the time when we may choose to add more functions to the package, which can be named EXC 3, EXC 4, and so on.

7. The interpreter must recognize an op-code for EXIT to return to normal machine language. A logical choice here is HLT.

8. The interpreter requires its own pseudo-instruction counter (PIC). This is a single word of storage. By using extended addressing (i.e., 2 words per instruction) for all commands to be interpreted, we can avoid troubles in addressing.

9. As part of the package, we will store as constants the numbers $\pi$ and e (the natural logarithm base). Further, we will allow for zero-level addressing for certain op-codes, so that constants can be created within instructions. Thus, if the number stored at address XX is to be multiplied by 73, we can write these instructions:

$$\text{LDBE} \quad \text{XX}$$
$$\text{MULE} \quad 73$$

10. The package (but not the user) will need two more subroutines: PACK and UNPACK, to switch the form of numbers from their 25 word packed form to the 98 word form and back.

We will describe just one of these subroutines in detail. The complete package, in assembly source language, is reproduced in Appendix 5.

Floating addition is the most complicated arithmetic operation. Suppose that there is a number in PAC and the instruction

$$\text{ADDE} \quad \text{M}$$

is to be executed, where M is the address of the low-order word of a number M (that is, M occupies machine words M, M+1, . . . , M+24). The interpreter links to the floating addition subroutine, and the following events take place:

1. The number M is unpacked into a work area of 98 words. The logic of the signs is performed. If the two numbers have the same sign, then addition will be performed. If the numbers have opposite signs, then subtraction will be performed.

2. The difference between the two exponents is formed. If this difference is 0, then addition (or subtraction) can take place immediately. If the sum is 96 digits and the high-order digit is nonzero, then the result has the common exponent and can be moved to PAC, and the operation is completed. If the sum has 97 digits, it is rounded to 96 digits, the exponent is raised by 1, and the result is moved to PAC. If the sum has a high-order 0

digit, then the result must be normalized. In terms of 8 digit numbers, the situation is this:

$$12345678 \quad E03$$
$$-12349502 \quad E03$$
$$-00003824 \quad E03$$

which must be adjusted to the normal form:

$$-38240000 \ E\text{-}01$$

3.   If the exponents differ by more than 96, then the number with the larger exponent **is** the result.

(The number 0 forms an exception here, but the details of handling 0 are part of the task of the programmer who writes the interpretive package. The user need not worry.)

4.   If the difference between the exponents is greater than 0 and less than 97, then one of the numbers must be shifted relative to the other before the addition takes place. Again, in terms of 8 digit numbers, we have this situation:

$$32384626 \quad E01$$
$$97420755 \quad E\text{-}01$$

which must be treated as

$$32 \quad 384626$$
$$\quad 97420755$$
$$33 \quad 35883355$$

and the result must be rounded as

$$33358834 \ E01$$

As before, the result must be tested for number overflow, exponent overflow, exponent underflow, and nonnormalization.

In all cases, the final result is returned to the PAC. If the result is any form of 0, it must be put in standard form:

$$00000000 \ E00$$

To use the package, the programmer need only write a linkage to the interpreter:

$$\text{JMPM} \quad \text{FINT}$$

and then write his pseudo-instructions, ending with the HLT instruction that gets him out of the floating-point system.

To illustrate the use of the package, Figure 11.3 shows a program to calculate, correct to 96 digits, the real root of the equation

```
LINK    JMPM    FINT    Link to the floating interpreter
        LDAI    0       Zero to C
        STAE    C
        IME     1,X     Set initial value of X
REF1    LDBE    X
        MULE    X
        STAE    T1      X² stored at T1
        LDBE    T1
        MULI    2
        STAE    T4      2X² stored at T4
        LDBE    T4
        MULE    X
        ADDI    5
        STAE    T2      Numerator stored at T2
        LDBE    T1
        MULI    3       Form 3X²
        SUBI    2       3X² − 2
        STAE    T3
        LDBE    T2
        DIVE    T3
        STAE    X       This is the new X value
        LDAE    C       Add one to C
        ADDI    1
        STAE    C
        SUBI    4       Test for four iterations
        JAN     REF1    Jump back to repeat
        OME     1,X     Print final value of X
        HLT             Exit from interpretive system
        HLT             Normal machine halt
X       BSS     25
C       BSS     25
T1      BSS     25
T2      BSS     25
T3      BSS     25
T4      BSS     25
```

**FIGURE 11.3   Program to test the interpretive package.**

$$X^3 - 2X - 5 = 0$$

by the Newton–Raphson method, using $X_0 = 2.0945514815$ as a starting value. We must calculate

$$\frac{2X^3 + 5}{3X^2 - 2} \longrightarrow X$$

four times, to achieve 96 digit precision.

# 12

# FORTRAN

## 12.1  A Sample Problem

Fortran is both a language and a **compiler**. As a language, it furnishes us a new and better way to express what it is we want the machine to do. We write in Fortran at a higher level of symbolism than in assembly language, and our symbolic statements (they are no longer called instructions) must again be translated into the language of the machine. Most of Fortran deals with floating-point arithmetic, so we have at our disposal a complete floating-point package. Rather than having our statements translated at each execution, however, the translation is done in advance of execution, and just once.

We can best approach Fortran by considering a problem in probabilities. What is the probability that, of 20 cars passing at random, some 2 of them will have the same last 2 digits on their license plates? We'll get around to showing you how to solve that problem, but first we'll consider the problem in a slightly different form: For how many cars, passing at random, is there a 50% probability that some 2 of them have the same last 2 digits on their license plates?

Let's analyze this problem. We seek a probability, which is a number between 0 (representing an impossibility) and 1 (representing complete certainty). For example, the probability of getting exactly two heads on the simultaneous toss of two coins is 0.25. Many such problems are attacked by calculating first the probability of what we seek **not** happening; then the probability we seek is found by subtracting that result from **1**.

**130**

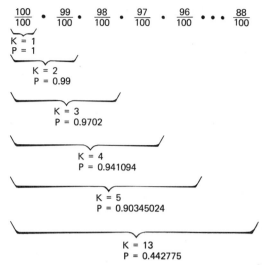

**FIGURE 12.1** Calculations for the license plate problem.

We start with 1 car. In counting cases, we then have K = 1, and the probability up to that point (that no 2 of the K cars have the same last 2 digits on their license plates) is 1; namely, complete certainty. We express this probability as 100/100, since there are 100 possible 2 digit numbers.

Now we advance to 2 cars. Whatever the 2 digits on the license plate of the first car, there are only 99 possible numbers for the second car in order that they be different. The probability up to this point is then given by

$$\frac{100}{100} \cdot \frac{99}{100} = 0.99$$

For the third car, we multiply the probability that was determined for 2 cars by 98/100 (there are 98 possible 2 digit numbers such that all 3 are different) to arrive at the probability for 3 cars, which is 0.9702. The calculations proceed as shown in Figure 12.1. We want to continue those calculations until the probability value becomes 0.5 or less, which occurs when we have 13 cars.

Figure 12.2 shows this logic in flowchart form. We have used N for numerator, D for denominator, P for probability, and K for a counter of the number of cars. Compare the flowchart to the hand calculations of Figure 12.1. The iterative loop begins at reference 2. To advance from car to car, we subtract 1 from the current numerator, tally 1 in K, and form the new probability by taking the previous probability and multiplying by N/D. Now notice several things:

1. Our hand calculations have already arrived at the answer, 13, so why

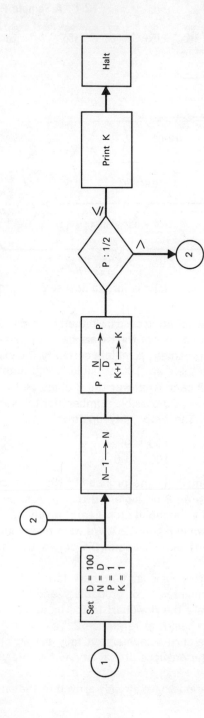

**FIGURE 12.2** The license plate problem.

should we do the problem on the computer? First, because it is a training exercise in Fortran, and it is wise to approach the use of a new tool with a situation that is firmly in hand — we are then studying the tool, rather than the problem. Second, our solution to this problem can be generalized to other cases. For example: What is the probability that, of K persons taken at random, some 2 have the same birthday? This is the same problem with D = 365 (366 if you prefer). The calculations for the birthday problem will be longer, but our computer solution will perform those calculations expeditiously. And, finally, for any computer solution, we must arrange to test the program before committing it to production. The license plate version provides a nice test case.

2.   The problem clearly involves fractions, and thus calls for either extensive scaling of the numbers N, D, and P, or else the use of floating-point arithmetic. Notice that K is a counter for the (integral) number of cars, and can and should be done in normal fixed-point arithmetic.

3.   If the problem is new to you, it might be difficult to predict the possible range of the numbers involved, particularly P. Again, floating arithmetic, with its tremendous range, relieves us of the burden of predicting that range precisely. We frequently assume (as in this problem) that the range will certainly be less than the allowable range of our available floating-point system, and so we can proceed with a solution without worrying about things like word size limits.

## 12.2   A Fortran Code

We will now proceed to code the flowchart of Figure 12.2 and explain the rules of elementary Fortran as we go.

This chapter is intended as an introduction to the Fortran language. There have been, to date, some 90 texts completely devoted to Fortran, not to mention complete Fortran reference manuals furnished by each computer vendor. Some of the better books on Fortran are listed at the end of this chapter. If you wish to explore the elaborate rules of the language, consult one of these books and coincidentally start writing some Fortran programs of your own.

Fortran is written in the form of statements, one per line, which will be transcribed (perhaps via punched cards) into machine-readable form. In terms of column positions on punched cards, all statements begin in column 7, as shown on a standard Fortran coding form in Figure 12.3. The printed form is handy, but not necessary, for Fortran work.

Columns 1–5 are used for statement numbers, which are to be **right**-justified. Any integers of up to 5 digit length may be used; they are arbitrary numbers used to provide a label for certain statements. We suggest that for

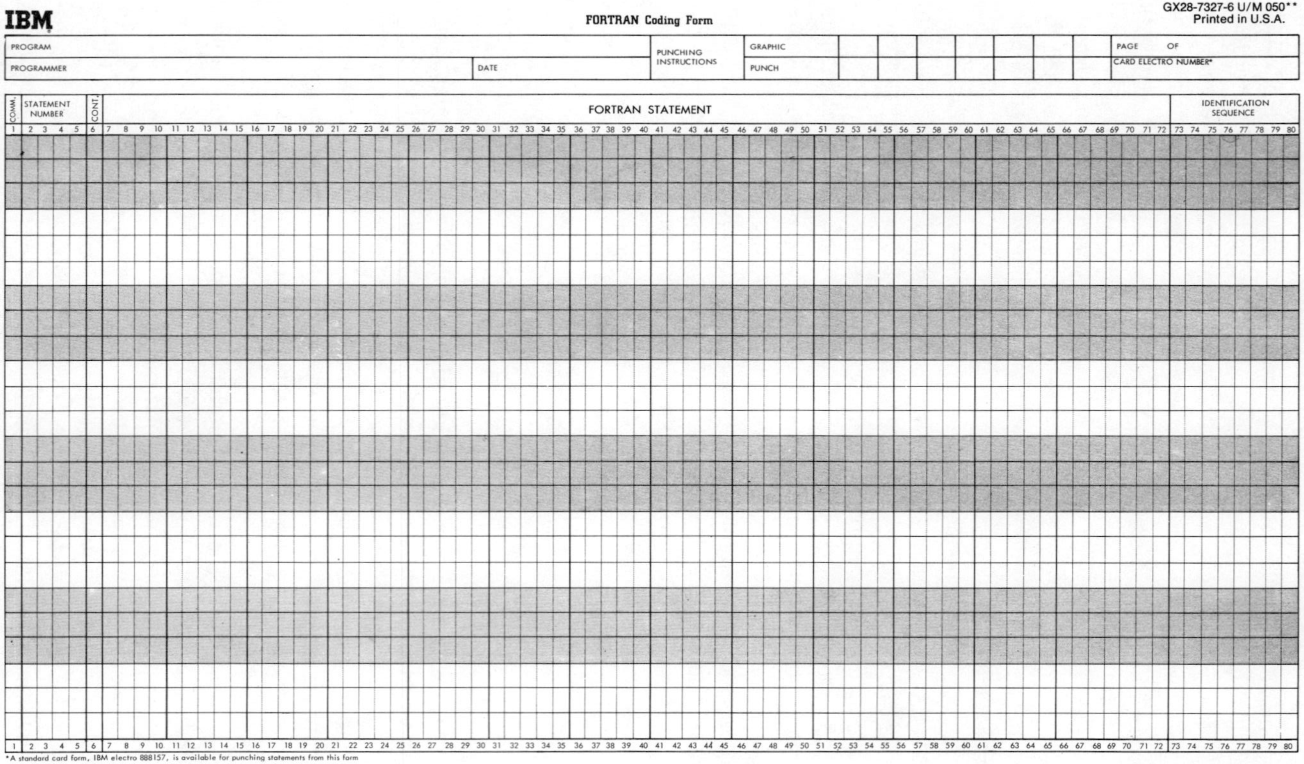

**FIGURE 12.3   Fortran coding form.**

short programs, the statement numbers be made to match the reference numbers on the flowchart.

So, following the flowchart of Figure 12.2, we will write our first Fortran statement:

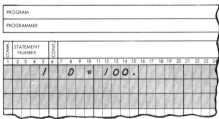

The statement is given the number 1, to agree with the flowchart. The statement itself seems much like its flowchart counterpart, but notice these points:

1.   We have used D to stand for denominator. We want D to be a floating-point number. In Fortran, initial letters of variable names signal the arithmetic mode. Initial letters I, J, K, L, M, N signify fixed-point numbers (i.e., integers). The other letters of the alphabet signify floating-point numbers. We could have called it DENOM if we wished. Keep the names less than seven characters long; make sure the first character is alphabetic.

2.   The constant 100 is written with a decimal point. Fortran demands this convention for floating-point numbers. We have told Fortran twice that we mean to use floating arithmetic for the variable D.

3.   The flowchart might have been written 100 → D, and we would like to write D ← 100 in Fortran (this only changes the form of the English sentence from "100 replaces D" to "D is replaced by 100"). Fortran wants single variables on the left. Since our keypunches lack the left-pointing arrow, the equals sign is used. It is **not** an algebraic equals sign; think of it as "is replaced by."

The second statement of our program ought to be just as easy to write, but due to the I, J, K, L, M, N rule, we must invent a new name for the numerator of our fraction. How about using TOP? We can now write

| COMM. | STATEMENT NUMBER | | CONT. | 7 | 8 | 9 | 10 | 11 | 12 | 13 | 14 | 15 | 16 | 17 | 18 | 19 | 20 | 21 | 22 | 23 |
|---|---|---|---|---|---|---|---|---|---|---|---|---|---|---|---|---|---|---|---|---|---|
| | | 1 | | D | = | | 1 | 0 | 0 | . | | | | | | | | | | |
| | | | | T | Ø | P | | | = | | D | | | | | | | | | |
| | | | | P | = | | 1 | . | 0 | 0 | 0 | | | | | | | | | |
| | | | | K | = | 1 | | | | | | | | | | | | | | |

and again we note:

4.  Spaces are meaningless to the Fortran compiler (in fact, during the translation phase, the compiler will delete all the spaces from your statements before processing them). The characters you write will come back to you on your printout, including the spaces, but they have no use other than to make your statements pretty and readable. So, if we choose, we can spread a statement out, as shown in our second line of code.

5.  The third statement shows this notion again, and also that the trailing 0s of the number 1.000 don't hurt, nor do they help. The only significant digit is the **1.** The choice of the letter P for probability is logical.

6.  The variable K is used to count cars. Since counting is an integral process, we do **not** want floating arithmetic, and the choice of the letter K is appropriate.

We are now at reference 2 of the flowchart. Let's proceed with our code.

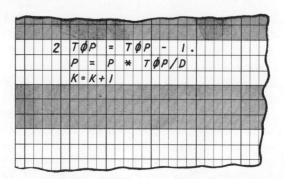

7.  Notice that decimal points are used with care. Our fifth statement (the first one shown above) needs one, since all its variables are in floating-point. The seventh line must not have a decimal point in its digit.

8.  On the flowchart we used the mathematician's centered dot for multiplication. Again, the limitations of the keypunch preclude that usage, so the asterisk is used to denote multiplication.

9.  The sixth statement is not ambiguous, but there would be no harm in writing

$$P=P*(TOP/D)$$

The rule is: When in doubt, parenthesize. If we wanted to express the following operation

$$Q = \frac{A + B}{C + D}$$

we would **have** to use parentheses, like this:

$$Q=(A+B)/(C+D)$$

to make the meaning clear.

10. At any place in a Fortran program, we can insert comments (corresponding to REMARKS on an assembly language code) by writing a line with a C in column 1. The entire line will be ignored by the compiler (but it will appear on the listing). Thus, we could have begun the whole program with lines like

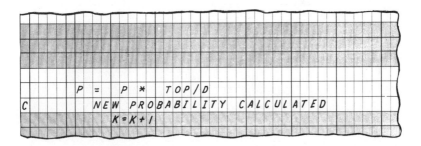

and thus label our printouts. The line ends at column 72.

Similarly, between our statements 6 and 7 we could include a comment:

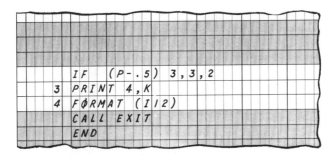

A line bearing only the C in column 1 will simply provide vertical space on the listing and may dress it up for ease in reading. Use comments lines liberally to explain what you think your statements should do.

Now we come to the decision box on our flowchart. The remainder of the code is

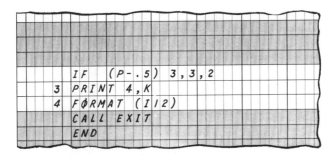

11. The word IF has its English meaning, and is thus a **reserved word** in Fortran; that is, you should not call some variable by the name IF.† During executions, the expression in parentheses in the IF statement is evaluated and control passes to one of the three statements given after the parentheses, according to whether the evaluation comes out less than, equal to, or greater than 0 (always in that order). Thus, in our problem, control passes to statement 2 if (P—.5) is greater than 0, but to statement 3 if (P—.5) is negative or 0.

12. Statement 3 calls for printing. It is tied to statement 4, which indicates how we want to print whatever the print statement calls for. The last statement is the Fortran analog of HALT. The words PRINT, FORMAT, and CALL EXIT are also reserved words.

The print statement specifies (in this case) that one number, K, should be printed. The format statement specifies that K should appear as an integer (by the use of the letter I) and should occupy the first 12 printing positions of our output paper. In our problem, the total output will thus be the number 13, printed on a line with ten spaces to its left. If we had written instead

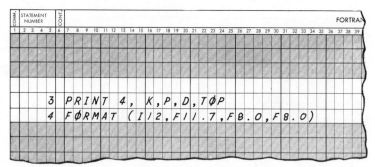

then we would be calling for four numbers to be printed across the page like this:

13      .4427750      100.      88.

The notation in the format statement of F11.7 means floating-point, eleven printing positions, and seven decimal places. Leading 0s are suppressed in the printing. Similarly, F8.0 means floating-point, eight printing positions, and no decimal places.

## 12.3   Running the Program

The birthday problem resulted in 12 statements (the complete program is given in Figure 12.4). These make up the **source code.** They constitute the

---

† The word is reserved only in the sense that you shouldn't use it for some other purpose. You **may** name a variable IF, but it would be foolish to do so.

FORTRAN Coding Form

GX28-7327-6 U/M 050**
Printed in U.S.A.

```
C     PROGRAM TO CALCULATE BIRTHDAY
C     PROBABILITIES, BY HENRY GIBSON
C     MARCH 12, 1983, TRY NUMBER THREE
1     D = 100.
      TOP = D
      P = 1.0
      K = 1
2     TOP = TOP - 1.
C     NEW PROBABILITY CALCULATED
      P = P * (TOP/D)
      K = K + 1
      IF (P - .5) 3,3,2
3     PRINT 4, K
4     FORMAT (I12)
      STOP
      END
```

FIGURE 12.4  The complete Fortran program for the problem posed in Section 12.1.

input to the Fortran compiler. If there are no syntactical errors that the compiler can detect, the code will be translated into machine language and executed. All necessary linkages to the appropriate subroutines will be furnished by the compiler, as well as the subroutines themselves. The possible syntactical errors correspond to the mechanical bugs that an assembler can detect, and if there are any, there will be error messages, and execution will be inhibited.

Our program contained its own data. If external data is needed in a program, it is called for by statements like

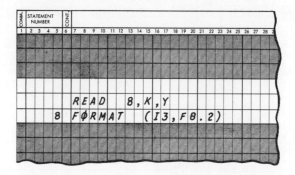

And when the READ statement is executed, data is to be inputted; in this case, data like

$$98712345678$$

which will load a number K with the value 987, and a number Y with the value 123456.78 (the latter in floating form).

## 12.4   The License Plate Problem Extended

The license plate problem, as we have presented it, would hardly consitute good use of a computer (reread Section 2.7). If we coded and ran the Fortran solution, our total output would be the number 13. How would we be sure that the solution is correct, other than by performing the calculations by hand (or desk calculator) in order to check?

Suppose, however, that we modify the program slightly. After calculating and printing the K value for D = 100, we let D+50 → D, test for D not exceeding 2000, and calculate the K values for every D from 100 to 2000 by 50s. Now we have a computer problem.

## EXERCISE

**285.** A group of K persons each wears a wristwatch. At a given signal, each person notes the position of the second hand on his watch. What is the probability that some two of the watches have their second hands in synchronization within 1 second?

This is the license problem again, with a population of 30, rather than 100. The resultant probability should be at 0.5 for K around 6. What value of K will give a probability of 0.8? (The value 0.8 here refers to the probability of the original problem; in our calculation, we would seek the point at which P falls below 0.2.)

The last question in Exercise 285 suggests that we can introduce another parameter into the problem. The original form carried the calculation to the point where the probability level reached 0.5 or less. We can vary the probability level **and** the values of D, so that our problem could involve thousands of calculations. Eventually, we can get around to the **real** problem, which is to acquire insight into what is going on.

## 12.5   Fortran DO Loops

Suppose we have a block of data stored in a Fortran atmosphere. If the data is in floating-point form, we can no longer refer to it as residing in words, since each floating-point number may occupy as many as three machine words. Each number must have a name, but we can still assign these names in relative form. We might wish to use the mathematical notation $X_i$, with the subscript i running from 1 to 100 (for 100 numbers). Again, the limitations of keypunches forced a new notation; in Fortran we write X(1), X(2), X(3), . . . , X(100). Notice that now we start counting from 1, where, in assembly language, we used a notation like X, X+1, X+2, . . . , X+99 (that is, numbering from 0).

For such a block of 100 numbers, let us devise a Fortran program to sum the squares of the 100 numbers and put the sum into a word called S.

## EXERCISE

**290.** Draw a flowchart for the logic of forming the sum of squares of a block of 100 numbers addressed at X(1), X(2), X(3), . . . , X(100), with the sum to be placed at S.

A Fortran routine for the logic of Exercise 290 could be

| COMM. | STATEMENT NUMBER | | | | CONT. | | | | | | | | | | | | | | | | | | | | |
|---|---|---|---|---|---|---|---|---|---|---|---|---|---|---|---|---|---|---|---|---|---|---|---|---|---|---|
| 1 | 2 | 3 | 4 | 5 | 6 | 7 | 8 | 9 | 10 | 11 | 12 | 13 | 14 | 15 | 16 | 17 | 18 | 19 | 20 | 21 | 22 | 23 | 24 | 25 | 26 | 27 |
| | | | | | | S | = | 0 | . | 0 | | | | | | | | | | | | | | | | |
| | | | | | | I | = | 1 | | | | | | | | | | | | | | | | | | |
| | | | 2 | | | Y | = | X | ( | I | ) | * | X | ( | I | ) | | | | | | | | | | |
| | | | | | | S | = | S | + | Y | | | | | | | | | | | | | | | | |
| | | | | | | I | F | | ( | I | - | 1 | 0 | 0 | ) | 3 | , | 4 | , | 4 | | | | | | |
| | | | 3 | | | I | = | I | - | 1 | | | | | | | | | | | | | | | | |
| | | | | | | G | Ø | | T | Ø | | 2 | | | | | | | | | | | | | | |
| | | | 4 | | | | | | | | | | | | | | | | | | | | | | | |

In this routine there are a few new features to note.

The reserved words GO TO are the unconditional jump of Fortran.

The third and fourth statements could be combined into one:

$$S = S + X(I) * X(I)$$

and, in fact, Fortran statements can be made quite long. Column 6 is used for continuation numbers for statements that exceed the allotted space of one line (72 characters on the Teletype, for example). Statements should be short, however. It is usually better to write several short statements, rather than one long, complicated statement.

The short routine is a loop, and it has all five parts of a loop in evidence. The first 2 statements are the housekeeping and initialization. The next 2 are the DO block. The IF statement is the TEST, and statement number 3 is the MODIFY. The GO TO is the jump back to the DO block.

The loop can be expressed in much neater form, as follows:

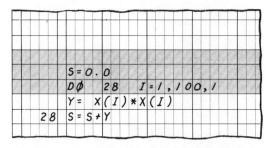

This is a Fortran DO loop. The second statement provides the compiler with this directive: Create a loop to execute all statements from the one following the DO, down to and including the **target** statement (numbered 28 here), controlled by the index I which should run from 1 to 100 by 1s. The DO **statement** combines four of the parts of a loop, leaving only the DO **block** itself to be written. The DO loop facility is probably the most powerful, and certainly one of the most attractive, features of Fortran.

## 12.6 Bracketing

With Fortran at our disposal, we can explore more realistic and useful problems and new techniques. One such technique is known, for lack of a better name, as **bracketing.**

The general idea is this: We know that the solution to a problem lies, say, somewhere between 1 and 100. (See Exercise 51, Chapter 2, for example, which called for calculating the fifth root of 100.) We will search that range, taking big steps in the independent variable. The critical stage in the bracketing process is our ability to determine, for any suggested value of X, whether X is too small, too big, or just right. If it is just right, we are done. If it is too small, we continue the search. And if it is too big, we step back and cut down the size of the step. The example should make this notion clear.

We will establish a variable, X, initialized to 0. We let X increase by an amount D, initialized to 1. For each new value of X, we test $X^5$ against 100, which is the critical stage in the bracketing process. See the flowchart logic of Figure 12.5. If the test comes out less than, we return to increase X by another D. If the test comes out equal, we have found the required root. And if the test comes out greater than, then we have gone too far. We back off one full step (at reference 3 of Figure 12.5), cut D down by a factor of 10, and tally 1 in a counter, K. Each traverse of the logic at reference 3 improves our result by one decimal digit; we count to 50 in K.

The pattern shown in Figure 12.5 is quite general, and has wide applicability. It is a rather crude and inefficient process, but has the virtue of being easily coded in any language.

Reference 4 is not needed on the flowchart; it is added only to enable us to mention that we do not expect ever to get there. The number we seek is irrational, so we should not expect to find a value of X that will exactly produce 100 when raised to the fifth power. Nevertheless, we must arrange for some positive action for each outcome of the comparison.

The step at reference 3 (back off one full step) can cause trouble in some situations. It is always safe to use X−2D→X, but sometimes the 2D is not needed. In other words, although the bracketing process is fairly canonical, it should not be applied blindly. Let's make that statement even stronger: **No** algorithm should be applied blindly. The intelligent computer user should know what he is doing at all times.

In order to conform to Exercise 51 (Chapter 2), the flowchart was written to seek a 50 digit solution. If the available tool (Fortran) is restricted to 8 digit precision, the last comparison should be changed to K:8.

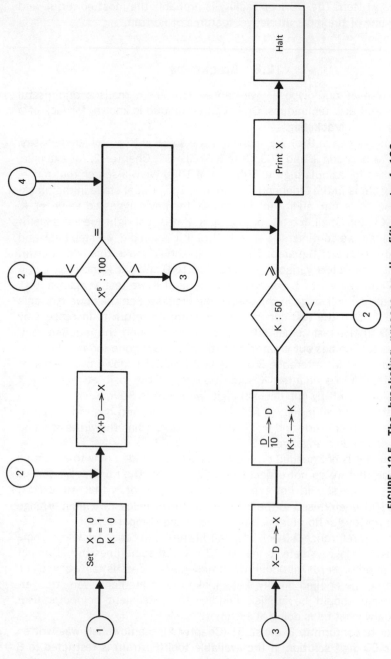

**FIGURE 12.5** The bracketing process on the fifth root of 100 problem.

The ability to search for a result by this process of bracketing is a powerful tool, unique to the computer. Consider a simple, old problem. Divide the number 10 into two parts, such that the product of each part plus its square root is the number 23. In other words, solve for X:

$$(X + \sqrt{X})(10 - X + \sqrt{10 - X}) = 23$$

There are many ways by which the root of such an equation can be calculated; for example, the Newton–Raphson scheme. But such schemes lead to very messy equations to handle, and the bracketing process is easy to program. Using bracketing, and the high-precision package described in Appendix 5, the root is found to be

$$X = .9370103835130287 1730392748 \ldots$$

## 12.7    Fortran Limitations

Fortran comes close to being the universal computer language. It is available on every computer in some form. The language is well-defined and a set of standards for a Fortran compiler exists. Since most U.S. computer manufacturers offer a Fortran compiler that supposedly adheres to these standards, it follows that a program written in Fortran should compile and execute on any computer and produce the same results. Alas, we are a long way from that dream.

First of all, anyone may write a compiler and call it Fortran. If it conforms to most of the standards that have been established, but fudges some of them, there is no recourse. This is not to imply maliciousness or carelessness on the part of the compiler writer, but only that the writing of a compiler, which may involve 10,000–30,000 instructions, calls for the making of several thousand decisions, and different programmers will make them in different ways. It is only natural, for example, to take advantage of the peculiar features of the machine that the compiler is written for. Consider the implementation of the Fortran statement

which is the Fortran notation for raising to a power; that is, this is the way to express $Y = A^3$. Probably, the machine code for this operation would involve multiplying A by itself three times. On the other hand, the statements

| | | | | | Y | = | A | * | * | 3 | 7 | | | | | | | | | | | | | | | |
| Q | = | B | * | * | 3 | . | 8 | 2 | 7 | 5 | | | | | | | | | | | | | | | | |

1  2  3  4  5  6  7  8  9  10  11  12  13  14  15  16  17  18  19  20  21  22  23  24  25  26  27

*A standard card form. IBM electro 888157, is available for punching statements from this form

would be implemented through logarithms. Now, where should the line be drawn? For the calculation of Q, logarithms must be used. But the calculation of Y could be done with 36 multiplications. The compiler writer must decide where to use one method and where to use the other. No two systems programmers make such decisions the same way. Or, consider the implementation of a set of nested DO loops. They could be set up using address modification or index registers. Suppose there are three such loops and the machine has only one index register. Again, there are decisions to be made. Someone has made them for you (and you normally don't even see the results), and left very little trail behind him.

The following is a famous Fortran program:

```
       DO   44   K = 1 , 10 , 1
       K = K + 1
       PRINT   17 , K
  17   FORMAT  ( I 5 )
  44   CONTINUE
       END
```

What would you expect Fortran to do for you if you submitted that program? What you would really like is an error message that says "You have altered the index of a loop within the loop" (which the Fortran reference manual says you shouldn't do), with another message telling you that, because of the error you have committed, execution has been inhibited. Most Fortrans will compile that program and execute it, printing 2, 4, 6, 8, and 10. Some will print 1, 3, 5, 7, and 9 (it depends on whether the loop is set up to modify before test or test before modify). Still others print 1, 2, 3, 4, 5, 6, 7, 8, 9, and 10. The universal language is something less than universal.

Again, consider this complete program:

```
       A = B
       PRINT   5 , A
  5    FORMAT  ( F 13 . 6 )
       END
```

What we would like is an error message that says "B has not been defined." Most Fortrans give no error message; computation takes place; and any value left over in storage is assigned to B. No one would write a program like that, of course. What happens is that in writing a long program over a period of months, the programmer thinks that he has defined B, and now wants to set A equal to B. He has a right to expect his compiler to detect such things.

There are hundreds of such things lying in wait to trap you. This is not to denigrate Fortran; it is a powerful tool, widely used, that can help you. But be warned. You are buffered from the machine with thousands of instructions of **support software** that you didn't write that contain decisions you know nothing about. The solution to the problem is (a) to gain experience with the new tool and learn something of its weaknesses and limitations; (b) to become familiar with the well-known traps it contains; and, above all, (c) to learn to test your programs so that you know that they do what you intend they should do. In the exercises at the end of this chapter, we suggest some problems that lend themselves to Fortran solution.

## BIBLIOGRAPHY

Blatt, J. M. *Introduction to Fortran IV Programming.* Pacific Palisades, Calif.: Goodyear, 1971.

Dimitry, D. and T. Mott, Jr. *Introduction to Fortran IV Programming.* New York: Holt, Rinehart and Winston, 1966.

McCracken, D. D. *A Guide to Fortran IV Programming.* New York: Wiley, 1968.

Organick, E. I. *A Fortran IV Primer.* Reading, Mass.: Addison-Wesley, 1966.

Weiss, E. *360 Fortran Programming.* New York: McGraw-Hill, 1969.

## EXERCISES

**295.** Write a Fortran code that follows the flowchart of Figure 12.5 and debug and execute it.

**297.** The product of the annual interest rate (compound interest) and the number of years it takes for money to double is fairly constant; it forms the "rule of 72." Thus, at 6% interest, compounded annually, money doubles in about 12 years; at 8%, in 9 years; at 9%, in 8 years, and so on. Compound interest can be calculated from the formula

$$F = A(1 + i)^N$$

where F is the final amount; A is the initial amount; i is the interest rate; and N is the number of period of time (in this case, years). If we always start with A = 1, we seek the value of N for which F will be 2. Our formula then becomes

$$N = \frac{\log 2}{\log(1 + i)}$$

So, for 5%, we can calculate

$$N = \frac{\log 2}{\log(1.05)} = \frac{0.3010}{0.0212} = 14.2$$

(a) Write a Fortran program to calculate and print values of N for i = 0.01(0.005)0.06(0.01)0.10. This notation is a compact way of stating that i should vary from 0.01 to 0.06 by increments of 0.005 and from 0.06 to 0.10 by increments of 0.01.

(b) The rule of 72 applies only to **annual** compounding. If interest is compounded semiannually, or quarterly, or monthly, the constant 72 must be replaced by some other number. Write a Fortran program to find the constant for one of these other periods of compounding. Notice that the N in the compound interest formula relates to periods of time. Thus, for quarterly compounding at 6%, the formula becomes

$$F = A \left(1 + \frac{0.06}{4}\right)^{40}$$

for 10 years (at i = 0.06/4 per period).

**300.** We wish to construct a cylindrical can which will contain 1000 cubic centimeters and will be the shape that will use the least amount of tin. We can find the proper shape by the bracketing process. You are to draw a flowchart. Let us help you get started.

First, we should make a few hand calculations to get some feel for the problem. The radius of the can is the thing we can vary. For a radius of 1 centimeter, and a fixed volume of 1000 cubic centimeters, the height, H, can be calculated from

$$V = \pi R^2 H$$
or
$$1000 = \pi \cdot 1 \cdot H$$
AND
$$H = \frac{1000}{\pi} = \text{about 318 centimeters}$$

This is a tall, narrow can, and its surface area is given by

$$S = 2\pi R^2 + 2\pi RH$$
$$= 2\pi \cdot 1 + 2\pi \cdot H$$
$$= \text{about 2006 square centimeters}$$

Let's try the other extreme, with R = 10. Now H is about 3.18 centimeters (a low, flat can) and S is about 662 square centimeters. The value of R that we seek is somewhere between these extremes. Apply the bracketing process on R. A possible flowchart is given in Appendix 3.

**305.** In Exercise 230 (Chapter 9), multiple precision was used to calculate the Fibonacci sequence. With floating-point arithmetic, this sequence could be extended much further, but with only perhaps 8 significant digits for each term. Write a Fortran program to calculate and print the first 100 terms of the Fibonacci sequence.

**310.** The series

$$\frac{1}{2} + \frac{1}{3} + \frac{1}{4} + \frac{1}{5} + \frac{1}{6} + \cdots + \frac{1}{K}$$

is well-known, in mathematics, to diverge; that is, the sum will increase without limit as K increases without limit. If the series is summed in any system of arithmetic in which the precision is finite (e.g., in 8 digit floating-point arithmetic), then for some value of K, the number 1/K will no longer contribute anything to the sum, and the series will converge. Converge to what? Before attempting to find the answer by the simple method of writing a Fortran program and running it, first estimate for what value of K the sum will cease growing. Then write the Fortran program, but don't run it.

**315.** A circle of radius 1 is circumscribed around an equilateral triangle. A square is now circumscribed around the circle, and a second circle is circumscribed around the square. The second circle will have a radius of 2. The process is continued: a pentagon, a third circle, then a hexagon, then a fourth circle, and so on. Will the successive radii converge, and if so, to what? Can we arrive at either answer with a Fortran program?

**320.** The formula

$$D = \sqrt{1.5H}$$

is a remarkable approximation formula for the distance to the horizon, D, in **miles,** for a height above the earth's surface, H, in **feet.** Thus, a man whose eyes are 6 feet above ground, standing at the ocean's edge, sees 3 miles to the horizon. Or, in an airplane flying at 20,000 feet, one can quickly calculate that the horizon is $\sqrt{30{,}000} = 173$ miles away. The formula is remarkable because it is surprisingly accurate for being so simple, and it is all mixed up in its dimensions. The exact formula for the same function is

$$D = \sqrt{H^2 + 2RH}$$

where all values are in miles, and R = 4000 is the radius of the earth.
Write a Fortran program to evaluate both formulas for values of H from 1000 feet, in increments of 1000 feet, to the height at which the approximation formula is in error by 2% or more.

**325.** Exercise 320 will locate the 2% error point in the formula for the distance to the horizon within 1000 feet. To locate the height within 1 foot, the bracketing process can be used. Write a Fortran program to do this.

# 13

# MORE ON FORTRAN

## 13.1   Fortran's Built-in Functions

In Chapter 11 it was pointed out that whenever a package of subroutines is made up for a system of arithmetic, it is customary to include, besides the arithmetic operations, the elementary functions of square root, sine, cosine, arctangent, logarithm, and exponential. This is true of Fortran. The angles involved in the trigonometric functions are expressed in radian measure. Logarithms are to the base e; that is, natural logarithms. The exponential function is the antilogarithm; that is, it yields powers of e.

The Fortran statements below show examples of these functions:

| COMM. | STATEMENT NUMBER | | | | CONT. | | | | | | | | | | | | | | | | | | | | | | | | | | | |
|---|---|---|---|---|---|---|---|---|---|---|---|---|---|---|---|---|---|---|---|---|---|---|---|---|---|---|---|---|---|---|---|---|
| 1 | 2 | 3 | 4 | 5 | 6 | 7 | 8 | 9 | 10 | 11 | 12 | 13 | 14 | 15 | 16 | 17 | 18 | 19 | 20 | 21 | 22 | 23 | 24 | 25 | 26 | 27 | 28 | 29 | 30 | 31 | 32 |
| | | | | | | A | = | | 0 | . | 7 | 8 | 5 | 3 | 9 | 8 | 1 | 6 | | | | | | | | | | | | | |
| | | | | | | B | = | | 2 | . | 7 | 1 | 8 | 2 | 8 | 1 | 8 | | | | | | | | | | | | | | |
| | | | | | | C | = | | 2 | . | 0 | | | | | | | | | | | | | | | | | | | | |
| | | | | | | X | = | | S | I | N | ( | A | ) | | | | | | | | | | | | | | | | | |
| | | | | | | Y | = | | L | Ø | G | ( | B | ) | | | | | | | | | | | | | | | | | |
| | | | | | | Z | = | | E | X | P | ( | C | ) | | | | | | | | | | | | | | | | | |
| | | | | | | D | = | | A | T | A | N | ( | C | / | 2 | ) | | | | | | | | | | | | | | |

After execution, the variables should have these values:

$$X = 0.70710675 \quad \text{(sine of } \pi/4\text{)}$$
$$Y = 1 \quad\quad\quad\quad \text{(log}_e \text{ e)}$$
$$Z = 7.3890559 \quad \text{(e}^2\text{)}$$
$$D = 0.78539816 \quad \text{(the angle whose tangent is 1)}$$

Each of the built-in functions has certain restrictions, and violations of these restrictions will result in errors during execution:

1.   SQT will not accept a negative argument.
2.   LOG will not accept a negative argument.
3.   SIN and COS, while not restricted in most Fortrans to any given range, will probably not yield functional values that are correct for values of the argument beyond some reasonable point, say, 1000 radians.
4.   ATAN produces a result (the principal value) in the range from $-\pi/2$ to $\pi/2$.

## 13.2   The Facilities of Fortran

In addition to the built-in functions, Fortran offers many other facilities.
1.   Subroutine capability. The user may write his problem solution as a set of subroutines; each subroutine is called by the following mechanism: We have a subroutine for random number generation, for example, called by the statement

CALL   RNG(X)

2.   Double precision. Fortran IV offers double-precision arithmetic in both fixed- and floating-point modes. This allows integer capability up to $2^{30}$, or floating-point precision up to 15 decimal digits (the range of the exponent is not affected).
3.   Choice of output formats. Information that is stored may be printed in a variety of ways. Figure 13.1 shows examples. In each case, the format description shown is placed in a FORMAT statement, matching one-for-one with the stated variables in a PRINT statement. Thus, if variables A, B, K, D, and E are to be printed, the FORMAT statement could be

FORMAT(F16.3, E12.4, I7, 2D17.8)

which would call for A to be printed in floating-point; B to be in exponential form; K to be in integer form; and both D and E to be printed in double precision. In the figure, the letter b denotes "blank." The "General" format is designed to adjust the output to fit the number being printed; it combines the E and F formats and uses the one that is appropriate.

| Information in storage | Type | FORMAT description | Printed output |
|---|---|---|---|
| A = 1234.56 | Floating | F8.2 | bb123.56 |
| B = 789.6 | Floating | F12.3 | bbbbb789.600 |
| K = 31416 | Integer | I8 | bbb31416 |
| C = ABCDE | Alphabetic | A7 | ABCDEbb |
| A = 100000. | Exponential | E12.4 | bb1.0000Eb05 |
| B = −.0123 | Exponential | E15.2 | bbbbbb-1.23E-02 |
| X = 9.6327542163 | Double precision | D20.12 | bbbbbb9.632754216300 |
| | Hollerith | 16HTHISbISbH-FORMAT | THIS IS H-FORMAT |
| A = .TRUE. | Logical | L3 | bbT |
| A = 3.14159 | General | G14.6 | bb3.141590bbbb |
| B = 1000001. | General | G14.6 | bb1.000001Eb06 |

FIGURE 13.1 Fortran FORMAT possibilities.

## 13.3   Fortran Fine Points

Fortran is a rich and viable language. Like other living languages, it tends to become idiomatic and it develops interesting quirks. We will mention a few of these points, together with hints for better Fortran work.

  1.  The Fortran furnished with the Varian machines is Fortran IV. In Fortran IV, mixed-mode statements are legal; that is, fixed-point and floating-point variables may occur in the same statement. Despite this forgiveness on the part of the compiler, it is good coding practice never to mix modes, except when a statement is written to deliberately float a fixed-point number. Mixed-mode expressions generally indicate muddled thinking, and hence poor computing.

  2.  The two statements

$$Y = B*B$$
$$Y = B**2$$

should be logically equivalent, and the compiler probably creates the same machine code in both cases. Similarly, the statements

$$X = A*A*A*A$$
$$X = A**4$$

should be logically equivalent. At some point, the writer of the compiler must decide where to draw the line. For the statement

$$Z = C**123$$

it would be foolish for the compiler to set up 122 multiplications; it is easier to go to log and exponential operations, and all Fortrans will do just that. The point is this: The programmer should use the form that will be most efficient. Certainly for squares and cubes, the multiplication form for the arithmetic is better than the exponential form (with the two asterisks).

  3.  Fortran IV allows the use of the assigned GO TO. That is, a statement like

$$GO\ TO\ K,\ (6,7,8,9)$$

is legal, and the value of K at the time of execution should be a valid statement number. Thus, the device could be used as a multiple switch (see also Section 13.4). If control in the program is to go to statements 6, 7, 8, or 9 at various times, then K can be given one of those values. But this is a slippery tool. What if K acquires some other value inadvertently during execution? (And such things do happen.)

  4.  Never use constants as arguments in a subroutine call [e.g., CALL ALPHA (35)]. The called subroutine can alter the "constant" for you, as in

```
SUBROUTINE ALPHA (K)
K = 1234
RETURN
```

5. Tests for equality of floating-point numbers can be misleading. The statement

```
IF (A − B) 3,2,3
```

may not get you to statement 2 as you had planned. This statement will:

```
IF (ABS(A − B) − 1.0E−8)2,2,3
```

6. Test for the case of zero iterations prior to a DO loop. Fortran always performs at least one iteration of a DO loop. Try this:

```
    IF ((K − J)/I)1,1,2
  2 DO 6 M = J, K, I

  6 CONTINUE
  1 CONTINUE
```

7. Watch for unneeded expressions inside loops, as in

```
     DO 25 J = 1, 2500
     C = 0.0
  25 A(J) = 6.0
```

8. An integer can be tested for odd–even by this statement (going to 1 on even and 2 on odd):

```
IF (MOD(K,2))2,1,2
```

9. To zero a multidimensional array, the scheme

```
     DIMENSION A(60,60,60), B(21600)
     EQUIVALENCE (A(1,1,1), B(1))
     DO 10 I = 1, 216000
  10 B(I) = 0.0
```

is quicker than

```
     DIMENSION A(60,60,60)
     DO 10 I = 1, 60
     DO 10 J = 1, 60
     DO 10 K = 1, 60
  10 A(I, J, K) = 0.0
```

## 13.4  Switches

A programmed switch is a device for storing a decision. The decision itself is made at one place in a program, but its effect take place at another. Figure 13.2 shows some of the possibilities and their flowchart notation.

The top section of the figure shows the action of a one-time switch. The two sides of the switch are arbitrarily called "ON" and "OFF." The switch is initialized to its ON side, in the housekeeping phase of the program. At the switch point, the program will proceed to reference 6, where the switch is turned to OFF. The action indicated by "DO something" will be done just once. When the program returns to reference 8 again, the one-time action will be bypassed; we thus have a "slam-the-door" switch.

The middle portion of the figure shows a switch used to form a flip-flop. On each passage through reference 2, actions A and B will be taken alternately.

In the bottom portion of the figure, this notion is extended to three courses of action. The switch could have more than three exits, if desired.

Figures 13.3, 13.4, and 13.5 show possible Fortran codes for each of these switch actions.

The one-time action switch could be used in a subroutine, for example, to execute some action that is to be done the first time the subroutine is called, and only the first time.

A use of the flip-flop might be in the implementation of a formula like Simpson's rule for numeric integration:

$$S = \frac{h}{3}[y_0 + 4y_1 + 2y_2 + 4y_3 + 2y_4 + \cdots + y_k]$$

where the first and last ordinates have coefficients of 1, and all the rest have alternate coefficients of 2 and 4.

Be wary of switches. They are attractive and useful, but it is easy to overdo their use. As a general rule, **one** switch in a program is the maximum number to use. If you find yourself using several switches (and especially if you are tempted to use switches that control other switches), it is likely that your analysis of the problem is getting muddled.

### EXERCISES

**330.**  Suppose that the Gross National Product (GNP) of the United States in 1972 is 1 trillion dollars (1.E12 in floating decimal notation) and is increasing at a constant annual rate of 3%. Suppose also that the gross output of the computing industry in 1972 is 10 billion dollars (1.E10) and is increasing at a constant annual rate of 9%. In what year will the gross

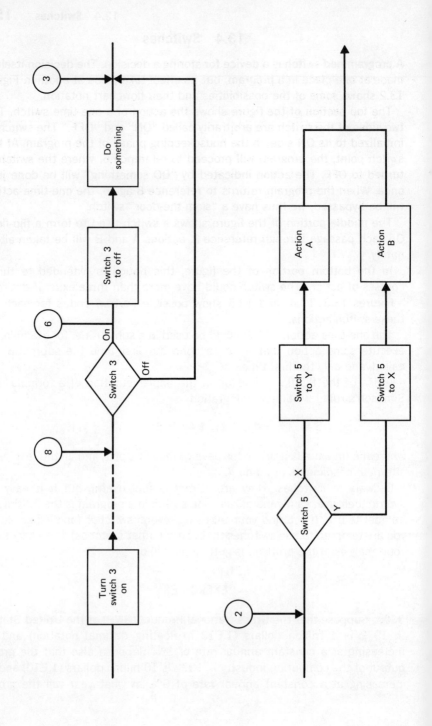

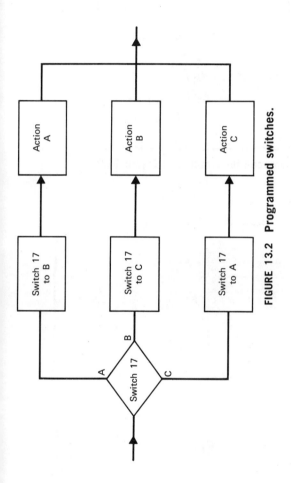

FIGURE 13.2 Programmed switches.

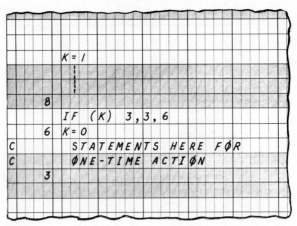

FIGURE 13.3  Fortran code for switch 3 of Figure 13.2.

```
C  | STATEMENT NUMBER | C | FORTRAN STAT
 1 | 2 3 4 5 | 6 | 7 8 9 10 11 12 13 14 15 16 17 18 19 20 21 22 23 24 25 26 27 28 29 30 31 32 33 34 35 36 37 38 39 40 41 42

C  |        |   |      THE  IF  STATEMENT  IS  THE  SWITCH
   |        |   | IF  (M) 8,8,7
   |     7  |   | M = 0
C  |        |   |      THIS  IS  THE  Y  SIDE
C  |        |   |      PUT  ACTION  B  HERE
   |        |   | GO  TO  9

   |     8  |   | M = 1
C  |        |   |      THIS  IS  THE  X  SIDE
C  |        |   |      PUT  ACTION  A  HERE
   |     9  |   |
```

FIGURE 13.4  Fortran code for switch 5 of Figure 13.2.

```
 C            THE IF IS THE 3-WAY SWITCH
              IF (J) 9,10,11
       9      J = 0
 C            PUT ACTIØN A HERE
 C            SWITCH SET TØ B BY LINE 9
              GO TØ 5
      10      J = 1
 C            PUT ACTION B HERE
 C            SWITCH SET TØ C BY LINE 10
              GØ TØ 5
      11      J = -1
 C            PUT ACTION C HERE
 C            SWITCH SET TØ A BY LINE 11
       5
```

**FIGURE 13.5** Fortran code for switch 17 of Figure 13.2.

output of the computing industry exceed the GNP of the nation? (The result is nonsense, of course, but the nonsense has been built into the problem.) Write a Fortran program and run it.

**335.** With the same conditions as in Exercise 330, find the year in which the amount of **growth** in computing during the year exceeds the growth in GNP for that year. This is not the same year as in Exercise 330.

Should this exercise be a separate Fortran program, or could it be calculated at the same time? Which year will come first? Must you know in advance? Would a switch be useful?

**340.** Given a number X, it is easy, in a Fortran program, to calculate

$$Y = X^X$$

It is not quite as easy, given a value of Y, to calculate the corresponding X. The calculation of X, given Y, calls for inverting a function. The bracketing process offers a solution to this problem, and can be used, in fact, to invert almost any function. To be specific, we wish to calculate values of X for all integral values of Y from 1 to 100. Draw a flowchart, and write and run a Fortran program for these 100 results.

# 14

# BASIC

## 14.1 The BASIC Language

BASIC (standing for **B**eginner's **A**ll-purpose **S**ymbolic **I**nstruction **C**ode) is a language based on Fortran, originally intended, as the name implies, for student use in learning computing. It appears simpler than Fortran, but do not be misled. Over the years, BASIC has developed into a powerful but easy to use language.

There can be BASIC compilers, but on many machines the language is executed interpretively, as it is on your mini.

One outstanding feature of BASIC is its modularity. It is not necessary to learn all of BASIC in order to make good use of it; you can learn a small subset of the language and do useful work, and pick up the fine points later.

We will describe the rules and uses of BASIC in terms of its implementation on the Varian machine. The particular BASIC that you may use may differ in its details. Be sure you have the BASIC reference manual that goes with your machine. If you intend to make extensive use of BASIC, by all means consult a text on that language. There are several excellent ones; a list of some is found at the end of this chapter.

## 14.2 A Problem in BASIC

Since BASIC much resembles Fortran, in order to understand BASIC we need only dwell on the differences between the two languages. A large portion of the differences can be shown by exploring a simple problem.

**160**

```
10   LET A = 100
20   L  E  T  K    =    0
30   LET A = A*1.03
40   PRINT A
50   LET K = K + 1
60   IF K = 100 THEN 80
70   GO TO 30
80   END
```

**FIGURE 14.1   A program in BASIC.**

We want to calculate the compound interest on $100, at 3% annual interest, for 100 years. A BASIC program to perform that calculation is shown in Figure 14.1. Follow the comments below with the program at hand.

1.   Every statement is numbered. It is common practice to number by 10s. Regardless of the order in which they are typed, the statements will be executed in ascending order of the statement number. Thus, if we have to patch by inserting a statement between those we have numbered 50 and 60, we can use a number in the range 51–59 for the insertion.

2.   The statements are similar to those in Fortran; that is, they are English sentences, but in capital letters only and with no period at the end of the sentence. If the statement is in equation form, read the equals sign as though it were a left-pointing arrow; i.e., "is replaced by."

3.   In the equation type of statements, there must be a single variable on the left of the equals sign and an expression on the right. Statement length is limited to the width of the line on the Teletype (say, 72 characters, counting everything that can be typed).

4.   As in Fortran, spaces in the statements are a matter of appearance and readability only. Thus, in statement 20, the extra spaces are of no consequence to BASIC.

5.   The IF statement at 60 is simpler than its Fortran counterpart. The statement to go to if the condition is met is stated explicitly. If the condition is not met, control will proceed to the next statement in numerical sequence.

6.   Printing is greatly simplified in BASIC. All numbers are in floating-point, and the format will be selected by BASIC. Small numbers will be printed in fixed-point format; large numbers will appear in scientific notation. The position on the page is selected by BASIC.

7.   Since all numbers in BASIC are in floating-point, there is no true integer capability, and the I, J, K, L, M, N rule does not apply. However, if the translating program is well-written, it is feasible to count in floating-point (a procedure that is not recommended in Fortran). All variables are named with either single letters or a letter followed by a digit.

8.    BASIC is usually used at a time-shared terminal (although your use may be at a Teletype with a dedicated computer). Thus, BASIC is highly **conversational.** This means that syntax errors in your statements will be detected as you make them, and will be reported back to you immediately. You are on-line with the system, and it is said to be interactive. This is a great blessing, since you are then informed of mechanical errors at the time they are committed; you are in context with your problem at that time, and can correct the error and drive toward your solution at a faster pace.

9.    BASIC also lets the user execute direct commands, which turns the terminal into a kind of huge printing desk calculator. A statement that is not numbered will be executed immediately, so that one can call for

PRINT SQR(2)

and get back immediately:

1.41421

## 14.3    The Birthday Problem Again

Let's repeat the generalized birthday problem (first considered in Section 12.1 and Exercise 285, p. 230) in BASIC. The flowchart is shown in Figure 14.2, and the BASIC program is given in Figure 14.3. As before, study the two figures in connection with the following observations.

1.    Comments in BASIC are indicated by the word REMARK or REM. They can be inserted anywhere in a code. They are not executable statements and will have no effect on the running of the code.

2.    The program calls for printing 19 lines (check that), with two numbers on each line.

3.    The printing position across the page is set by BASIC. If we wish to dress up our printed output, we could insert the statement

25   PRINT   "D", "K"

which will fall between statements 20 and 30 and cause printing of column headings. These headings will be properly spaced (or nearly so) because of the orderly way in which BASIC normally prints results.

4.    All the data for the problem was generated by letting D have the value 100 and incrementing D by 50s. Suppose we wished to run the same program for specific values of D, such as 30, 60, 144, and 365. These specific values can be entered in a DATA statement (anywhere in the code):

155   DATA 30,60,144,365,0

(The 0 at the end of the list is a sentinel to signal the "out-of-data" condition.) Then our program can be altered as follows:

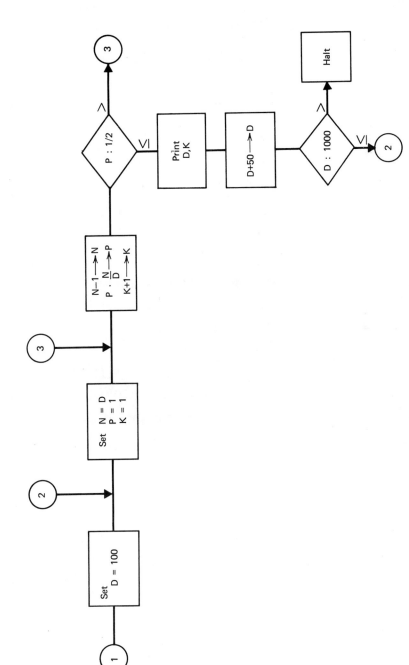

FIGURE 14.2  The generalized birthday problem.

```
10   REM BIRTHDAY PROBLEM
20   LET D = 100
30   LET N = D
40   LET P = 1
50   LET K = 1
60   LET N = N-1
70   LET P = P*N/D
80   REM NEW PROBABILITY
90   LET K = K+1
100  IF P > .5 THEN 60
110  PRINT D,K
120  LET D = D+50
130  REM TEST D FOR LIMIT
140  IF D > 1000 THEN 160
150  GO TO 30
160  END
```

FIGURE 14.3  **BASIC code for the birthday problem.**

```
20   READ D
```

and each time statement 20 is executed, D will be assigned the next available value in the data stack. In our example, this can occur five times:

```
25   IF D = 0 THEN 160
```

This statement tests the sentinel and terminates the program when the useful values of the data stack are exhausted.

Statements 120, 130, and 140 should now be deleted, and statement 150 should be changed to

```
150   GO TO 20
```

The program has now been altered to handle the new situation.

5. Alternatively, statement 20 could be changed to

```
20   INPUT D
```

and values of D could be fed in on demand from the Teletype each time statement 20 is executed. Nothing else in the program would have to be altered in this case.

## 14.4   More Tools in BASIC

Consider this short program segment in BASIC:

```
200  FOR K = 1 TO 7
210  LET A(K) = B(K)*C(K)
220  NEXT K
```

First, we see a form of subscript notation. We can name variables B1, B2, C6, A7, and so on, but the notation B(I) lets us assign names more systematically.

The FOR . . . NEXT notation is BASIC's way of looping (corresponding to the Fortran DO loop facility). The program shown will operate on two lists, B and C, each of 7 numbers, and form their product by pairs, putting the seven results into list A; K is stepped by 1s. We could also write

$$200 \quad FOR\ K = 1\ TO\ 106\ STEP\ 7$$

to send the loop through 16 iterations, ending with K = 106.

BASIC offers ten built-in functions: square root (SQR), natural logarithm (LOG), exponential or antilog (EXP), absolute value (ABS), sine (SIN), cosine (COS), tangent (TAN), arctangent (ATN), integer (INT), and random number generation (RND). Most of these should now be familiar from their use in Fortran, but some are new. The ABS function furnishes the absolute value of the argument. The statement

$$10 \quad LET\ A = ABS(-B*B+C)$$

for B = 5 and C = 4 will furnish A = 21.

The INT function furnishes the integer part of a number:

$$20 \quad LET\ A = INT(SQR(10))$$

will yield A = 3. The statement

$$30 \quad LET\ A = INT(.2+.8)$$

should yield A = 1. This statement and ones like it [e.g., INT(1.2+.8)] furnish tests of the INT function, and not all BASIC translators give the results you might expect. Indeed, all of the built-in functions should be suspect until you personally test them. We expect COS(3.1415927/2) to be 0, for example, and we have reason to expect that ATN(SIN(A)/COS(A)) will yield A itself for any reasonable value of A. But these niceties depend on how the functions are calculated. Before relying on any function, be sure you subject it to your own thorough tests.

The function RND is unique. Each time the statement

$$53 \quad LET\ A = RND(X)$$

is executed, A will be assigned a new random number of the form .XXXXXX (that is, a 6 digit number lying between 0 and 0.999999). The scheme of generation is hidden from you. The generator may be sophisticated and good, or it may not be. The same rule applies: Test it carefully in your BASIC system to guarantee, to your satisfaction, that it does what you wish.

In addition to the ten built-in functions, BASIC makes provision for user-defined functions. Suppose, for example, that we are doing some work that requires angles in degrees. The conversion from radians to degrees is simple enough (i.e., multiply the radian measure by $180/\pi = 57.2957795$), but we may have to do this many times. We can define a function called D by

$$116 \quad \text{DEF FND(K)} = \text{K} * 57.2957795$$

where K is a dummy argument that will not appear in the use of the function. If we must add two angles, A and B, in degrees, we can write

$$232 \quad \text{LET C} = \text{FND(A)} + \text{FND(B)}$$

BASIC also makes subroutining easy. Given a set of BASIC statements (numbered, say, 9000–9150) that form the subroutine, we can involve that subroutine at any other statement by writing

$$570 \quad \text{GO SUB 9000}$$

provided that the last statement of the subroutine (number 9150 in our example) is written

$$9150 \quad \text{RETURN}$$

The subroutine will be executed at statement 570, and control will return to the next statement in sequence (most likely numbered 580).

## 14.5 Extended BASIC

All the features that have been outlined so far apply to nearly every BASIC implementation. There are more features in what is called Extended BASIC. The line of demarkation between elementary BASIC and Extended BASIC keeps changing, as the extra features become standard items.

The ON statement provides a multiple branch of control. For example, the statement

$$200 \quad \text{ON A GO TO 50,150,280,360,27}$$

causes control to pass to one of the given numbered statements, depending on the value of A at the time of execution. If A is 3, control will pass to statement 280 (the **third** specified statement). The integer value of A is used. If A has a value greater than 5 (in this example), an execution error message will result. For A, any valid expression can be used.

Character **strings** can be set up and named by attaching the symbol $ to a normal name. Thus, we can write

>315   LET Q5$ = "JULY 22, 1972"
>325   LET Q6$ = "JUNE 17, 1973"

and such strings can be manipulated as though they were variables. Thus, we can utilize statements like

>576   IF Q5$ < Q6$ THEN 160
>610   LET X3$ = Y3$
>666   IF A$ <> B$ THEN 400

A normal PRINT statement like

>123   PRINT A,B,C,D,E

causes printing at fixed positions across the page, usually 15 characters apart. The statement

>123   PRINT A;B;C;D;E

Adjusts the horizontal spacing according to the width needed by each variable value. Both of these forms of printing are standard in all BASICs. Extended BASIC also offers the ability to control horizontal spacing even more. Thus, the statement

>123   PRINT TAB(23);A;TAB(65);B

causes the values of A and B to be typed at positions 23 and 65, in much the same way as the tab stops on a typewriter function. The statement

>213   PRINT TAB(X);"*"

causes typing of an asterisk in position X across the page. Proper use of this device allows for plotting results.

The most powerful of the extra features provided in Extended BASIC is the set of matrix operations. Since a matrix is simply an array of numbers, there is no new problem in getting a matrix into and out of storage. Special instructions are provided, however, to make reading and printing of matrices easy. In addition, the operations of adding, subtracting, and multiplying two or more matrices are available. Thus, statements like the following can be written:

>100   MAT INPUT B,C,D,E
>120   MAT A = B+C
>130   MAT F = A*E

All of these operations could be performed also by simple loops. The real power of the system lies in the **inverse** function:

$$140 \quad \text{MAT} \quad G = \text{INV(F)}$$

The inverse of the matrix F is calculated and furnished as a new matrix, G. Since the operation of inverting a matrix is quite equivalent to solving a system of simultaneous equations, the operation INV offers a lot of computing power in one instruction.

Other matrix operations are those of TRN (the interchange of rows and columns in a matrix, called the transpose); CON (for constant, to make all elements of a matrix equal to unity); IDN (identity, in which the main diagonal elements of a matrix are set to 1 and all off-diagonal elements are set to 0). A combination of operations:

$$123 \quad \text{MAT} \quad A = \text{INV(B)}$$
$$133 \quad \text{LET} \quad C = \text{DET}$$

provides the capability of calculating the determinant of a matrix; this is another complicated function that is compressed into a single handy BASIC command.

## 14.6 Summary

We have done little more than list the features of the BASIC language. Since there are at least ten books devoted exclusively to the rules and uses of the language, there is obviously much that can be learned about it. If your mini offers access to BASIC, then the proper way to learn is to apply the language to problem situations.

### BIBLIOGRAPHY

Coan, J. S. *Basic BASIC*. New York: Hayden, 1970.

Farina, M. V. *Programming in BASIC*. Englewood Cliffs, N.J.: Prentice-Hall, 1968.

Gruenberger, F. *Computing with the BASIC Language*. San Francisco: Canfield Press, 1972.

Hare, V. C., Jr. *BASIC Programming*. New York: Harcourt Brace Jovanovich, 1970.

Kemeny, J. G., and T. E. Kurtz. *BASIC Programming*. New York: Wiley 1965.

Sharp, W. F., and N. L. Jacob. *BASIC*. New York: Free Press, 1971.

Spencer, D. D. *A Guide to BASIC Programming: A Time-Sharing Language*. Reading, Mass.: Addison-Wesley, 1970.

## EXERCISES

**345.** Run the BASIC program given in Figure 14.3. For the 19 values of D that are generated, values of K are calculated for which the probability is .5; that is, the probability level that forms an even-money bet. Alter the program to form a 2:1 bet. This means a probability level of .666667 in favor of the event; in our calculation, we must test for P = .333333.

**350.** Write and run a BASIC program for the flowchart of Figure 12.4 (the fifth root of 100, found by the bracketing process).
   The bracketing scheme shown in Figure 12.4 called for 8 digit precision. If your BASIC system operates to only 6 digit precision, be sure to change the logic of your solution accordingly. If you left the test for convergence at 8, your BASIC program would hang up in an endless loop. Can you see why?

**355.** Write and run BASIC programs to explore various aspects of the rule of 72, described in Exercise 297 (Chapter 12).

**360.** Given 500 feet of fencing with which to fence off a rectangular field along a straight river; the river forms one boundary of the field. What are the dimensions of the field, if it is to have the maximum possible area?
   The area of the field can be expressed as the product of the width, X, by the length, 500 − 2X. A bracketing scheme can be set up, letting X vary from 0 to 250 until the maximum area is found.
   Write a BASIC program for this problem in bracketing.

**365.** The field of Exercise 360 is to be constructed beside a circular lake of radius 1 mile. Find the dimensions of the new field.
   Exercise 360 is a trivial problem in differential calculus, and the point of the exercise in this text is the ease with which we can substitute the power of the computer for the advanced knowledge needed to apply the calculus. We expect the result from the bracketing process to agree with the analytic solution, so that we gain assurance that our new tool works. (If you explore the mathematics deeply enough, it seems that the methods of the calculus **are** processes like bracketing carried to their mathematical limit.)
   Now, Exercise 365 is not a trivial problem. The fact that one boundary of the field is part of a circle introduces new elements of complexity. If we try to flowchart a solution by bracketing, we will come to the critical step "calculate the area of the field."
   Draw a flowchart for the bracketing process; include the step just described. Now consider that step as a subroutine and draw a new flowchart for the logic of finding that area. It would help greatly to make a few calculations for special cases, such as for the answer to Exercise 360 (length 250, width 125). And here is where a language like BASIC is priceless. While you

are solving the larger problem, and have isolated a particularly sticky small problem, BASIC is there to help by making it easy to perform routine calculations along the way to aid your thinking. Further suggestions about this problem can be found in Appendix 3.

**370.** Repeat Exercise 305, Chapter 12 (the Fibonacci sequence), in BASIC.

**375.** Repeat Exercise 310, Chapter 12 (the sum of the harmonic series), in BASIC.

**380.** Repeat Exercise 315, Chapter 12 (the circumscribed polygon problem), in BASIC.

**385.** Repeat Exercise 320, Chapter 12 (the distance to the horizon problem), in BASIC.

**390.** Repeat Exercise 340, Chapter 13 (inverting the function $X^x$), in BASIC.

**400.** Section 12.7 contained two famous Fortran problems that usually lead to misleading or incorrect results. Run those programs in your BASIC.

**403.** See Exercise 222 (Chapter 8). The $10 \times 10$ array of numbers is awkward to manipulate when the symbolic addresses are B, B+1, . . . , B+99. In BASIC, we may use double subscripts, so that the array is more conveniently described with the notation B(I,J) where I and J run from 1 to 10. A cell in the array, B(I,J), now has for its eight neighbors the cells B(I−1, J−1), B(I,J+1), and B(I+1,J−1), B(I−1,J), B(I+1,J), B(I−1,J+1), B(I,J−1), and B(I+1,J+1), for any values of I and J. If the $10 \times 10$ array is considered as being embedded in a $12 \times 12$ array, then there are no exceptions, and the averaging process can sweep over the entire array in two simple FOR . . . NEXT loops. Write a BASIC program to make one averaging sweep over the $10 \times 10$ array.

**405.** Play with your BASIC system to find some of its weaknesses and limitations. The following program, for example:

```
10  LET X = 2
20  LET X = 2*X
30  PRINT X
40  GO TO 20
50  END
```

will help establish for you the limits of the floating-point system by developing a table of powers of 2 until the system overflows, at which point you will receive an error message.

Now repeat this program with statement 20 replaced by

```
20  LET X = .5*X
```

to find the lower bound on the floating-point system, and the action that results.

In particular, explore carefully the INT function. Study carefully the following program:

```
10  LET X = INT(.5+INT(.5 + INT(1.5)))
20  PRINT X
30  END
```

and predict what you expect to see printed; then try it out.

In the equation

$$A = (SQR(EXP(TAN(ATN(SIN^2 X + COS^2 X)))))^2$$

the value of A should be e = 2.71828 for any value of X. Write a BASIC program to evaluate A for values of X between 0.1 and 3 in steps of 0.1. For all 30 values of output, the system should produce the value e.

Finally, explore the action of your BASIC system in handling numbers for which the conversion from decimal to binary is not exact:

```
10  LET S = 0
20  LET X = .2
30  FOR K = 1 TO 500
40  LET S = S + X
50  NEXT K
60  PRINT S
70  IF S > 1000 THEN 90
80  GO TO 30
90  END
```

This program adds the number .2 to itself 500 times and then repeats this action 10 times. One might expect to get as output the numbers 100, 200, 300, . . . , 1000. But the exact decimal number .2 must be represented in a binary machine as the repeating fraction .001100110011 . . . , which is not exact. Try this program in your BASIC system.

# 15

# SOME LARGER PROBLEMS

## 15.1 Background

Most of the problems considered so far have been small and somewhat artificial, in order to demonstrate some new technique. In this chapter, we will consider some larger problems, to furnish you with something challenging to work on. For each problem, enough information will be furnished to get you started, but not so much information as to spoil the fun of really learning computing, which can only be done by doing it.

The choice of language (assembly, Fortran, or BASIC) is yours. For problems involving nonintegers, or where the range of values is large, either Fortran or BASIC would be called for. For problems that involve only integers, assembly language would be suitable. You should not consider yourself in any way adept at computing until you have mastered the use of one high-level language (e.g., Fortran) **and** assembly language.

For each problem presented here, a great deal of the analysis has already been done for you. For example, the basic decision as to whether or not the problem is a good computer problem has already been made, as has the choice of machine. The problems require no knowledge of advanced mathematics.

**172**

## 15.2  Gauss' Lattice Problem

If a circle of radius R is drawn on a lattice, with its center on one of the lattice points, how many of the lattice points are in or on the circle? Figure 15.1 shows the situation for R = 1, 2, 3, and 4. For these cases, one can count the number of points by eye; there are 5, 13, 29, and 49 points, respectively. We wish to extend this table of values, perhaps up to R = 1000.

A brute force approach might be to let two variables, A and B, take on all integral values independently from −R to R, and for each pair of values determine whether

$$A^2 + B^2 \leqslant R^2$$

If so, the point (A,B) satisfies, and should be counted; if not, the point (A,B) is rejected. This approach will work, but it is grossly inefficient. Examine the part of Figure 15.1 for R = 4. Clearly, for a large block of points within the

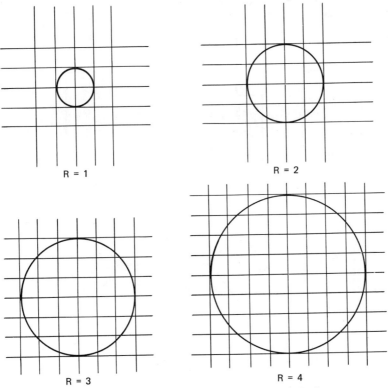

R = 1

R = 2

R = 3

R = 4

**FIGURE 15.1  The lattice problem for R=1, 2, 3, 4.**

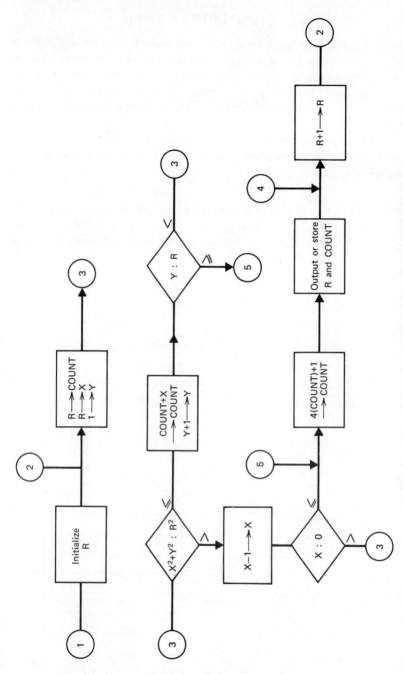

**FIGURE 15.2  The lattice problem (solution by Richard Sandin).**

circle, the determination of being selected is trivial. Moreover, the picture is symmetrical, so we should be able to work in just a quarter of the circle. The problem really reduces to decisions about the points that lie near the circle.

Figure 15.2 shows a flowchart for a possible scheme. Your chief problem will be to determine how to handle the numbers when $R^2$ becomes greater than 32,767. Do not try to use floating-point arithmetic; this is a problem in integers. (The integer facility of Fortran on the Varian 620 allows for a range of 32,767, however.)

The problem is interesting because it is believed that there is no simple formula that yields the number of points for any value of R. As R gets large, however, the number of points should be close to $\pi R^2$, as you can check.

Notice that the flowchart is drawn as an endless problem. A test for some limit can be inserted at reference 4.

## 15.3  Pythagorean Triplets

Figure 15.3 shows the start of a table of primitive Pythagorean triplets; that is, sets of integers that satisfy the Pythagorean relationship, $X^2 + Y^2 = Z^2$. Each set of values X, Y, and Z is called primitive because X, Y, and Z have no factor in common.

Theory tells us that we can generate all such triplets systematically if we can generate values of R and T having three properties simultaneously:

1.   R is greater than T
2.   R and T have no factor in common; that is, R and T have a greatest common divisor of 1
3.   R and T are of opposite parity; that is, if one is odd, the other is even

Given values of R and T that satisfy all three conditions, we are guaranteed the values of X, Y, and Z by the equations

$$X = R^2 - T^2$$
$$Y = 2RT$$
$$Z = R^2 + T^2$$

| R | T | X | Y | Z |
|---|---|---|---|---|
| 2 | 1 | 3 | 4 | 5 |
| 3 | 2 | 5 | 12 | 13 |
| 4 | 1 | 15 | 8 | 17 |
| 4 | 3 | 7 | 24 | 25 |
| 5 | 2 | 21 | 20 | 29 |
| 5 | 4 | 9 | 40 | 41 |
| 6 | 1 | 35 | 12 | 37 |

**FIGURE 15.3**   **The start of a table of Pythagorean triplets, X, Y, and Z.**

The problem, then, is that of generating the R and T values systematically. Figure 15.4 shows one such scheme. Again, there is no end indicated for the problem; a limit test may be inserted after the "calculate and print" box. Notice the notation in the bottom rectangle. It is understood that when several actions are called for within one rectangle, they are to be performed in the given order. Thus, if we enter the box with R = 66, the new R value will be 67 and the new T value will be 66.

## 15.4 The Hexagon Problem

Figure 15.5 shows a pattern of seven hexagons. (See also Exercise 60, Chapter 2.) Each hexagon is labeled, from A to G, and each hexagon has numbers on its six edges. The hexagons are movable, but the numbers within each hexagon are to remain fixed. The problem is to rearrange the seven hexagons in a pattern like the one shown but such that each pair of numbers at the adjacent edges has a greatest common divisor of **1**.

Figure 15.6 lets us establish some notations for this problem. For the pattern as a whole, and for the orientation of each hexagon, let us use the wording suggested. Thus, the southwest hexagon in the original pattern is hexagon F; the northeast edge of hexagon G bears the number 15, and so on. The circles on Figure 15.6 show the 12 places where pairs of numbers should each have a GCD of 1. In the original pattern, test position 3 shows a pair of numbers having a GCD of 5. Test position 8 shows a pair of numbers whose GCD is 1. What we want is an arrangement of the hexagons such that **all** 12 test positions show a GCD of 1. The problem is due to Lee Morganstern and has a unique solution.

The positions of the seven hexagons can be permuted in (7!), or 5040, ways. For each such permutation, the hexagons can be rotated in $6^6$ ways. And for each of these arrangements (235,146,240 of them), 12 pairs of numbers must be tested. The total is nearly 3 billion tests. At least, that's how the first rough try at the problem appears. Even on a machine that can perform a complete operation in 3.6 microseconds, this brute force approach might consume several hundred hours of main frame time.

The problem must be cut down to size. No solution will be offered, but some suggestions are in order.

Refer to Figure 15.5, which shows one of the 5040 permutations of the placing of the seven hexagons. For this particular permutation, there are $6^6$ rotations possible. Think of the seven hexagons as a set of rotating dials, forming a 7 place counter for which hexagon A is the high-order "wheel"; hexagon B is the next lower wheel; and so on to hexagon G, which is the low-order wheel of this base 6 "counter." We can perform all the necessary rotations by moving these wheels as a counter. That is, we will rotate G first;

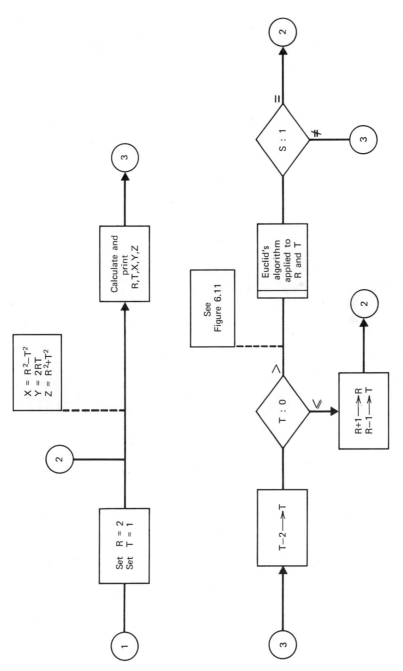

**FIGURE 15.4 Generating Pythagorean triplets.**

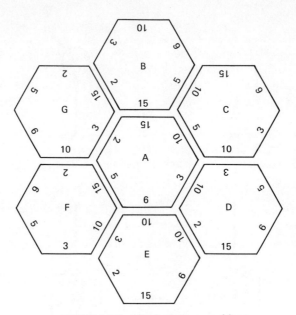

**FIGURE 15.5  The hexagon problem.**

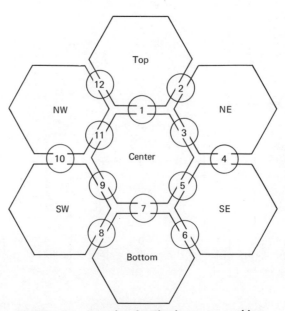

**FIGURE 15.6  Notation for the hexagon problem.**

when it has made a complete revolution, F rotates one position. When F completes a revolution, E rotates one position, and so on.

Now, for each new arrangement, we will make 12 tests, as indicated in Figure 15.6. Suppose that tests 1, 2, 3, and 4 are passed, and the first test that fails is number 5. All the rotations that involve the hexagons that follow (namely, E, F, and G) have no further effect. At this point, then, we should rotate only wheel D for subsequent testing. As soon as wheel D reaches a position for which test 5 is passed (and while hexagon D is being rotated, tests 1, 2, 3, and 4 need not be repeated), the test procedure can go on to tests 6, 7, . . . , 12.

Looked at this way, with the rotations reduced to those that are necessary, the total number of configurations to be tested is cut down to 50,000 or so, and for each configuration, only three or four tests for the GCDs are needed.

## 15.5 The No-Right-Triangles Problem

Consider a 32 × 32 lattice (that is, a graph of dimensions 32 by 32 in which the only points of interest are the 1024 points where the grid lines cross). (See Exercise 65, Chapter 2.) It is easy to locate 3 points on the lattice that do not form a right triangle; the points (15,16), (16,15), and (18,16) will do. How many more points can be found on the lattice, starting with those three, such that no 3 points form a right triangle?

The answer to that question is not known (the number is somewhere around 33).

To find a pattern of such points, you will have to pick some scheme for scanning the lattice; that is, a plan for selecting individual points one after the other. Given the three starting points, then each successive selected point must be tested against **each pair** of previously selected points to determine whether or not a right triangle exists. Thus, for the fourth trial point, there will be three pairs of points to test with the fourth. For each set of 3 points, calculate the square of the distances between them, and then test to see whether or not any square is the sum of the other two. For the fifth point, there will be six sets to test; for the sixth point, there will be ten sets to test; for the seventh point, there will be fifteen sets to test; and so on.

One simple scanning scheme would be to select points at random. Given a random number (generated by the package described in Chapter 9), its low-order 10 bits can be used as two sets of 5 bit numbers which are the coordinates of a point in the 32 × 32 lattice.

Another possibility is to scan the lattice systematically in a pattern like the one shown in Figure 15.7. Figure 15.8 shows the logic of a subroutine

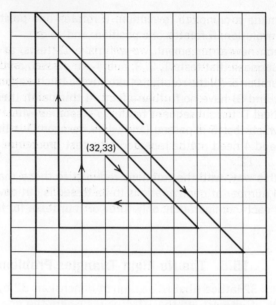

(32,33)

**FIGURE 15.7   A plan for scanning a lattice.**

that will generate this scan. In the flowchart, the variables LX, LY, and LD refer to the lengths of legs in the X, Y, and diagonal directions. XC, YC, and DC refer to counters for the traverses in the X, Y, and diagonal directions. At the start of the scan, the switch should be set to D. The variables should be initialized in the housekeeping part of the program as follows:

$$Set \quad LX = 3$$
$$LY = 4$$
$$LD = 2$$
$$XC = 0$$
$$YC = 0$$
$$DC = 0$$
$$Set\ the\ switch\ to\ D$$

and

$$Set \quad X = 32$$
$$Y = 32$$

The cover of this book shows one such pattern made into an artistic painting. The computer program that produced the pattern had the following features:

1.   All points, including the starting points, were selected at random.

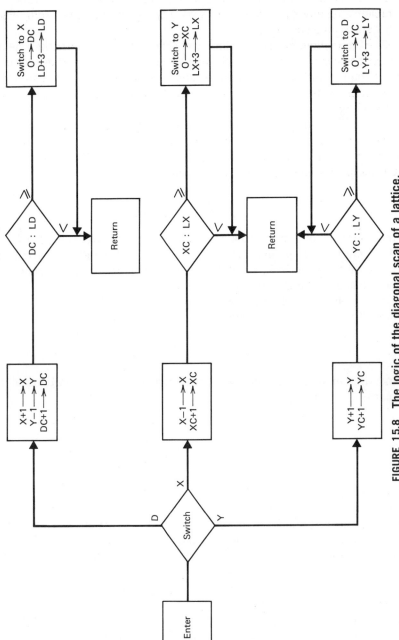

**FIGURE 15.8** The logic of the diagonal scan of a lattice.

2.  In addition to finding all points on the lattice that satisfy the problem's requirements, the results were typed out in graphic form. Figure 15.9 shows one such graph.

3.  The random choice of points will select many that must be rejected, either because they have already been selected, or because they do form a right triangle with some previously selected pair. The program counts how many trial points were considered for each selected point, and outputs this information.

4.  When the number of trial points reaches 3072 (three times the square of the lattice size), the program switches over to a systematic scan of the lattice, so that when the pattern is graphed, we know that, for the given starting points, we have found all possible points.

## 15.6    Permutations

In the problem of Section 15.4 there is a subproblem involved; namely, that of generating the permutations of 7 things systematically. Let these 7 things be the digits 1–7; we wish to generate all possible arrangements of those digits, and there are $7! = 5040$ of them.

We can solve this problem by working up from the bottom. The permutations of two things are limited to these cases: 12 and 21. For three things, we can similarly write down immediately all possible cases:

$$123 \quad 132 \quad 312 \quad 213 \quad 231 \quad 321$$

And without much difficulty we can record all the permutations of four things:

| | | | | | |
|---|---|---|---|---|---|
| 123<u>4</u> | 1324 | 3124 | 2134 | 2314 | 3214 |
| 12<u>4</u>3 | 1342 | 3142 | 2143 | 2341 | 3241 |
| 1<u>4</u>23 | 1432 | 3412 | 2413 | 2431 | 3421 |
| <u>4</u>123 | 4132 | 4312 | 4213 | 4231 | 4321 |

This has been done in an orderly fashion. The first column above was formed by taking the first permutation of three things (namely, 123) and passing the next character, 4, through it from right to left, as shown by the underscores in the first column. The second column was similarly formed by taking the second of the listed permutations for level three (132) and passing the 4 through it from right to left.

This scheme is readily extended to any level we might wish. If we have available the 24 results at level 4, then the 120 permutations at level 5 can be generated by taking each of the level 4 results and passing a 5 through them. Thus, the first five results at level 5 can be formed as follows:

**FIGURE 15.9   One solution for the no-right-triangles problem.**

$$1234\underline{5}$$
$$123\underline{5}4$$
$$12\underline{5}34$$
$$1\underline{5}234$$
$$\underline{5}1234$$

Assume that the 24 level 4 permutations are stored. This might be done most conveniently by using 4 words of storage for each permutation. We can write a subroutine for which each call will yield a new permutation of five things. See the flowchart of Figure 15.10. We will set up 9 words of storage, as shown. Another word, P, contains an address; it is a pointer to one of the 9 words. Words T+1, T+3, T+5, and T+7 contain one of the level 4 permutations; initially, these words will contain the numbers 1, 2, 3, and

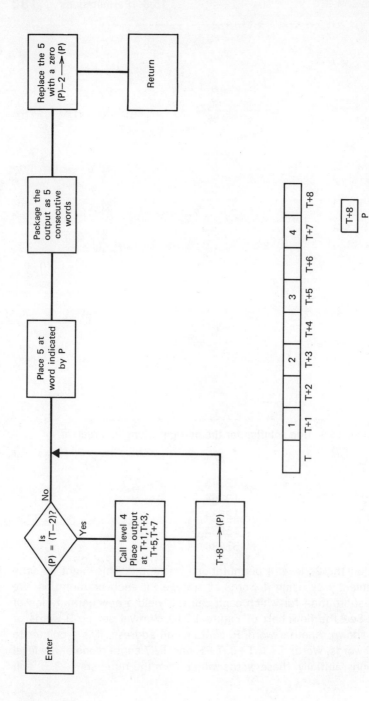

**FIGURE 15.10  A subroutine to generate permutations of five things.**

4. Word P indicates where the number 5 is to be placed. After each call of the subroutine, the address in P is decremented by 2. When P contains T−2, it is time to call on level 4 again, restore the contents of P to T+8 and move the 5 through the next set of five permutations. The calls to level 4 should be circular; that is, after the permutation 4321 has been called, the next call should fetch 1234 again. Thus, our level 5 subroutine will output the 120 possible permutations endlessly.

We can similarly create a subroutine for level 6. Its work area will be 11 words long; it will need a pointer P2 to indicate where the 6 should be placed; and it will call the level 5 subroutine as needed. Other than that, its logic is identical to that shown in Figure 15.10.

A third subroutine can be written for level 7. It will need 13 words in its work area, and it will call on the level 6 subroutine as needed. With all three subroutines working properly (and with the 24 permutations for level 4 in storage), we have the mechanism for generating the 5040 possible permutations of seven things.

Clearly, this scheme could be extended to level 8 and higher, by writing still more subroutines. At some point it should become apparent that we are doing the same work over and over; these subroutines are all alike. It should be possible to write one subroutine that can function at any level. Such a subroutine would be **recursive,** since at certain times it will have to call itself. The creation of such a recursive subroutine is a nontrivial task.

## 15.7 The 3X + 1 Problem

This problem was introduced in Section 8.2, and Figure 8.2 shows the basic logic. As stated then, the problem was to calculate, for all values of N up to 500, the number of terms, A, that are generated when the given algorithm is carried out.

Now let us introduce three new problems based on this procedure.

1. Will the algorithm always get us to 1? In other words, will the process always converge?

2. When N equals 1 or 2, the number of terms generated is the same as N. For values of N greater than 2, will A ever equal N again?

3. Can we get any given value of A? The answer to this question is yes. If we want an A value of 137, for example, let $N = 2^{136}$. So the real problem is this: Given a value of A, is there an **odd** value of N that will produce that value of A?

Martin Gardner's column in the June 1972 issue of *Scientific American* reports that all values of N up to 60 million have been tested for problem 1 above.† This proves nothing, but makes plausible the conjecture that the process will always converge. The values of A increase very slowly; for example, the largest A up to N = 4,993,366 is 597. As a consequence of this observation, it is doubtful that A will ever equal N again – but this has not really been proved, of course.

For problem 3 above, it would be necessary only to exhibit one value of A that cannot be produced by any odd value of N. This is not hard to do. For example, an A value of 3 can be produced only by N = 4, but 4 is not odd. An A value of 7 can be produced by N = 64 or by N = 10, and by no other value of N. When the A values in question become larger, there are more possibilities to consider. Nevertheless, it is clear from the given counterexamples that not every A is possible for odd values of N. The actual pattern of As that will be missing as N increases has not yet been explored.

So what computer problem do we have? Problem 1 could be extended to new heights (the values of X in the algorithm will require at least triple precision to extend N beyond 200 million). Problem 3 is settled mathematically, but it might be interesting to calculate what values of A appear and what values of A do not, as N increases.

As a matter of interest, we have listed the first appearance of each larger value of A, together with the value of N that produces it. These calculations were made using only odd values of N.

| A | N | A | N |
|---|---|---|---|
| 1 | 1 | 128 | 231 |
| 8 | 3 | 131 | 313 |
| 17 | 7 | 144 | 327 |
| 20 | 9 | 145 | 649 |
| 21 | 19 | 171 | 703 |
| 24 | 25 | 179 | 871 |
| 112 | 27 | 182 | 1161 |
| 113 | 55 | 183 | 2223 |
| 116 | 73 | 209 | 2463 |
| 119 | 97 | 217 | 2919 |
| 122 | 129 | 238 | 3711 |
| 125 | 171 | 262 | 6171 |

† This calculation has been extended, on our Varian machine, to N = 200 million. The algorithm itself is fast, since the calculation of X/2 involves only a right shift, and the calculation of 3X+1 can also be done using shifts. Even so, the calculation can be greatly speeded up by observing that (a) only odd values of N need be considered, provided that one proceeds steadily upwards; (b) it is not necessary to test for X equal to 1, but only X less than N; and (c) a little algebraic analysis reveals that only every other odd value need be tested, since numbers of the form 4K+1 will always converge, again provided that the search is conducted for all values, working upwards. We have here a delightful example of how a very fast calculation can be made approximately eight times as fast with a little thinking.

| A | N | A | N |
|---|---|---|---|
| 268 | 10971 | 509 | 626331 |
| 276 | 13255 | 525 | 837799 |
| 279 | 17647 | 528 | 1117065 |
| 282 | 23529 | 531 | 1501353 |
| 308 | 26623 | 557 | 1723519 |
| 311 | 34239 | 560 | 2298025 |
| 324 | 35655 | 563 | 3064033 |
| 340 | 52527 | 584 | 3542887 |
| 351 | 77031 | 597 | 3732423 |
| 354 | 106239 | 613 | 5649499 |
| 375 | 142587 | 665 | 6649279 |
| 383 | 156159 | 686 | 8400511 |
| 386 | 216367 | 689 | 11200681 |
| 443 | 230631 | 692 | 14934241 |
| 449 | 410011 | 705 | 15733191 |
| 470 | 511935 | 706 | 31466383 |

## 15.8 A NIM-like Game

A game known as Tsyanshidzi goes like this. Two players have before them two stacks of counters. When it is a player's turn, he may remove any number of counters from one stack, or the same number of counters from both stacks at once. The player who first faces empty stacks loses, since he cannot make a move.

The player who faces stacks of 1 and 2 counters loses. Try it: Whatever you do, your opponent could present you with 0,0. Similarly, the player who faces 3,5 will lose. The combinations (4,7), (6,10), and (8,13) are also losing positions.

The problem is to extend this list indefinitely, and thus derive a formula for winning against an opponent who does not know the pattern.

## 15.9 The Reciprocal Problem

Figure 15.11 shows the reciprocals of some small integers and the lengths of their periods of repetition. We wish to find the smallest integer, N, for each possible period from 1 to 100. The figure shows that we have already found the values of N for periods of 1, 2, 3, 6, 16, 18, 22, and 28. In the desired range, we have not yet found an N whose reciprocal has a period of 4, 5, 7, 8, and so on. The flowchart of Figure 15.12 shows the required logic.

| N | Length of period | Reciprocal |
|---|---|---|
| 3 | 1 | .3333333... |
| 7 | 6 | .142857142857... |
| 9 | 1 | .11111111... |
| 11 | 2 | .090909... |
| 13 | 6 | .076923076923... |
| 17 | 16 | .05882352941176470588... |
| 19 | 18 | .052631578947368421052639... |
| 21 | 6 | .047619047619... |
| 23 | 22 | .043478260869565217391304349... |
| 27 | 3 | .037037... |
| 29 | 28 | .0344827586206896551724137931... |

FIGURE 15.11 Some periods of reciprocals.

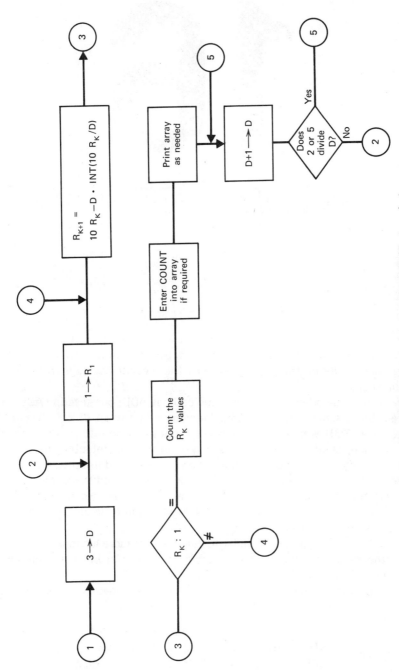

**FIGURE 15.12** Finding reciprocals with specified periods.

# 16

# PROGRAM TESTING

## 16.1   What Is Testing?

After a program has been written, say in assembly language, it is submitted to the machine for processing. The first few tries at assembly will be debugging passes. During this phase, we seek the mechanical bugs in the program, such as:

1.   Illegal op-codes. If we wanted the op-code ADD, but keyed in ADE, we expect the assembler to detect this blunder and notify us of it. Notice that if we keyed SUB, which is a valid op-code, but we **meant** ADD in the logic of our problem solution, the assembler has no way of detecting that fact.

2.   Undefined symbols. If an instruction has for its address REF2, but we have not labeled any instruction REF2 as a location, then the symbol is undefined; the assembler will inform us of this. Even if we have a line labelled REF2, but for some reason that line is itself illegal or incorrect, then the symbol is still undefined.

3.   Ambiguous symbols. If we try to define two or more locations as REF2, then the symbol is ambiguous. This bug is also referred to as multiply-defined symbols.

4.   Illegal operations. Things like the following are mechanical errors that will be caught during assembly:

| | | |
|------|-----------|-------------------|
| LDA  | TABLE,I   | Improper indexing |
| STA  | SUM+ 1    | Space not allowed |
| JMP  | I = LIMIT | Improper equals sign |
| DATA | 12345678  | Too large |

| BSS | 638592 | Too large |
| JMP | REF 2 | Space not allowed |

Similar mechanical errors can be made in Fortran and BASIC.

5.  Illegal symbols. Assemblers allow for considerable freedom in the invention of symbolic addresses and locations, but not complete freedom. Thus, most assemblers require that these symbols begin with a letter and not contain punctuation marks. Symbols like 2REF and REF3,5 are not allowed, and their attempted use triggers error messages.

6.  A really good assembler will detect impossible paths in the program; that is, the presence of instructions for which there is no way to get to them. For example, an unlabeled instruction just after an unconditional jump may be legal, but it is most likely a coding error, and should be noted during the translation process of the assembly.

When all such bugs are found and corrected, to the point at which assembly or compilation proceeds with no error messages, then debugging is completed. The program may now execute, and in some sense can be said to solve some problem. The question is, what problem? We would like it to be solving the problem we started out with. It is at this point that program testing begins.

The objective in program testing is to have the programmer reach a level of confidence that his program works correctly and will continue to work correctly with any data. Notice that this implies that the programmer is the one who does the testing.

There are no rules for program testing; it is an art, not a science. Every problem is different, and a test procedure must be devised afresh for each program. *No program should be committed to a production run without being tested.* We can present some guidelines and precautions, but the capability for program testing is acquired only through practice.

## 16.2   A Simple Example

Review at this time Exercise 220 (Chapter 8) and its suggested solution.

The logic has been developed to accept a sequence of values, F, and calculate and print F, and its first, second, and third differences. A program has been written and debugged that follows that logic. The program should be able to accept any sequence of numbers and produce the correct differences. To test the program, we can, in this instance, control the data. As was suggested, we might try using data for which the third differences are all the same; a table of cubes is one such possibility. Figure 16.1 shows the expected results from that data. The cubes of the numbers from 1 to 10 form the input data, and the differences that we expect are shown. The places indicated by the circles will be filled with irrelevant numbers.

| Input values | First differences | Second differences | Third differences |
|---|---|---|---|
| 1 | ◯ | ◯ | ◯ |
| 8 | 7 | ◯ | ◯ |
| 27 | 19 | 12 | ◯ |
| 64 | 37 | 18 | 6 |
| 125 | 61 | 24 | 6 |
| 216 | 91 | 30 | 6 |
| 343 | 127 | 36 | 6 |
| 512 | 169 | 42 | 6 |
| 729 | 217 | 48 | 6 |
| 1000 | 271 | 54 | 6 |
| EOF | | | |

FIGURE 16.1   Test data for the differencing problem.

If we run the program with that data, and get those results, our confidence level concerning the validity of the program might be quite high. But notice that we have tested the program only with positive numbers, and only increasing values. Our confidence level might increase somewhat if we made a second run with some negative numbers and decreasing values, as shown in Figure 16.2.

Would still another run with other data increase our confidence level significantly? Probably not. It is an important characteristic of a good test procedure to know when to stop testing.

## 16.3   Suggestions for Testing a Program

1. If the program being tested operates on stored data or on data read in from an external device (e.g., the Teletype), then test data can be devised that you control. As a general rule, the data numbers should all be different. All-alike data is always weak for test purposes.

2. Test data that can be **generated** is advantageous, since it makes your work easier. The test data for Figure 16.2 was generated by evaluating the expression $X^3 - 3X^2 - 6X + 8$ for values of X from $-4$ to $+5$.

3. If the test data is systematic (rather than erratic or random), then we can frequently calculate the expected results by some formula. Our program may perform the calculation the long way (since it must operate on any set of data ), but during testing we control the data.

4. Avoid the temptation to alter the program being tested simply to make the test easier. You must test the program being tested. If the program is built to operate on 6000 words of storage, then the test procedure must use 6000 words of data. If the program deals with hexagons, then the

| Input values | First differences | Second differences | Third differences |
|---|---|---|---|
| −80 | | | |
| −28 | 52 | | |
| 0 | 28 | −24 | |
| 10 | 10 | −18 | 6 |
| 8 | −2 | −12 | 6 |
| 0 | −8 | − 6 | 6 |
| − 8 | −8 | 0 | 6 |
| −10 | −2 | 6 | 6 |
| 0 | 10 | 12 | 6 |
| 28 | 28 | 18 | 6 |
| EOF | | | |

FIGURE 16.2  More test data.

test should concern hexagons, not pentagons. (A first test might involve pentagons, if that's easy to do, but the original program is not thoroughly tested until the data conforms to the program.)

5.  The results of a test run must be predictable and be predicted. We must know what we expect to see as output before we get it. If you try it the other way around ("check to see that the results are correct") you may be deluded by the neat appearance of computer output.

6.  There must be positive feedback, which means that the test procedure must produce printed results. Exercise 433 at the end of this chapter illustrates this principle.

7.  Test calculations that lead to a result of 0 are generally weak; 0 is a number that is too easily obtained by accident.

8.  You cannot rely on reading many printed results and checking them. As a general rule, a test procedure should involve only a few printed numbers, say six. If your test procedure calls for reading 5000 numbers by eye, it is probably worthless. You can always arrange to sum the 5000 numbers and print the sum, which is **one** number to read.

9.  It is not a valid test procedure to "run the program on another machine and check that the results are the same." That would be testing machines, and we are concerned with testing program logic.

10.  The ultimate goal of testing is to make sure (to some reasonable extent) that our programs work correctly. Keeping in mind that the program you write may some day be used by someone else, you want to reach that level of confidence that will let you put your name and your telephone number in the run book, with the understanding that you can be called anytime, day or night, if your program blows up.

## 16.4 System Testing

While you are learning the basics of computing, your contact with the art of program testing will be limited to small, self-contained problem situations, such as those given in the exercises at the end of this chapter. If you don't learn to test small programs, you may never become accustomed to testing anything. From the time you write and debug your first loop or subroutine you should plan ahead — how will I test this so that I can put it into production with confidence?

In practical computing work, either in science or industry, we seldom enjoy the luxury of programming small, isolated, well-defined problems. We must deal with **systems,** which involve large programs for ill-defined problems and usually involve the work of a team of programmers. Each member of the team will write subroutines, and each subroutine will be debugged and tested as an independent program. Eventually, however, all the pieces must be brought together to form the system that was contemplated in the first place. Even if each of the components has been thoroughly tested, the system may not function properly, or even function at all.

Consider, for example, the high-precision package outlined in Chapter 11. It requires eighteen subroutines, each of which is clearly defined and can be carefully tested. But in the package that the programmer will use, these subroutines will interact with each other. Strange and wonderful things can and will happen. If it is a difficult task to devise adequate test procedures for small problems, then it is so much the greater task to test a system. You have already used such systems — your assembler and Fortran compiler are fine examples. Would you judge that they were system-tested adequately? Few programmers have ever been satisfied with the systems they work with.

### EXERCISES

*In the exercises that follow, assume in every case that a correct flowchart has been developed and that a program has been written and debugged that follows that flowchart. Your task is to devise, in outline form, a test procedure for each problem situation.*

**410.** A loop is written to sum the contents of the words addressed at B, B+1, B+2, . . . , B+499, with the sum placed in the word addressed at B+500. Outline a test procedure.

After completing Exercise 410 and before proceeding further, read the discussion on this exercise in Appendix 3.

**415.** The loop of Exercise 410 is changed to produce the sum of the squares of the numbers in the B block. Write a test procedure.

**420.** Given two blocks of storage, addressed at A through A+99 and B through B+99. The numbers in these blocks are to be multiplied by pairs and the products are to be stored in a block of words addressed at C through C+99. That is,

$$
\begin{array}{ll}
\text{(A)} \quad \text{(B)} & \rightarrow \text{(C)} \\
\text{(A+1)} \ \text{(B+1)} & \rightarrow \text{(C+1)} \\
\text{(A+2)} \ \text{(B+2)} & \rightarrow \text{(C+2)} \\
\qquad \qquad . \\
\qquad \qquad . \\
\qquad \qquad . \\
\text{(A+99)(B+99)} & \rightarrow \text{(C+99)}
\end{array}
$$

Write a test procedure for this loop.

**425.** (See Exercise 160, Chapter 8.) For a block of words addressed at G through G+999 we are to count how many of the numbers are (a) 0, (b) positive and nonzero, (c) even, (d) greater than +100, and (e) negative and odd. How can this loop be tested?

**430.** A block of storage addressed at K through K+1999 is to have its contents reversed; that is,

$$
\begin{array}{ll}
\text{(K)} & \leftrightarrow \text{(K+1999)} \\
\text{(K+1)} & \leftrightarrow \text{(K+1998)} \\
\text{(K+2)} & \leftrightarrow \text{(K+1997)} \\
\qquad . \\
\qquad . \\
\qquad . \\
\text{(K+999)} & \leftrightarrow \text{(K+1000)}
\end{array}
$$

(For example, if the contents of the K block is originally in ascending sequence, then after running the loop, the contents will be in descending order.) Outline a test procedure for the loop.

**433.** Consider the following test procedure for Exercise 430:
  (a)  Generate the numbers 1–2000 in block K.
  (b)  Run the program **twice.**
  (c)  Check, with a loop, that the numbers in the K block are now the consecutive numbers from 1 to 2000.

What is wrong with that as a test procedure?

**435.** (See Exercise 90, Chapter 4.) A program has as input three integers, P, Q, and R, taken to be the lengths of the three sides of a triangle. The program is to print out P, Q, and R, and one of the following indicators: non-triangle, equilateral triangle, isosceles triangle, or scalene triangle. After the program has been debugged, how shall it be tested?

**440.** (See Exercise 40, Chapter 2.) A program is written to calculate the elapsed time in days between two given dates. What pairs of dates would you use to convince yourself that the program functions correctly? Assume that all dates involved are in the twentieth century.

**445.** (See Section 6.13). A subroutine has been written to calculate the greatest common divisor of two integers. Outline a test procedure for the subroutine.

**450.** (See Exercise 180, Chapter 8.) A block of words addressed at A through A+19 is used as a set of 320 triggers. We want to count the number of bit positions that contain **1s** in these 20 words, and put this count in word A+20. The result, then, could be any number between 0 (i.e., the 20 words contain no 1 bits) and 320 (the 20 words contain all 1 bits). Outline a test procedure for this program.

**455.** (See Exercise 200, Chapter 8.) A program has been written and debugged that will accept any date from our current calendar and output that date and its day of the week. How many dates would you submit to this program to satisfy yourself that it works correctly? Several test dates were furnished in Exercise 200 — were they sufficient? If we added one more (February 29, 1960 was a Monday), would we then have enough? If you wanted more test cases, where would you go to get them?

**460.** Suppose we write a loop to add the contents of all 16,384 words of storage. (The sum would overflow many times, of course. We could write the program to ignore the overflows, so that our sum would represent only the 16 low-order bits of the true sum.) How could we test such a program? Notice that the final sum includes the words of the program itself.

**465.** (See Exercise 275, Chapter 9.) A program has been written and debugged to calculate an approximation to $\pi$ by a Monte Carlo technique. How could we test this program?

**470.** (See Section 15.3.) A program has been written and debugged to calculate and print sets of primitive Pythagorean triplets. Indicate how such a program could be tested.

**475.** (See Exercise 195, Chapter 8.) A program has been written and debugged for the sets-of-four problem, in which each of 240 sets of 4 words are to be checked to make sure that each of four types, A, B, C, and D are present and in that order; for any set in which the four types are not all present, the set number is to be printed. Outline a procedure to test this program.

**476.** Suppose you are given a subroutine that purports to calculate the tangent of an angle. In the calling sequence for the subroutine, you specify an angle (in radians, of course), and the subroutine will RETURN with the value of the tangent of that angle. You have already been admonished to test such a package for yourself before you place any faith in it. In this case, assuming that the subroutine works at all, the chief worry is about the **range** of the subroutine. Its author may have designed it to work only for small angles. Devise a test procedure for the subroutine. What would you expect the subroutine to do with the argument $\pi/2$? Notice that no such number exists in any computer, but we can come close to it. How about an angle like $1000\pi$, or $1000\pi + \pi/4$? What would you like to have the subroutine do in those cases?

# 17

# THE COMPUTING ART

## 17.1   What Comes after an Introduction?

It has been the intent of this book to introduce you to computing under the assumption that you have access to a mini computer and have used it. The key word is "introduce." We want to show you the basics of the art — to get you started. There are many topics left that surely qualify as "introductory," and you should be informed about the broad topics that lie ahead if you wish to continue learning the computing art.

## 17.2   Documentation

Documentation is the sixth listed stage of the seven stages in a computer solution (the last stage is production). By listing it as a stage, there is an implication that documentation is isolated from the other things we do; by deferring mention of it until now, there is also an implication that it is a minor topic. Both of these implications are wrong. The topic is vital, but has been deferred while you worried about more immediate problems (like how a computer works and how you get it to work). And documentation isn't done in isolation (or as an afterthought), but should be done in parallel with all the other stages of the problem solution. *The solution isn't completed until it's documented* — that's the watch word.

For training problems, which are by their nature small and self-contained, the documentation can be minimal. But supposedly you are preparing yourself for real-life use of a computer. For problems that have some significance, the documentation of the solution should include the following:

**198**

1. *English statement of the problem.* What is it that you intend to do? What are the available inputs and what are the expected outputs?

2. *Analysis.* Is it a good problem for computer solution? That is, does it fit all six of the criteria outlined in Section 2.7? Is there an algorithm available, or can you devise one? Have you made some preliminary calculations by hand to validate your method? Are there prior results that can be checked?

3. *Flowchart(s).*

4. *Code.* The code will be handwritten, but every assembly (or compiler) run will give you a new printed listing of your code. The last of these (that is, the one that worked) should be included. And it should be internally documented with liberal use of Remarks or Comments.

5. *Test Procedure.* You should have fabricated a test procedure for your debugged code. Describe it, with samples of the runs made with test data. It is particularly important to specify the acceptable range for the input data for which your program will function properly.

6. *Results.* Show printed results that came from real data (as opposed to test data, although sometimes these are the same).

7. *Range and limitations.* If someone else (who may be you, a year later) is to use this program, for what range of values is it **not** valid?

8. *Run procedure.* Describe how the program is to be used, so that someone else can operate with it without confusion.

9. *Conclusions.* What can you conclude from the running of this program (other than "I found it interesting").

As a model, let us outline the documentation that might accompany the solution to the 3X+1 problem given in Section 8.2.

1. The English statement of the problem is given in Section 8.2. The specific problem we are doing is this: for successive values of N, we want to investigate the growth of A. So we modify the solution shown in Figure 8.2 to print N and A whenever A is larger than any previous A.

2. The problem solution fits the six criteria (if we make the assumption that it is useful to us as a learning tool). We have a method; namely, to implement the algorithm of the problem itself, and test each A value against the largest A found so far. A previous run or a hand calculation has produced some A values for consecutive Ns and we thus have some results to check against. We are assured that the scheme will converge for any N less than 200 million.

3. A modified form of Figure 8.2 is the flowchart we will work from.

4. We will code in assembly language, and one of our later symbolic listings will show our annotated code in detail.

5. The previous runs have provided us with sufficient test data so that we can assure ourselves that our new solution is proceeding correctly.

6. Our new run will cover values of N from 2 to 1 million and we display

these results. If the problem is to be picked up and extended to $N = 2$ million, these results provide new test data for the extended run.

7. We used double-precision arithmetic for the values of X in the solution. Thus, X must never exceed the limits of double-precision arithmetic (i.e., 1073741823).

Here is where you should see how good documentation interacts with all the other stages. What happens if X **does** exceed $2^{30} - 1$? Was a safeguard inserted into the program? Shouldn't it have been? Of course it should, and we now back off to stage one (analysis) and patch that safeguard into our program. And we note **here** that the safeguard exists, so that another user is duly warned. (Notice that this says nothing about the allowable range on N — only that an overly large X value will trigger a halt.)

8. The run procedure specifies the mechanics of loading the program (say, via paper tape) into the computer and the setting of switches and registers to initiate a run. If the program includes a restart procedure (in order to start it from some arbitrary value of N), the details of that procedure are particularly important. Have someone who is totally unfamiliar with these procedures carry them out. Indicate any unusual things that can happen during a run and any interrupt procedures that exist. For example, "The following message will type if X overflows," or "Depressing sense switch 3 after a halt, with the Teletype on-line, will cause punching of a restart tape."

9. "Preliminary runs indicated the need for double precision for X. The observed growth in A indicated that, for the allowable range in N, single precision for A was adequate. At the start of each run, several new A values will type out very quickly, followed by long periods of computation with no output. If this problem is to be run beyond $N = 2$ million, recoding will be necessary. If we were to redo the entire problem, we would add the following features." And so on.

## 17.3 The Decline in Assembly Language Coding

We have dealt essentially with only one higher-level language, Fortran. Much of what we have discussed is in terms of assembly language. Assembly language is highly machine-dependent. The DAS assembler functions only on the Varian machines; even for another mini, a different language and a different translating program must be used. While assembly language gives the programmer closer control of the machine, and some programmers prefer to work in it, the fact is that little day-to-day work is done that way. Not only do most people prefer the additional power and freedom of a compiler language, but the semi-machine-independence of a language like Fortran provides strong motivation to use it.

This expansion to higher-level languages can go much further. Business applications lend themselves to COBOL (**CO**mmon **B**usiness **O**riented Language), which is another compiler. (But note that few minis offer COBOL.) Starting in 1965, a group of people from IBM and SHARE (SHARE is a user's group devoted to large IBM machines) devised a new language, PL/I which is supposed to combine the best features of both Fortran and COBOL. The hope at the time was to phase out the two languages in favor of the new single language. The fate of PL/I is still undecided.

But all these languages are procedural; that is, the programmer using them must spell out in detail just what the machine is to do. If two numbers are to be added together, then the programmer must specify the operation ADD in some form and the names or addresses of the two operands. This might be fun, or it might be unbearably tedious; it depends on what you want to get done and how you enjoy working. Now, step this up to a higher level. Suppose we want to sort a set of records. There are many algorithms for sorting, but in a procedural language we will have to program the algorithm we select in detail. What we want to do is specify "SORT," and indicate the parameters of the sort: how many things to be sorted; ascending or descending order; and on what key. To be sure, we can do all this with subroutines, but it would be even nicer if the language had the verb SORT as one of its op-codes.

This kind of thinking leads to even higher levels of language. We can design a generalized **program** (as opposed to a subroutine) that will perform any sorting task. While we are at it, this program can be made to do other stock business jobs, such as file maintenance (merging, purging, adding to a file, deleting from a file, selecting records from a file), and report writing. Such a program becomes quite large (called a File Management package) and soon leads to a language of its own. In such a language, the verbs will include SORT and SELECT and MERGE and the like; the procedural details are left up to the master program, and the user need only specify files and records by name and indicate what it is he wants done.

There are specialized languages for many broad task areas: simulations, machine tool control, and algebraic manipulation are three examples. The day is past when programmers have to write specific instructions for tasks that can be generalized, parameterized, and packaged.

## 17.4   The Storage Size Barrier

We have indicated ways by which the word size, integer, and language barriers can be surmounted. That leaves only one big barrier to being able to manipulate numbers with freedom. Our machine (any machine) is limited in the size of its central store. If the core size is 16,384 words, then, at any one time, we can have no more than 16,384 instruction and data words in core. How can we handle problems that involve more than 16,384 words?

The key to that is the phrase "at any one time." If the proposed solution can be broken into distinct parts, then we can run each part as a separate program, arranging to punch some output from part one to be input for part two, and so on. With a little more effort, this procedure can be made continuous and automatic, so that instructions in part one call for inputting new instructions for part two. Each new set of instructions coming in overlays some older instructions whose use has been exhausted.

It would help such procedures greatly if we did not have to depend on a paper tape reader for input and a paper tape punch for output. Suppose we attach a disk drive to our computer, or a magnetic tape drive. Now, after loading central storage and the disk, say, with all the words of our problem (a set of disks can store a million words), new sections of the program can be called into core at high speed, and intermediate results can be stored on the disks.

Let's go further. By the time we write our third large program to handle this machinery, we would have discovered that most of our effort was spent on the overlays and the sheer mechanics of keeping things straight. As we have noted in several other situations, a human is doing work over and over that should be done only once. In other words, we want to back off and write a control program that will do all the bookkeeping that is involved; moreover, we would like to have this control mechanism transparent to the user.

Advances along these lines lead to the concept of **virtual memory.** On a machine whose core size is N words, access to 100N words is made automatic. The programmer need not see (or even be aware) of the mechanisms that control the movement of stored words. All he sees is his facility for functioning as though the central storage were considerably larger than it really is. For the present, virtual memory is available only on large machines, but there is nothing in the concept to prohibit its use on a mini.

## 17.5 The Broad World of Computing

Let us conclude by listing, in no special order, some of the topics that cannot be covered in an introductory text, but which make up the new discipline called computing.

1. *Numerical methods.* This is the computing analog of the time-honored subject called numerical analysis. The numerical analyst is concerned, for example, with methods for finding the roots of an algebraic equation. These methods are firmly grounded in theory and on the tacit assumption that numbers behave the way mathematicians want them to. But in the world of computing, all numbers have finite precision, and most real numbers do not even exist. The number 3/7 exists in mathematics, and can

be shown to be less than 42/97 and greater than 427/997. None of these numbers can exist in a computer.

The notion of **continuity** (which means, in crude terms, that except for passing through values that attempt division by 0, a small change in the argument should lead to a small change in its function) which is at the heart of many derivations in numerical analysis, becomes somewhat meaningless when dealing with numbers in a computer.

Again, mathematically a matrix is singular or nonsingular (i.e., the determinant of the matrix is 0, or nonzero). In computing we must deal with the notion of "not 0, but too small."

Or, the number system in mathematics is uniform and homogeneous. The floating-point number system of computers is not; the numbers are closely packed near 0 and widely spaced at the upper limit of the system.

Finally, the mathematician is free to speak of "the sum of the infinite series . . . ." There are no infinite series in computing (see Exercise 310, Chapter 12).

What all this means is that both subjects cover the same ground (e.g., roots of equations, numerical integration, Fourier analysis, etc.) but from radically different points of view. The serious student of computing should consider taking courses in both subjects.

2. *Graphics.* Working with a mini computer is limited to text input and output. We can enter characters that can be created by keys, and we can print much the same set of characters. This is unfortunate, since all too frequently we want to see our results in graphic form. Moreover, we may want to enter information into the machine graphically. The field of computer graphics concerns both these concepts. Graphic input is possible through devices like light pens or tablets; graphic output can be achieved with plotters, or cathode ray tube displays. At the far edges of this field, graphic output can be produced in three dimensions and in color.

3. *On-line computing.* Generally, you have operated your computer in pure batch mode; that is, each problem to be run has taken over the entire machine. Your use of BASIC may have been conversational, in the sense that you could obtain an immediate response from the machine while you were at the Teletype.

Any mode of operation of a computer that yields a response time that is less than the response time for pure batch mode is said to be an on-line use of the machine. Usually "on-line" implies a quick response, but all such time measurements are relative. If the turnaround time in pure batch mode is, say, 24 hours, than a 1 hour response time is on-line.

In the early days of computing, users were on-line with the machine in the sense of taking it over; the programmer was the operator. Except for this case, on-line mode was achieved by the technique called time-sharing. In time-sharing mode, many users can function on-line at once, and the central processor services them in turn, according to some scheduling algorithm. The simplest scheduling algorithm is first-in–first-out; that is, care for requests strictly in the order in which they enter the queue. A slight variation of this calls for giving highest priority to requests that can be completely disposed of in some minimal time (say, 500 milliseconds), after which all other requests are serviced in turn, allocating a time slice of perhaps 2 seconds to each user.

The two concepts of on-line and time-sharing are independent, however. It is possible to be on-line with a dedicated machine, as you are when you are running a BASIC program by hand at the Tetetype. It is anticipated that a large portion of the eventual use of mini computers will be in on-line mode, with the entire machine dedicated to one user.

# Appendix
# 1
# GLOSSARY

**Accumulator.** One-word storage device in which most of the computer's work is performed. Nearly all the possible arithmetic or logical operations produce their results in the accumulator. The name is misleading, since it is only a storage device.

**Address.** (Noun) Place where information may be found. Each word in main storage of a computer is given a numerical address in order to locate that word precisely. The address specifies **where** something is; not **what** it is. An address such as 03485 tells where to go for information, but provides no clue as to what is stored in word 03485. The sequence of addresses in all machines start at 0. (Verb) Act of specifying where some information is located. Core storage, for example, is addressed by number. A disk storage device is addressed by specifying the disk surface, the band, and the sector within the band. Tape storage is addressed either by the position of the tape record or by its identifying key.

**Address (portion).** (Noun) The part of an instruction word that specifies where the operand is. In normal addressing, the operand is somewhere else; it is one level away from the instruction itself.

**Address modification.** Characteristic of a computer whereby the address portion of an instruction can be modified by other instructions or by indexing. The effective address (that is, the one that is actually executed) is the stated address in the instruction plus one or more modifications that take place as the instruction moves from storage to the decoder.

**Algorithm.** "A method." Step-by-step plan for solving some problem. An example is an algorithm for extracting square roots of numbers.

**Algorithmic.** Problem-solving by the use of algorithms, as opposed to solution by Monte Carlo techniques or by heuristics.

**Alteration switch.** *See* Sense switch.

**Argument.** Independent variable in a tabulated function. In a table of squares, for example, for the entry

$$17 \quad 289$$

17 is the argument; 289 is the functional value.

**ASCII.** American Standard Code for Information Interchange. A set of codes for the symbols used by computers and peripheral devices. For example, the ASCII code for the letter W is octal 327.

# 206 Appendix 1

**Assembler.** 1. Language for expressing instructions, using symbolic locations, mnemonic op-codes, and symbolic addresses. 2. Program used to translate from the symbolic language into binary machine instructions. The language follows the format of the instructions of a particular machine, and hence assemblers are machine-dependent. The symbolic language and the resulting machine language tend to a 1:1 ratio; that is, each line written by the user translates into one machine instruction.

**Batch processing.** Mode of computer operation in which independent jobs are saved up for execution. Jobs submitted all morning, for example, could be batch processed starting at noon. The antithesis is on-line (which see).

**Bit.** Smallest unit of information, usually expressed as 1 or 0. The word can refer to positions (as in "16 bit word length") or to the individual symbols ("the word contains seven 1 bits"). Bit is the binary analog of "digit" in decimal notation.

**Bootstrap.** A short routine that causes a longer routine to be loaded. A bootstrap routine on paper tape, for example, is a few words at the start of the tape. The bootstrap can be loaded by executing a few instructions manually at the console, and the bootstrap routine will then load the entire contents of the roll of paper tape.

**Bracketing.** Numerical procedure in which the result desired is searched for, first by incrementing the independent variable in large steps, and then in successively smaller steps as the location of the result is approached.

**Buffer.** Device to make compatible two other devices that work at highly disparate speeds. The buffer in a computer is a storage unit of 1 word size, located logically between storage and the registers. It can accept 1 word of information from storage at (slow) storage speed and pass it on to the accumulator, say, at (fast) accumulator speed. In this way, repeated accesses to the same storage word (as is needed during the process of multiplication, for example) need not slow down the accumulator to the relatively slow speed of core storage.

**Calculator.** Device for computation that falls short of being a computer. The line of distinction lies in the ability of a true computer to have an internally stored instruction operate on another instruction. Calculators may be simple (as in a desk calculator), or may include sequencing and storage, but they lack the capability of address modification.

**Calling sequence.** A linkage (which see) plus the arguments (or the addresses of the arguments) needed by a subroutine.

**Character addressable.** Type of machine organization in which the word length is one character long. On the IBM 1620, for example, the word length is 6 bits, which is sufficient to hold one decimal digit. Numbers larger than one digit are then formed by combining adjacent words.

**Character set.** Collection of symbols that a computer can accept (from cards, tape, or a keyboard) and store (that's the internal set), and collection of symbols it can similarly output to a peripheral device (that's the external set). These two sets, on a particular machine, may not be the same.

**Coding.** Writing of specific instructions (in an assembly language) or statements (in a compiler language) to carry out the intent of the user in the solution of a problem.

**Collating sequence.** Ordering of the internal character set of a computer that is dictated by the bit configurations chosen to represent the characters. For example, if the computer accepts ASCII coding, then its collating sequence will be as follows: blank !"#$%&'()*+,−./0123456789:;<=>?@ABCDEFGHIJKLMNOPQRSTUVWXYZ[\]↑

**Compiler.** **1.** Language in which statements written by the user express, in a high level of symbolism, the desired action by the machine. The language relates to a broad problem area. Thus, we have scientific compilers (e.g., Fortran, PL/I, JOVIAL, MAD), business compilers (e.g., COBOL), and specialized compilers (e.g., SIM-SCRIPT for simulation applications). **2.** Program used to translate from the language described above into binary machine instructions. The language does not have the format of the instructions of any machine, and hence tends to be machine-independent. For example, to a large extent a Fortran program can be compiled on nearly any computer, and will, on execution, deliver the same results.

**Complement.** (Noun) Number formed by differencing each digit with 9 in a decimal counter, or by changing 0s to 1s and 1s to 0s in a binary counter. Thus, the complement of 0036802 is 9963197 (decimal); the complement of 00010110101 is 11101001010 (binary). (Verb) To form the complement of a number.

**Computer.** Device for computation that has its instructions internally stored; that can be sequenced; and that can have instructions treat other instructions as data.

**Consecutive number check.** Specialized sequence check in which it is determined not only that successive words or records are in order, but also that the keys for each two words or records differ by exactly **one.**

**Conversational computing.** Form of on-line computing in which the user carries on an interactive dialog with the machine. Various languages (JOSS, RUSH, MAC, and conversational BASIC) have been designed for this purpose. In conversational mode, the user gets an immediate response to syntax errors, and may call for execution of any part of his program as he proceeds.

**Core dump.** Printed listing of all or part of central storage, usually in octal (or, on larger machines, in hexadecimal) notation.

**CPU (Central Processing Unit).** Main frame of a computer, including storage, all the registers, the arithmetic and logical circuitry, and the console. The CPU does not include peripheral devices.

**Data.** Numbers to be operated on by the computer as specified by the instructions. (Pronounced DAY-TAH in the computing industry.) Although technically the word is plural (the singular form being DATUM), it is used by computer people as both singular and plural.

**Debugging.** Process of finding and removing the mechanical errors from a program. The mechanical errors include such things as illegal op-codes, undefined symbols, ambiguous symbols, violations of the rules of the language being used, etc. Debugging should be kept distinct from testing. Debugging is not concerned with the logic of the problem solution, but only its mechanics.

**Dogear.** Address of the word just before the start of a table. The first word of the table is thus at address DOGEAR+1; the kth word of the table is at address DOGEAR+K, and so on.

**Double precision.** Arithmetic that is performed on numbers that occupy two computer words. On a 16 bit word machine, double precision involves 32 bit numbers. The concept can be extended to 3 word precision or higher (i.e., multiple precision).

**Dropout.** Bit error on reading or writing information. For example, a single hole punched on paper tape should cause a 1 bit to enter storage. If the bit position in storage then contains a 0, a dropout has taken place.

**EAM.** Electric Accounting Machine; IBM's term for punched card equipment.

**EBCDIC.** Extended Binary Coded Decimal Interchange Code. (*See also* ASCII.) In EBCDIC, the letter W is coded as $E6)_{16}$ or $230)_{10}$ or $346)_8$.

# 208   Appendix 1

**Elapsed time.**  Time between the original statement that a problem exists and delivery of the required results. Distinct from programmer time, CPU time, turnaround time, response time, etc.

**Emulation.**  Hardware-assisted simulation. An electronic device used in simulation of machines to speed up the process. For example, a simulation program for the IBM 360, designed to make it act like an IBM 1401, might use an emulator to implement certain op-codes of the 1401, like MULTIPLY and DIVIDE.

**Execution.**  Phase in problem solution following translation, in which the instructions are carried out as dictated by the user. (*See also* Translation.)

**Exponent overflow.**  In floating-point arithmetic, the generation of a result that exceeds the capacity of the floating-point system. For example, if the range of the system is such that 99999999E38 is the largest possible number, then attempted multiplication of the number 12345678E25 by itself will cause exponent overflow, since the multiply subroutine will try to develop a product with an exponent of 50. Usually, this condition would imply an error from which there is no recovery.

**Exponent underflow.**  (*See* Exponent overflow.) Under the same conditions, the attempted multiplication of the number 12345678E-25 by itself would result in an exponent underflow. The system may be programmed to treat this condition as a mild error, and return a true zero as the result.

**File.**  Collection of related records. For example, a reel of magnetic tape can contain all the payroll records of a plant for a given pay period; this is a file.

**Firmware.**  Sets of instruction, forming a subroutine, that have been cast into hardware. Double-precision and floating-point subroutines are the commonest examples.

**Floating-point.**  System of number representation and arithmetic based on scientific notation, in which each number has four parts: the first K significant digits; a power of a base factor; the sign of the number; and the sign of the power. In floating **decimal,** the factor is 10.

**Hang up.**  An undesired (and usually unexpected) termination of a program's action. The commonest hang up is an endless loop.

**Hardware.**  Physical parts of the computer: storage, registers, console, readers, printers, tape drives, and so on. As opposed to software (which see).

**Heuristics.**  Technique for problem-solving that attempts to mimic the way a human would attack the problem. Thus, for example, some chess-playing computer programs are written heuristically.

**Hexadecimal.**  Base 16 notation. Since base 16 needs 16 symbols, the letters A, B, C, D, E, F are usually used to denote 10, 11, 12, 13, 14, and 15, respectively. Thus, $1000)_{10} = 1750)_8 = 3E8)_{16}$. Binary notation converts to hexadecimal by taking 4 bit positions at a time.

**High-order, low-order.**  Extreme ends of a number. The high-order digit of the year 1973 is 1; the low-order digit is 3.

**Hollerith.**  Codes used to represent information on a punched card. Thus, the letter W in Hollerith code consists of a 0 punch and a 6 punch in the same card column. By extension, similar codes in core storage.

**Index register.**  Electronic device which modifies an instruction address (usually by addition) as the instruction word moves from storage to the decoder. Special op-codes are provided to operate on the index registers, to load or store them, and to test and modify them.

**Indexing.** Address modification that is performed by index registers.

**Instruction counter.** Device that keeps track of the current location of the instruction to be executed. In a machine with 16,384 words of central storage, the Instruction Counter (I.C.) is a 14 bit device that functions in the range 0–16383 (decimal) or 0–37777 (octal) or 0–11111111111111 (binary).

**Interrecord gap.** Space on paper or magnetic tape between successive records. On magnetic tape, there is usually a gap of ¾ inch of blank tape between every two records.

**Jump.** Op-code that operates **on** the Instruction Counter. Every computer has an unconditional jump command, plus an assortment of conditional jumps (jump on minus, jump on zero, jump and mark, etc.). Called also (on other machines) branch or transfer.

**Justified.** Alignment of data. Typewritten pages are usually left-justified. Typeset pages are usually both left- and right-justified. In a telephone directory, the names are normally left-justified in each column; the phone numbers are right-justified.

**Key.** The part of a record that is used to control processes like sequence checking or sorting. For example, payroll records are processed through most of the payroll procedures on employee number as the key.

**Levels of addressing.** Extent to which desired information is remote from the instruction that requires it. In zero-level addressing, the required information is in the instruction (as in SHIFT RIGHT 7). Normal first-level addressing specifies the required information one step away (as in LOAD ACCUMULATOR with the contents of word T). In second-level addressing, the address specifies a word whose contents is the address of the required word.

**Linkage.** Instructions that perform a jump to a subroutine and record somewhere the information needed to return from the subroutine to the correct location in the main routine.

**Load and go.** Procedure whereby, when the translation phase of an assembly or compile run is completed without error, the translated program is executed immediately. The alternative is to output a machine language program that is in shape to be reloaded and executed. The programmer frequently has the option of one or the other of these modes of operation, or both.

**Loading.** Process of putting information into storage. At the start of a problem, all the instructions and data are loaded into storage from an external device such as a paper tape reader or a card reader.

**Location.** Address of an instruction. In a 32K machine, there are 32,768 words of core storage, each of which can hold one instruction. We refer to addresses of data words, but locations of instruction words. This minor matter of semantics is quite useful.

**Loops, programmed.** Set of instructions for performing a repetitive task by using the same instructions for each case. A loop always has five parts: initialization; DO (the instructions for one case); test (for the last case); modify (to proceed from case to case); and jump back to the DO block. Programmed loops are one of the two basic building blocks in programming.

**Low-order.** *See* High-order, low-order.

**Machine-readable.** Information that can be entered into a computer without human actions. Punched cards are machine-readable, as are test scoring sheets. Information that is not machine-readable will have to be keyed, as on a keypunch or paper tape punch.

**Macro.**   Instruction in a source language (for example, in assembly language) that produces a specified sequence of machine language instructions. We could have the macro instruction READ (referring to a paper tape reader) that the assembler would translate into several machine instructions to cause tape reading and also take care of read errors, end-of-file conditions, and so on.

**Memory protect.**   Devices to allow portions of storage to be "locked" so that they cannot be altered. Sometimes done by adding an extra bit to each word in storage; if the bit is set to 1, the word can be read, but not written, with normal instructions. Special privileged instructions are used to set the extra bit and to alter those words when the alteration is required.

**Merge.**   Process of combining two or more sets of sequenced data into a new set which contains all the data in sequence. For example, two lists of names, both in alphabetical order, can be merged into a combined list which will also be in alphabetical order.

**Monte Carlo.**   Technique for problem solving in which the problem is turned into a game, and the playing of that game provides an approximation to the desired result. The Monte Carlo technique usually involves the use of random numbers.

**OEM.**   Original Equipment Manufacturer. The term is widely used in the literature on mini computers, since large numbers of them are sold to other manufacturers (e.g., the makers of key-to-disk equipment).

**On-line.**   1. Peripheral devices that are physically connected to the CPU. We speak of an on-line paper tape reader, for example.   2. Mode of computer operation in which the response time is lower than for pure batch processing. Thus, a user executing a BASIC program at the console is said to be on-line with the machine.

**Op-code.**   The part of an instruction word that specifies the operation to be performed.

**Open subroutine.**   Set of instructions that is inserted in-stream as needed in a program. For a short subroutine (e.g., ten instructions or less), it may be more efficient to insert it as an open subroutine than to link to it as a closed subroutine.

**Overflow.**   Generated information that exceeds the capacity of a storage device. A single addition in a 16 bit accumulator can result in a 17 bit sum, which is then an overflow.

**Pass.**   One use of a computer, in which input data is processed to produce output information. We speak of one pass of an assembly, or one pass of a production run. Synonymous with "run."

**Patching.**   Technique for making a correction in an operating routine whereby an old instruction is overlaid (stepped-on) by a jump to an unused area of storage; the stepped-on instruction is replaced there; the correction is added; and a jump is made to the location following the overlay. Sometimes called "out to the woods and back."

**Peripheral devices.**   Any device that is electrically connected (that is, on-line) to the CPU. Peripherals include tape readers, card readers, card punches, typewriters, line printers, disk drives, drums, and display devices. (The definition can be extended to include an off-line tape-to-printer, or card-reader-to-tape, setup.)

**Program.**   (Noun) Set of instructions or statements. Loosely synonymous with "routine" or "code" used as nouns.   (Verb) To plan the computer solution for a problem

Programming includes analysis, flowcharting, coding, debugging, testing, and documentation. The term is frequently applied to just the coding phase of the work.

**Programmed switch.** A software concept; a decision point in a program for which the decision is made somewhere else in the program than at the switch point itself. A device for storing a decision.

**Pseudo-op.** Operation code (in an assembly system) that has no direct machine op-code counterpart. For example, if the machine op-codes include jumps on minus, zero, and positive, the assembler might include a jump on positive-and-greater-than-zero as a convenience to the user. In the assembly process, the pseudo-op is translated into the two or three existing machine op-codes that effect the desired result.

**Queue.** Collection of items waiting to be serviced. The queue at a theater box office is a familiar example. In a time-sharing computing system, there is at nearly all times a queue of terminals (and their users) seeking service. There is a large body of knowledge called queueing theory that concerns methods of disposing of a queue systematically, to conform to some established criteria of optimization.

**Record.** (Noun) Group of related words that are handled as a unit. A payroll record, for example, might be several hundred words long, but each record is processed throughout the payroll procedure as an entity. (Verb) To write information from storage to a peripheral device such as a magnetic tape.

**Recursion.** Iterative equation or operation. For example, the basic equation for congruential random number generation, $X_{n+1} = M\,X_n \bmod P$, forms a new X value from an old one, and the process then repeats, or recurses.

**Redundancy.** Extra information that is inserted to guard against error. Examples: parity bits in tape records; check bits added to computer words.

**Registers.** The following components of the computer are called registers: accumulator(s), MQ, adder, instruction counter, buffer, decoder, and index registers.

**Relocatable.** Machine code that can be executed regardless of where it is located in storage. If the code is dependent on its machine location (as would be true, for example, with instructions that modify other instructions directly), it is not relocatable.

**Response time.** Time between a user's request for computer action and the receipt of the results. In batch processing, the response time might be measured in hours. In on-line processing, the response time might be measured in seconds.

**Restart.** Procedure inserted into a program to facilitate new runs that pick up where a previous run ended, or where it was interrupted.

**ROM.** Read-Only Memory. Refers to storage that can be read but not written. Such storage devices are cheaper to make than those that can be both read and written, and hence many computers offer, say, 2048 words of ROM as standard equipment.

**Scaling.** Process of keeping track of decimal points (or binary points) while using fixed-point integer arithmetic to calculate results with numbers that have a variable position for the decimal point. For example, to calculate what the user thinks of as $1/7 = .142857$, the calculation must be set up as $1000000/7 = 142857$, and the proper **scale factor** must be noted in the result (the scale factor here being $10^{-6}$).

**Sense switch.** A physical toggle switch on the console of a computer whose position can be interrogated by a program. Thus, the user can write an instruction to effect "jump to REF8 if sense switch 3 is on," and the like.

**Sequence check.** Procedure to determine that a set of words or records is in sequence; that is, that each word or record is greater than (or less than) the one preceding it. For example, a tape reel bearing payroll records, which has been sorted on Social Security numbers, would be sequence checked on those numbers upon being read into a subsequent pass.

**Sequencing.** Capability of a calculating device to advance from one instruction to the next as specified by the ordering of the instructions written by the user.

**Simulation.** 1. Process of causing one computer to function exactly like another. 2. Process of programming a computer to duplicate (within certain limits) the action of some part of the real world. For example, a program to act like a hospital, or an airport traffic pattern, or the checkout lanes of a supermarket.

**Software.** Computer programs; the sets of instructions that the computer is to execute.

**Sorting.** Process of putting words or records into a specified order (e.g., ascending order). One of many known sorting algorithms may be used (e.g., interchange sorting).

**Straight-line (code).** Instructions that are to be executed in order without repetition, as opposed to instructions that are looped.

**Subroutine.** Set of instructions that may be used repeatedly by being called from within some other routine. A **closed** subroutine is completely self-contained; for example, it includes all its own constants. Examples: subroutines for cube roots; double-precision; floating division.

**Supplied address.** Address portion of an instruction that is written in dummy form (usually as 0s) but is filled in prior to execution by the action of some other instruction. The instructions in a loop that refer to variable addresses are usually written as supplied addresses, to be initialized and modified by other instructions in the loop.

**Switch, programmed.** *See* Programmed switch.

**Testing.** Stage in the computer solution of a problem that follows debugging. Testing is concerned with the logic of the solution. It involves the determination, to the programmer's satisfaction, that the program solves the problem it is intended to solve and will continue to do so when the data changes.

**Throughput.** Amount of work that passes through the computer. For example, one speaks of machine B having four times the speed of machine A, but having an increase in throughput of only 150%.

**Time-sharing.** Mode of computer usage in which more than one user is on-line with the machine, and each user is serviced in turn, according to some kind of scheduling algorithm. Each user is given the impression that he has complete use of the machine.

**Translation.** Process of converting symbolic notation into machine language. Thus, for example, the assembly language instruction

STA  SUM

is translated into 053746 if the op-code for STA is 05 and SUM is addressed at 3746. Translation takes place after loading is completed, in the sequence followed for a load-and-go assembly or compile run.

**Word.** Set of bit positions that can be directly addressed. A medium-sized mini computer might have 262,144 magnetic cores of storage, packaged into 16,384 words of 16 bits each.

**Work area.** Words in storage to which successive data values are moved in order to minimize address modification.

# Appendix

# 2

# ABOUT MINI COMPUTERS

There is no generally accepted definition of the term "mini" as applied to computers. There is nothing to prevent the maker of the smallest possible computer from calling it a large-scale processor, nor to prevent the maker of a million dollar machine from calling it a mini. To some extent, the classification is made on the basis of physical size; all the machines that the computing industry calls minis are desk-top machines. Their CPUs measure close to 19 inches wide, 10.5 inches high, and 21 inches deep.

Two other classification criteria could be applied; namely, word size, and dollar cost. Most of the minis being marketed in 1972 had a word size of 16 bits, at prices ranging from under $3000 (for their CPU) to as high as $33,000, with the mode around $10,000. But there were machines with 12 bit, 18 bit, and even 24 bit word sizes that were included in surveys of the minis. As soon as you try to pin the word "mini" down, exceptions will pop up. Printed surveys of the field (including this one) tend to get out of date quickly.†

A complete installation whose CPU is a mini can cost considerably more, of course. The addition of desirable peripheral equipment like card readers, line printers, and display units can result in total costs of $100,000 or higher.

Nevertheless, the mini market clusters around machines with 16 bit word lengths having 2048–32,768 words of core storage, speed in the range 200,000–1,000,000 additions per second, and much the same physical characteristics. Indeed, if the dozen or so most popular minis were photographed together, the casual observer would have difficulty in telling one from the other without looking closely at the nameplates. If a mini is being used as a stand-alone general-purpose machine, it will have next to it the ubiquitous Teletype and boxes full of rolls of punched paper tape. The use of paper tape as an input/output medium is one of the biggest drawbacks to suc-

---

† But an excellent survey is J. L. Butler, "Comparative Criteria for Minicomputers," *Instrum. Technol.* **17**, 67–82 (Oct. 1970). This paper is reprinted in a book: F. Coury (ed.), *A Practical Guide to Minicomputer Applications*, New York: IEEE Press, 1972. The book reprints twenty-eight articles on mini computers.

cessful proliferation of the minis as general-purpose computers. To be sure, every mini is capable of supporting more sophisticated input/output gear (e.g., punched card readers, line printers, and magnetic storage devices), but these peripherals are expensive in relation to the cost of the CPU. Given the financial resources to hang good input/output gear on a mini, most users would prefer to get a second CPU, or to increase the central storage capacity of the first CPU, and we're back to paper tape again. There is clearly a need for an inexpensive cassette tape drive, or something like it.

By and large, the minis are extremely reliable devices. The central processors can and do operate for months without any sign of trouble. This is in contrast to large machines, which require daily attention from service personnel. As the number of interconnected components increases, and the packing density of those components goes up, the troubles increase. Any individual component may have a mean time between failures (MTBF) measured in thousands of hours, but the greater the number of components (transistors, resistors, condensers, and leads between them), the greater the probability that the system as a whole will have an MTBF that is quite low; there will also be cross-talk between the supposedly distinct electrical impulses.

The argument has been advanced for many years that the way to cheaper computation lies with ever larger machines. It is certainly true that the cost of executing a given million instructions is less on a large machine than on a small one. But the net cost of delivering the results from those million executed instructions to the user may be enormous with the large machine. The reasons for this include the following:

1. Because of the large investment in securing and maintaining the large machine, there is heavy pressure to keep it operating at all times. Thus, we are led to the problem of establishing a steady flow of work to a machine that, by its very nature, is remote from its users.

2. To increase operating efficiency even further, the large machine is heavily buffered from the users with red tape, operating systems, and communications gear. For the million instructions that the user wants executed, a typical large-scale system will execute many millions more instructions that seem to be required to keep the system going.

3. All of this added complexity is designed by systems programmers who traditionally seem to take great pains to make their work obscure and unintelligible to the user. The output is normally cluttered up with great amounts of information that the user can't read and doesn't want.

Large computers, large airplanes, electrical generators, and home refrigerators are about the only mechanisms in our society that are felt necessary to be run continuously. Nearly every other device that we buy stands idle most of the time; no one worries about it. Your automobile is idle perhaps 97% of its life. An electric can opener operates as little as 0.1% of the time. So it goes. Even the refrigerator, although it is kept cycling all the time, actually runs less than one-quarter of the time. The other three items that were mentioned function around the clock largely because of the huge investment necessary to establish any usage at all. The term "large" in connection with computers refers to machines that cost $100,000 or more. An old rule in the computing game says that machine dollars must always be matched with people dollars. A machine that costs $100,000 will rent for around $2500 per month, and the rule says that it will require another $2500 per month in salaries of the people who operate it (programmers, keypunch operators, console operators, and so on).

The mini computers currently sell for around $10,000, counting everything that is needed to make them useful. The corresponding monthly rental figure is thus about

$250, and the matching amount for people will not buy one whole competent person.

What all this leads to is this: Mini computers, used as general-purpose machines, will cause a revolution in the way computing power is delivered to its users. We must begin to think in terms of the cost (per million executed instructions, say) to the user, rather than the cost of raw CPU time. Above all, we must begin to get used to the idea that an idle computer is not necessarily a bad thing, and may be quite a good thing.

The vendors will soon be producing minis in lots of 10,000 rather than lots of 100. What will these machines be used for?

1. As replacements for general-purpose time-shared terminals. Many users rent a terminal which is then used for small engineering calculations, using Fortran or BASIC. Much of this use can be done less expensively on a dedicated terminal (e.g., a mini plus Teletype). One of the advantages of the time-sharing approach is that the user can buy in at a low level, perhaps as low as $500 per month to start. The initial investment in a dedicated terminal is much higher, although there is no reason why dedicated terminals could not also be rented.

2. As replacements for special-purpose terminals. Many terminals (using time-sharing, and connected to a large computer) are rented for specific applications. An example of this is a terminal for a doctor's billing procedures. The central machine is programmed for medical paper work, and individual doctors subscribe to the service. Much the same software can be used if the terminal connects to a local mini. The main advantage thus gained is lowered cost. But there are other advantages. Security is improved; the medical records never leave the doctor's control. The interface with the telephone company is severed (which eliminates telephone line costs, at the least). Overall reliability goes up—a malfunctioning CPU affects one doctor, rather than fifty doctors.

Thus, we can expect to see mini computers in large numbers that are programmed for one specific task (medical filing and accounting; law office paper work; small engineering problems; small business inventory; and so on). For all these tasks, someone must create human-engineered software that is thoroughly debugged and tested and made idiot-proof.

A more complete overview of the role of mini computers can be found in "The Mini-Computer's Quiet Revolution," *EDP Analyzer,* 10(12) (Dec. 1972). The *EDP Analyzer* is a monthly magazine published by Canning Publications, Inc., 925 Anza Avenue, Vista, Calif. 92083. The December 1972 issue is entirely devoted to this one article.

# Appendix

# 3

# ANSWERS TO
# SELECTED EXERCISES

## Chapter 2

**25.** How much of this problem did you explore by hand? Is it clear that if you carried out the example shown in Exercise 25, you would already have verified 17 of the possible 100 cases?

**30.** The answer is no. Ultimately, there are only some 25 numbers that are even eligible; the proper tool to use is a table of squares, or possibly a desk calculator. Richard Andree, in his book *Computer Programming and Related Mathematics,* New York: Wiley, 1967, discusses this particular problem at length on pages 187–191. While we're at it, that book is highly recommended as a supplementary text to this one. Despite its formidable title, it is written for beginners, with great charm and wit.

**40.** Again, a sensible answer to this problem is best arrived at by trying some cases by hand. After you calculate some pairs of dates by hand, you will begin to devise a systematic method of the problem. About that time, your estimate of how many pairs it takes to constitute good use of a computer is likely to fall drastically.

**45.** If we did use a computer for this problem, we could readily generate the 100,000 cases and test each one for the required property (but notice that the problem is intrinsically decimal in nature, since it deals with the properties of **digits;** hence the programming for a binary computer might be tricky). There is a simple analytic solution. Suppose the number we are examining is of the form

ABCBD

where the letters stand for different decimal digits; in this example, the second and fourth digits are the ones that are alike. There are 10 possibilities for the first B, but only one possibility then for the second B. The possible values for A, C, and D are then as follows:

A  B  C  B  D
9  10  8  1  7

This gives 5040 possible numbers of this form. Now, the choice of the two identical digits becomes the number of ways we can select two things out of five. Here they are:

BBACD
BABCD
BACBD
BACDB
ABBCD
ABCBD
ABCDB
ACBBD
ACBDB
ACDBB

The total number of numbers of the type we seek is then $10 \times 5040$, or 50,400.

**50.** The answer is "maybe." A brute force solution by computer would consume, in all likelihood, thousands of hours of computer time. If the problem is ever solved, it will probably be by analytic means; moreover, it will probably fall out of some other research.

**51.** The fifth root of 100 is the astronomer's "order of magnitude." The problem is well-defined: We seek a number that lies between 2 and 3 that can be multiplied by itself five times to yield 100. There are many methods by which the calculation can be performed, such as an iteration on the formula

$$X_{n+1} = \frac{4X_n^5 + 100}{5X_n}$$

But no matter; whatever method is used, it will eventually require doing arithmetic to 50 digit precision. So the question is, to do something like 42 multiplications, 6 additions, and 6 divisions (which is what the analysis reveals is needed), all to 50 digit precision, is the computer the proper tool to use?

Our machine can perform 5 digit arithmetic directly. It will require some extensive programming to extend its capability to 50 digits (this is the subject of Chapter 9), but it can be done.

The criteria can all be applied only with considerably more knowledge of how computers are used. In other words, the problem asks you to make a value judgment based on incomplete information. At the moment, we are only suggesting things to think about. What are the alternatives in this problem? Could we find that fifth root by hand calculation, or with the aid of a desk calculator? If we could arrange to program our machine to do it, which might take days of work, then how much computer time would be expended in the actual solution of this problem? Would you guess that the answer to that question is measured in milliseconds or in years? Even if the answer is in the millisecond range, would the use of the computer be cost-effective? All these questions should become clearer later, as you advance through this book. For now, you should begin looking at every problem situation from the point of view of "Is this really a good computer problem at all?"

**60.** If we attack the hexagon problem by brute force, we may find ourselves writing a program to run through billions of cases. It could be that these billions of cases are all necessary, but you should learn to be suspicious of such solutions; the catchphrase is "cut the problem down to size." The hexagon problem is outlined in detail in Section 15.4.

**70.** The crossword puzzle problem could be a computer problem. The real problem involved here is that of **data representation;** that is, how are we going to get the 1000 patterns digitized and entered into a computer? (If we can once get the data entered into storage, then the problem reduces to one of sorting, searching, and comparing, for which we have many standard techniques.) So back off. Consider the real problem that is implied here, and then try to answer the original question.

# Chapter 4

**75.** See Figure A3.1.

**85.** See Figure A3.2.

**88.** See Figure A3.3.

# Chapter 5

**95.** We can go at this in two ways. We could take the result of the decimal analysis (which is 999,000) and convert it to binary; the result is then 20 bit positions.

Or we could analyze the whole problem in binary. Each of the numbers is certified to be less than or equal to 1111100111 (which is the binary version of the decimal number 999). There are 1000 of them, which is 1111101000 in binary. Again, considering the problem as the product of these two numbers, the result should have as many bit positions as the sum of the bit positions in each of the factors. Again, we reach the answer of 20.

**105.** The product of two decimal numbers has as many digits as the sum of the digits in the two factors, or one less than that number. Thus, the product of a 7 digit number and an 8 digit number must be 15 or 14 digits long. Only one of the four choices given qualifies.

Furthermore, the product of two decimal integers that end in 3 and 6 must be an integer ending in 8, and again, only one choice qualifies.

**110.** This is the inverse of the multiplication problem. The answer is $15 - 9 = 6$ bits. That is, the number of numbers we can add is expressed in 6 bits. The largest number that can be expressed in 6 bits is 63. So we can add 63 such words.

**115.** The number 16,384 is the fourteenth power of 2. Therefore, the addresses will have to be 14 bits long, ranging from 00000000000000 to 11111111111111. Notice that we will label the words in binary with addresses that range from 0 to $16,383 = 2^{14} - 1$.

**120.** One bit position is reserved for the sign of the number. That leaves 23 bit positions, and the largest positive number is thus $2^{23} - 1 = 8,388,607$. Notice that there can be $2^{23}$ different positive numbers, but the first of them is the number 0.

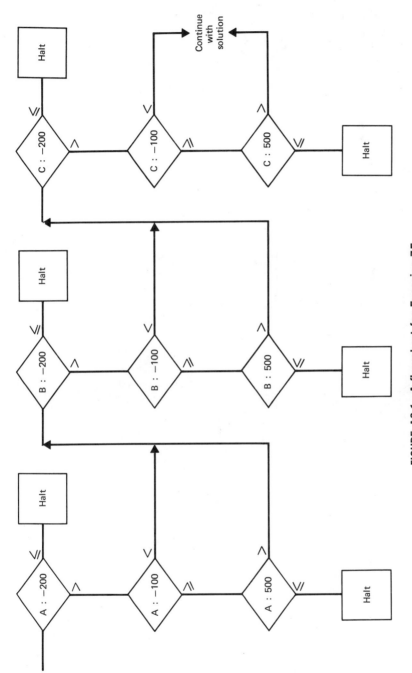

**FIGURE A3.1  A flowchart for Exercise 75.**

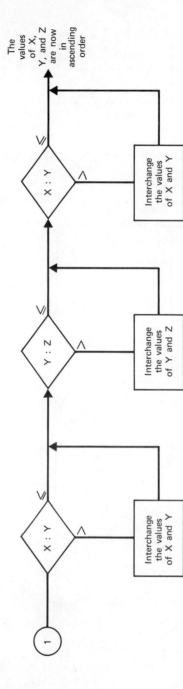

FIGURE A3.2 A scheme for sorting three numbers (Exercise 85).

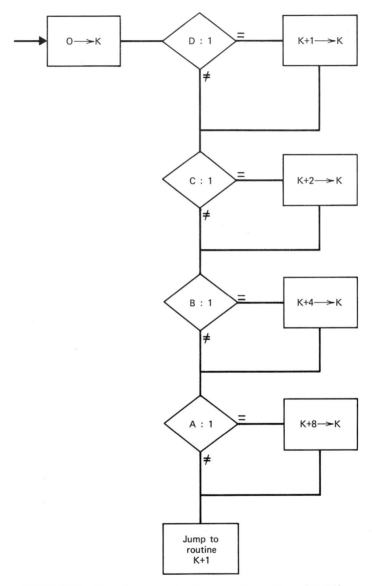

**FIGURE A3.3  Choosing one of sixteen routines (Exercise 88).**

# Chapter 6

**135.** You could probably connect to all the state senators (and to nearly anyone in the country as well) in at most third-level addressing. Fourth- or fifth-level addressing would take you to Lincoln, and perhaps no more than sixth-level would be required to get to Washington.

**140.** The flowchart of Figure A3.4 shows a scheme of a subroutine to advance the 3 word counter as a calendar. The logic is shown greatly condensed. The selection of the current month should probably be represented by 12 decision boxes, and the leap year decision might require a flowchart of its own. For the current four centuries, every year divisible by 4 is a leap year except the years 1800, 1900, and 2100.

**150.** Applying Euclid's algorithm to the pair of numbers 1638 and 10,920, we find that their GCD is 546. We now need only apply the algorithm a second time to 546 and 29,744. The answer is 26.

**155.** Figure A3.5 shows a possible scheme. Notice that in the first box X is an address, but in the first diamond we want the **contents** at address X. The parentheses are quite important to keep the meaning clear.

# Chapter 8

**160.** See Figure A3.6.

**165.** For the numbers from −500 to +499, the five counters should show 1, 499, 500, 399, and 250, respectively. With this data, and these results, we would have a pretty fair test procedure. Would it constitute a complete and valid test procedure? No; no test procedure could ever guarantee perfection. The goal is to achieve a level of confidence for the programmer. We could devise more elaborate tests, but we must stop somewhere and put the program into production.

**170.** See Figure A3.7.

**180.** See Figure A3.8.

**190.** See Figure A3.9.

**195.** See Figures A3.10 and A3.11.

**205.** See Figure A3.12.

**220.** The flowchart of Figure A3.13 shows one way to do the differencing problem. Words in storage are set up as indicated, with these meanings:

| | |
|---|---|
| F | The functional values that are read in |
| D1 | First difference |
| D2 | Second difference |
| D3 | Third difference |
| OF | "Old F"; the most recent value of the function |
| OD1 | Previous first difference |
| OD2 | Previous second difference |

The numbers being read into the machine are stored in F. The decision "EOF" means "end-of-file," a common notation for such work. As shown here, the program will produce some extraneous numbers in the difference columns on the first three lines of the output. We could, for some small effort, arrange to suppress the printing of

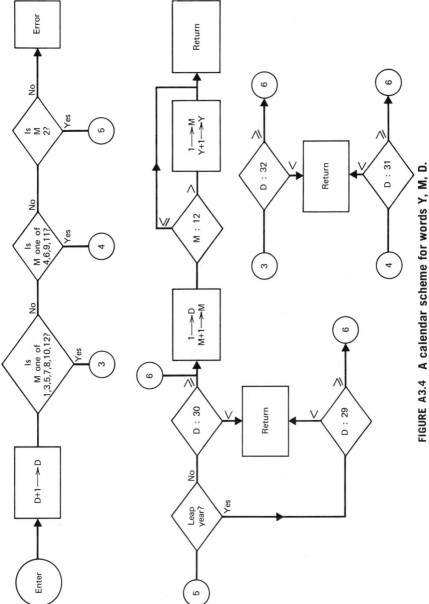

**FIGURE A3.4  A calendar scheme for words Y, M, D.**

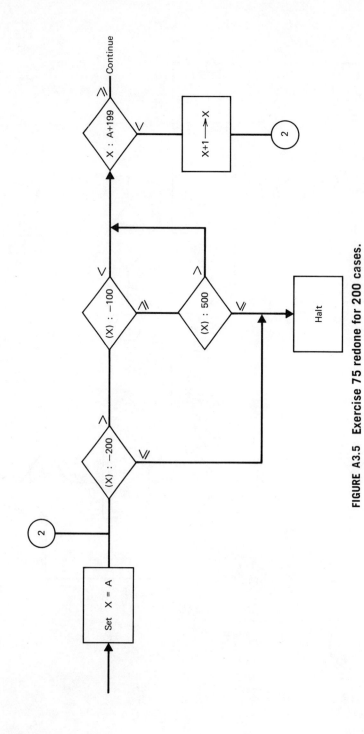

**FIGURE A3.5 Exercise 75 redone for 200 cases.**

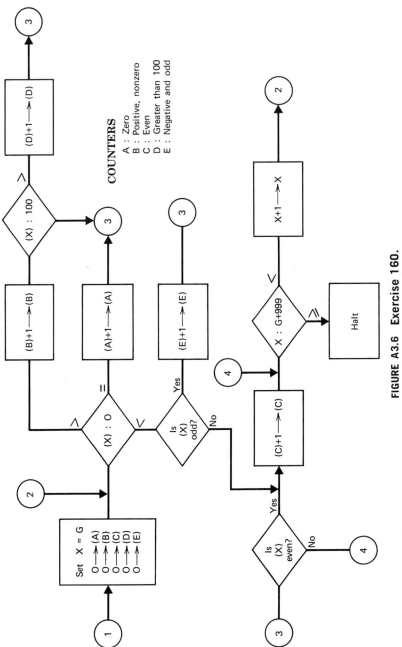

COUNTERS

A : Zero
B : Positive, nonzero
C : Even
D : Greater than 100
E : Negative and odd

FIGURE A3.6   Exercise 160.

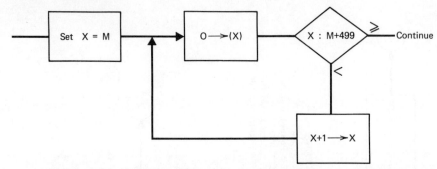

**FIGURE A3.7** **Exercise 170. A loop to clear a block of storage to 0.**

those extraneous numbers, but there is no rule against crossing them out with a pen on the printout.

To test the program, we should devise some input data for which the results can be predicted. How about using functional values whose third differences are all the same? Try the sequence 1, 8, 27, 64, 125, . . . , which is a table of cubes. This procedure is discussed more fully in Chapter 16.

# Chapter 9

**225.** For testing the square root procedure, you could arrange to compare the square of the result against N. This comparison will come out equal only for values of N that are perfect squares. For other values of N, the result squared will be less than N, but (result + 1) squared will be greater than N.

**230.** With double precision we could calculate the Fibonacci sequence to the forty-fourth term. For 100 terms (the one hundredth term is 21 digits long), we would need 3 word precision.

**235.** If we seek the cycle lengths of the low-order K digits of the Fibonacci sequence, the computer is a fine tool to use. Incidentally, the results are different if we seek the cycle lengths of the low-order **bits** of the sequence. This is one problem whose answers are dependent on the number base being used.

**245.** (*a*) The required range covers 219 numbers. Call the RNG subroutine, and reduce the output modulo 219, which yields a number at random in the range 0–218. Add 167 to that result; we now have random numbers in the range 167–385.

(*b*) Call the RNG subroutine and reduce the output modulo 259. If the sum does not exceed 385, use the sum. If the sum exceeds 385, then the difference should be added to 1279. Suppose that the random number is 14,793. The reduction modulo 259 yields 30. Adding 167 gives 197, which is less than 385, so we use 197. If the random number were 14,996, the reduction modulo 259 yields 233. When we add 167, we get 400. The difference between 400 and 385 is 15; add the 15 to 1279 to yield 1294.

(*c*) The output of the RNG subroutine can be reduced modulo 10,000.

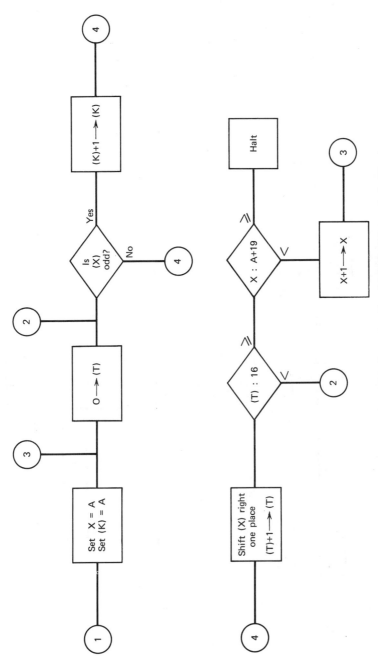

FIGURE A3.8  Exercise 180. Counting the 1 bits in 20 words in block A. The counter, T, counts the number of shifts.

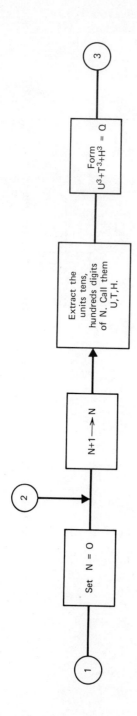
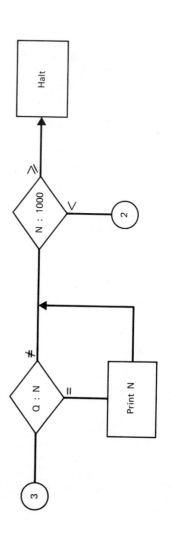

**FIGURE A3.9  Exercise 190.**

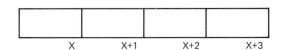

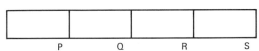

**FIGURE A3.10  The sets-of-four problem. For set N, the section of block T is shown (top). The words at X are a work area, as is the set of words P, Q, R, and S.**

## Chapter 10

**280.**  (a)  37987280 E02
   (b)  45534184 E00
   (c)  37862947 E02
(And no arithmetic was needed to produce this result.)

## Chapter 12

**300.**  See Figure A3.14. The number OS stands for "old S," initialized to some arbitrary high value. The critical step is the comparison of the current S to the previous S; we expect S to go down as we proceed to increase the R values. As soon as S increases, we have passed the minimum that we are seeking. We have arranged to calculate R to 8 significant digits.

## Chapter 13

**340.**  See Figure A3.15.

## Chapter 14

**365.**  The critical part of the area problem is the portion of the field of area X(500 − 2X) that is the cut off by the curve of the lake. Consider the case of the field of length 250. The sector of the circular lake then has a chord of length 250. The sector consists of two parts. One part is a triangle of sides 5280, 5280, and 250. The altitude of this triangle can be calculated as the square root of $5280^2 - 125^2$. Its area

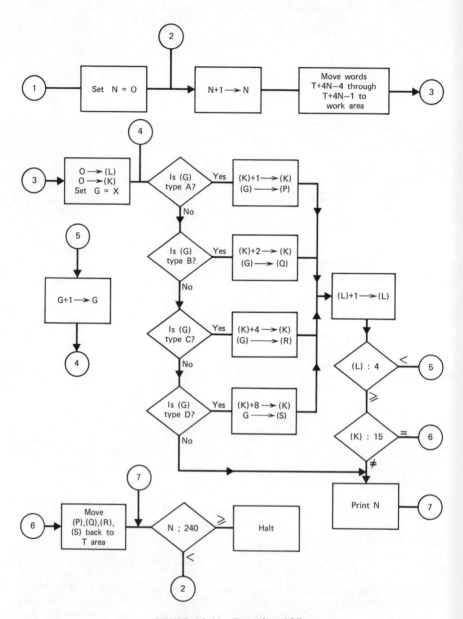

**FIGURE A3.11 Exercise 195.**

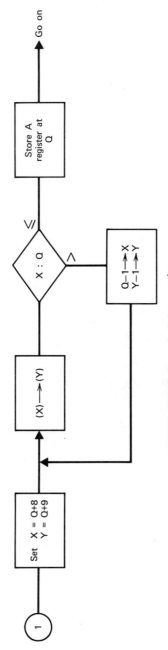

**FIGURE A3.12  A push-down routine.**

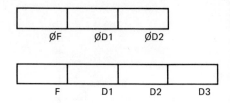

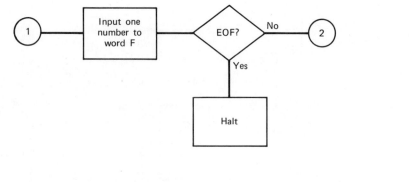

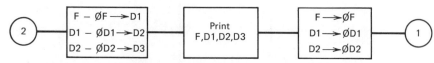

**FIGURE A3.13   A scheme for differencing.**

can be found if we know the central angle 2A, for which A is the angle whose sine is 125 divided by that altitude. The area of the entire sector is found by the ratio of 2A to 360° applied to the area of the lake. By this line of reasoning, we can establish a function (a BASIC user-defined function) for the area we want as a function of the field length. All of this is a new problem of some complexity. It is complicated, but straightforward, and BASIC lets us explore it in pieces, building up to a solution of the main problem without recourse to calculus.

## Chapter 16

**410.** We want 500 data numbers that are all different, are easily generated, and have a predictable sum. The numbers from 1 to 500 fit these conditions; their sum (by the formula for summing an arithmetic progression) is

$$\frac{1 + 500}{2} \times 500 = 125{,}250$$

This will not test the use of negative numbers. We could repeat the test, with the numbers from −1 to −500, with the predicted sum of −125,250. Or, we could have

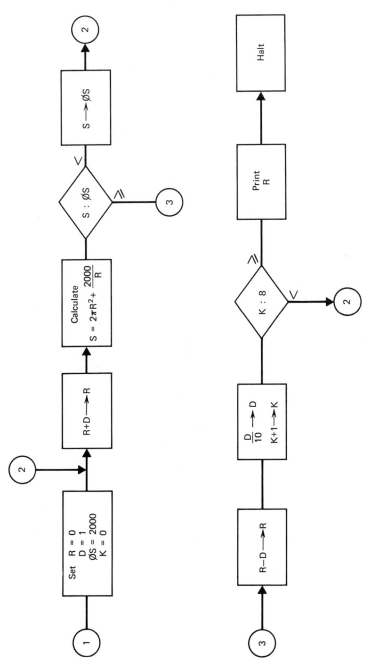

**FIGURE A3.14  The bracketing process for the tin can problem.**

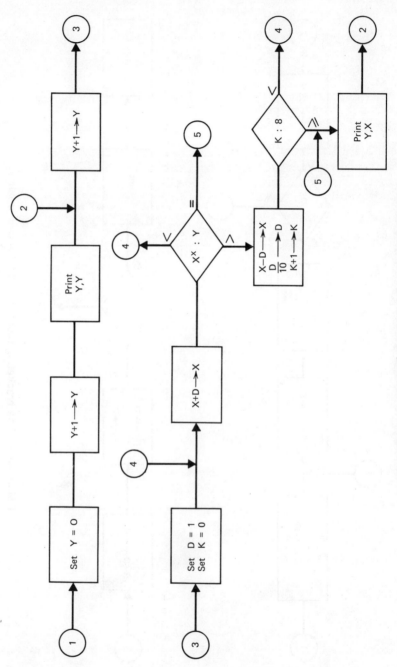

**FIGURE A3.15   A bracketing scheme for the $X^X$ problem.**

done both jobs at once with the numbers from −250 to +249, and a predicted sum of −250.

Using the latter set of data, a complete test procedure for the program should be written like this:

(a)  Generate the numbers from −250 through +249 in the block of words addressed at B through B499.

(b)  Run the program.

(c)  Print the contents of B+500, which should be −250.

Notice that the printing of (B+500) is part of the test procedure; it should not be made part of the program itself.

The requirement that test data consist of all different numbers ensures that the action of our loop is correct. If all 500 words were filled with the number 17 (leading to a predicted sum of 8500), we would not know whether we had added 500 numbers, or one number 500 times.

Our test procedure uses 500 numbers, which indeed tests the original program; it leads to **one** printed result; and the result, −250, is not likely to be produced by accident. Is the test procedure completely airtight? Not at all. No test procedure will ever be perfect. We have, however, reached a fairly high confidence level about the validity of our program.

**415.**  You may need the formula for the sum of squares of the consecutive integers from 1 to K:

$$\frac{K(K+1)(2K+1)}{6}$$

**420.**  If the A and B blocks are each loaded with the same sequence of consecutive numbers, then the sum of the numbers in the C block can be calculated from the formula given for Exercise 415.

**425.**  Just to make sure that you are catching on to the notion of a test procedure, we will outline a possible complete procedure for this problem:

(a)  Generate in the G block the consecutive integers from −499 through +500.

(b)  Run the program and print out the contents of the five counters.

(c)  Verify these results:

| | |
|---|---|
| zero count | = 1 |
| positive, nonzero count | = 500 |
| even count | = 500 |
| greater than 100 count | = 400 |
| negative and odd count | = 250 |
| sum of G block | = 500 |

**430.**  Suppose we load the K block with the numbers 1–2000. After running the program, we can predict the sum of the numbers in the K block, and also the contents of the words at K, K+999, and K+1999. These 4 words were chosen to represent the critical points in the loop.

A common error is to generate an ascending series in the block, run the program, and then write a loop to verify that the words now in the block are in descending order. Such a procedure lacks any feedback whatsoever. If the original program and the testing program both work, we get nothing back from the machine. If neither of the programs works (or, in fact, if the machine is down), we also get nothing back. This is no way to test anything.

**433.** Consider this rule: If any part of the flowchart of the original problem can be removed, and the test procedure still seems to work, then there is something wrong with that procedure. In this case, we could remove *the entire flowchart*. The test procedure works even if the program doesn't. Moreover, there is no positive feedback from such a procedure. If both the program and the test worked properly, we have nothing to show for it.

**435.** Your test procedure should account for all these cases:

(a) Nontriangle. This includes the case of 0,0,0, as well as that of negative numbers. For negative numbers, there should be three test cases (e.g., −7,5,4; 5,−7,4; and 5,4,−7) to ensure that the program tests for the negative number in any of its three positions. The other nontriangle case is represented by 3,4,7 and, again, should be tested in all three positions.

(b) Equilateral triangles. Only one such triangle need be included in the data.

(c) Isosceles triangles. This will also require at least three test cases.

(d) Scalene triangles. There should be three of these, too.

**440.** Start with the two extremes: the same date taken twice, for which the answer should be 0; and two dates at the extreme ends of the century, for which the answer should be 36,523. Then pairs of dates should be fabricated that are one week apart in the same month; one week apart in successive months; one year apart; one year apart involving a leap year; and so on. A thorough test would involve at least a dozen pairs of dates.

**445.** A person writing a subroutine for the greatest common divisor of two integers probably assumes that the user of the subroutine intends to use it sensibly. But strange things can happen in a computer; at the time of execution, numbers change rapidly. What will the subroutine do when presented with number pairs like (0,8), (5,0), and (0,0)? The term "greatest common divisor" has meaning only for nonzero integers. Nevertheless, the subroutine should be written to care for all cases. So the first three test cases are clearly indicated. Other interesting test cases are

$$(819,220) = 1$$
$$(997,512) = 1$$
$$(11934,4488) = 102$$

**450.** One possible procedure consists of loading the numbers 1, 3, 7, 15, 31, . . . into the A block, up to $2^{16} - 1$. In binary, these numbers are 1, 11, 111, 1111, etc., and the first 16 of them can be summed by formula (for a total of 136 bits). The last 4 words could be loaded with the (decimal) numbers 1, 2, 3, and 4, which add 5 more 1 bits, for a grand total of 141.

This is an adequate procedure for the stated problem. Consider, however, that the problem is not altered conceptually if we have 10,000 words in which to count the 1 bits. Now how shall we test it? If we load the block with the numbers 1–10,000, then our problem is how to **calculate** the 1 bits without having to write out 10,000 numbers in binary and counting the 1 bits. If we began that monumental task:

```
00001
00010
00011
00100
00101
00110
00111
01000
```

01001
01010
01011
01100
01101
01110

we could observe a pattern if we look at the columns of bit positions. The low-order column alternates 1s and 0s. For 10,000 consecutive numbers, that column will contribute exactly 5000 1s. The next column (what would be called the tens position in decimal notation) alternates 1s and 0s by twos. It will also contribute around 5000 1s, depending on how the pattern is interrupted at the end. Every column, in fact, exhibits a regular pattern; the trick is to calculate the remainders on dividing 10,000 by 4, 8, 16, 32, and so on. It is tedious, but much faster than any other method.

**455.** Every unabridged dictionary, as well as the *World Almanac,* contains a perpetual calendar that will furnish dates and days of the week over a 2000 year span.

**460.** This is a sticky problem in testing. The following procedure would do:
(a) Write a program located in the first few words of core that will store, in every word above the program itself, the address of the word in that word. For the Varian 620, such a program is

```
STX   0,1     075000
DXR           005344
JMP   0       001000
              000000
```

(and with the X register loaded with the largest possible address, which is 37777, octal, for a 16K machine).
(b) Now write the program to sum all words to be located also in the lower part of core. Again, a sample program is

```
ADD   0,1     125000
JXZ   *+5     001040   000006
DXR           005344
JMP   0       001000   000000
HLT           000000
```

(and with the accumulator set to 0, and the X register set to the largest possible address).
(c) The result can now be predicted. It will be the sum of all the words in the second program, plus the sum of the numbers from 7 to 37777 (octal), all reduced modulo 65536. For the Varian machine with 16,384 words, the result is 114365)$_8$.

**465.** Part of the $\pi$ calculation program is checked automatically by the known result. But before we commit such a program to production, we should still test its logic. The program uses the random number generator subroutine. Recall that this subroutine has a reproducible action; that is, if we reset its starting values to the same numbers, it will output precisely the same stream of results. Print some of these results and hand calculate their effect, to see how many points lie in or on the quarter circle. Then run the program with a limit inserted to act on the same number of points, and compare the results.

**470.** This is still another situation in testing. The program for Pythagorean triplets, after being debugged, will output as many sets of numbers, X, Y, and Z, as we please.

It does little good to verify that $X^2 + Y^2 = Z^2$, since the formulas for X, Y, and Z are essentially identities; that is, they will produce values that satisfy the Pythagorean relation regardless of what values of R and T are fed to them. Consider these three cases:

|     | R | T | X | Y | Z |
|-----|---|---|-----|----|----|
| (1) | 2 | 5 | −21 | 20 | 29 |
| (2) | 7 | 3 | 40  | 42 | 58 |
| (3) | 6 | 3 | 27  | 36 | 45 |

In case (1), R is not greater than T. In case (2), R and T have the same parity. In case (3), R and T have a factor in common. Yet in all three cases it is true that $X^2 + Y^2 = Z^2$. We do not want to produce such results. Case (1) produces a triangle with a negative side; case (2) is twice as big as the triangle 20,21,29 and is hence not unique; and case (3) is the 3,4,5 triangle again.

What we really want to test is that our program generates the R and T values properly. To test it, we should either do some extensive hand calculation, or compare the printed output of the program with a previously calculated table. Suppose we were to look up a prior table of such triplets that had been run to 1000 sets. If we were to adjust our program to calculate the first 1000 triplets and print just the last set, and it agreed, our confidence level would be fairly high.

The point here is that some programs cannot be tested by controlling the input data, nor are there predetermined results to check against. Every program is different, and in devising adequate tests, the programmer has his finest opportunity to demonstrate the superiority of his brain over the machine's brawn.

**475.** For the four types, there are 24 ways in which they can be arranged in any one set. Generate these 24 arrangements of valid data and store them in the data area, replicated ten times. Run the program with this data. No set numbers should be printed out, and all 240 sets should now have the four types in correct order. Print out enough sets to satisfy yourself that correct action has been taken.

With the original data, we next need to test the invalid combinations, such as

```
AABC
ABCA
ABAC
BAAC
ABBB
ACCA
ABCE
```

(The last case represents a number, E, which is not one of the four possible types.) Each such invalid combination should result in its set number being printed. The number of cases to consider is a function of your own confidence level, but you could hardly call the program tested with less than twenty or so such cases.

The general guideline says that your test procedure should not call for examining more than six or so numbers. It is only a guideline; not a rule. For this problem, you might have to check carefully several hundred printed numbers.

You are now learning computing, but some day you may use the computer professionally. In designing program tests, picture yourself in an atmosphere where you are paid to do things right. If you are going to err, let it be on the side of testing too much, rather than too little. The world is already overpopulated with people who commit untested or poorly tested programs to production.

# Appendix
# 4
# MACHINE OPERATING DIRECTIONS

The following sets of directions relate to the Varian 620, having an ASR 33 Teletype and a photoelectric paper tape reader. Your installation is probably different, and these directions do not apply in detail. They are given here as a model; you should arrange to paraphrase them to fit your installation.

## Using the DAS 8A Assembler

1.  Write the program.
2.  Punch the program on paper tape, either off-line or with an on-line editing routine.
3.  Load the assembler into a storage and set the options for pass I.
4.  Mount the source tape (from Step 2) and start the reader.
5.  The assembler now performs pass I: create a symbol table and check for any illegal conditions that appear in the source code. If requested, the assembler will output the symbol table at this time.
6.  Set options (console switches) for pass II.
7.  Again mount the source tape.
8.  The assembler now performs pass II, which will produce an object tape and a symbolic listing. (Some assemblers require a third pass of the source tape in order to perform all the required tasks.)
9.  Multiple assemblies are possible (that is, assembling more than one program at the same time), since the assembler can be reinitialized to perform each pass with different source tapes.

## Core Clear

1.  Press SYSTEM RESET.
2.  Set REPEAT key.
3.  Set U = 054000
    P = 000000
4.  Set A = 055000 and press STEP.
5.  Set A = 005144 and press STEP.
6.  Set A = 001000 and press STEP.
7.  Set P = 000000
    U = 000000
    A = 000000
    X = 000003 and press RUN.
8.  Set U = 054000
9.  Press STEP two times.
10.  Reset REPEAT key and clear all registers.

## Loading Memory

1.  Press SYSTEM RESET.
2.  Set REPEAT key.
3.  Set U = 054000
    P = starting address
4.  Set A = first (next) word to be loaded.
5.  Press STEP.
6.  Repeat Steps 4 and 5 until all words are loaded.
7.  Reset REPEAT key.

## Inspecting Memory

1.  Press SYSTEM RESET.
2.  Set REPEAT key.
3.  Set U = 014000
    P = starting address
4.  Press STEP.
5.  A register now contains contents of memory at location P.
6.  Repeat Steps 4 and 5 until all words have been inspected.
7.  Reset REPEAT key.

## Loading BLD II and AID II

1. Press SYSTEM RESET.
2. Follow the procedure given for loading memory and load the following:

```
007756:  102637
007757:  004011
007760:  004041
007761:  004446
007762:  001020
007763:  007772
007764:  055000
007765:  001010
007766:  007000
007767:  005144
007770:  005101
007771:  100537
007772:  101537
007773:  007756
007774:  001000
007775:  007772
```

3. Set X = 007000
   B = 000000
   A = 000000
   U = 000000
   P = 007770
4. Set sense switch 1 off, sense switches 2 and 3 on.
5. Position BLD and AID tape in high-speed reader.
6. Press RUN.

## Loading Programs

1. Press SYSTEM RESET.
2. Set P = 037600
   U = 000000
   A = 000000 for loading only or
   000001 for load and execute
3. Set sense switches as required by the program being loaded.
4. Position object tape in high-speed reader.
5. Press RUN.

# Dumping Programs

1. Press SYSTEM RESET.
2. Set P = 037404
    U = 000000
    A = first location to be dumped
    B = last location to be dumped
    X = 177777 if this is not the last segment to be dumped or program restart
       address if last segment (or only segment)
3. Press RUN.
4. Repeat Steps 2 and 3 as many times as needed.

# Display

If storage (of the Varian 620) is loaded as follows:

| | |
|---|---|
| 00000 | 005117 |
| 00001 | 005017 |
| 00002 | 005017 |
| 00003 | 005017 |
| . | . |
| . | . |
| . | . |
| 37775 | 005017 |
| 37776 | 001000 |
| 37777 | 000000 |
| P | 000000 |
| U | 000000 |
| A | 000000 |

then, on RUN, the display lights will exhibit a binary counter.

# Appendix

# 5

# A HIGH-PRECISION PACKAGE

The complete program for the interpretive package described in Chapter 11 is reproduced on the following pages. This interpreter permits floating decimal arithmetic on 96 digit numbers that are packed into 25 16 bit words.

For each number in the system, the first of its 25 words contains the sign of the number in the high-order bit position and a signed exponent in the range ±16,383 in the remaining 15 bits. The subsequent 24 words contain the first 96 significant digits of the number, packed 4 digits per word in binary coded decimal form.

The package contains the following facilities:

1. The arithmetic operations: addition, subtraction, multiplication, and division.
2. Input and output commands.
3. Square root and absolute value functions.
4. Unconditional jump, five conditional jumps, and one subroutine jump.
5. Zero-level addressing, permitting creation of constants in the range ±16,383 within one pseudo-instruction.
6. Pseudo-registers PAC (pseudo-accumulator) and PMQ (pseudo-MQ), both of 96 digit length.
7. A pseudo-index, PIN, which is a single machine word used for loop control.
8. Twenty-two miscellaneous instructions for ease in using the package.
9. The constants PI and E, correct to 96 significant digits.

The command list shows all the available op-codes for the package. The program is entered by linking to FINT (floating interpreter). Exit from the interpreter is by use of the pseudo HLT command. The program has been written in modular form to facilitate extension by the user (e.g., the addition of more functions).

Following the listing of the interpreter, there is a listing of a sample program that uses it, together with some of its output. The package itself, plus the user's program, assemble together under the DAS 8A assembler. The interpreter occupies 3039 words of core storage.

**243**

Timing is as follows:

| | |
|---|---|
| ADD, $2 + 3$ | 16 milliseconds |
| ADD, $\pi + e$ | 21 milliseconds |
| MULTIPLY, $2 \times 3$ | 611 milliseconds |
| MULTIPLY, $\pi \times e$ | 1207 milliseconds |
| DIVIDE, $6 \div 2$ | 607 milliseconds |
| DIVIDE, $\pi \div e$ | 2300 milliseconds |
| SQUARE ROOT, $\sqrt{2}$ | 20,982 milliseconds |

Subroutining instructions are used as follows: Given a subroutine called NEG in storage,

```
NEG   ENTR
      STAE    NEG1
      TZA
      SUBE    NEG1
      RETU*   NEG
NEG1  BSS     25
```

the subroutine can be called within an interpretive program by the instructions

```
LDAE   A
CALL   NEG
```

The instructions SOF (Set noisy mode) and ROF (Reset noisy mode) provide information about loss of significance. The normal floating-point action is to insert 0s at the low-order end of a number as the significance drops. For example, the addition of

$$\frac{\begin{array}{r} 12345678...5678E10 \\ -12341876...2345E10 \end{array}}{00003802...3333E10}$$

is normalized to 3802 . . . 3333E06 in normal operations. If noisy mode is set, then the interpreter feeds 9s rather than 0s into the low-order end during this normalization. If the same calculations are made in noisy mode and not in noisy mode, the difference between the results gives a measure of the loss of significance.

Noisy mode is reset whenever the interpreter is entered. Thus, if the user sets noisy mode, and then exits from the interpreter and reenters, he must reset noisy mode if he wishes to continue to use it.

The number 0 can be in any form and will be handled internally with an implied decimal point after the first digit.

Quotients are carried to 96 digits; they are not rounded from a 97th digit. The other three arithmetic operations are rounded to 96 digits if the operation yields more than 96 digits.

Input can be in any legal form and will be converted to the proper internal form. Invalid characters are ignored (and not even echoed on the Teletype). Input numbers may have more than 96 digits, but only the first 96 are used, and there is no rounding on input.

The PAC and PMQ are not initialized, but all the routines assume that these registers contain valid numbers. Therefore, unpredictable results will occur if arithmetic is performed before PAC and PMQ are loaded. This course of action allows the user to exit from interpretive mode, perform normal machine operations, and reenter the interpreter with previous numbers in PAC and PMQ undisturbed.

Negative numbers are stored in true (not complement) form.

The linkages to FINT, PI, and E are through machine words 010, 011, and 012, respectively. This information is needed if the program and the interpretive package are assembled separately.

## Command List

### Single word

| | |
|---|---|
| HLT | Exit interpreter |
| NOP | No-operation |
| TZA | Transfer 0 to PAC |
| TZB | Transfer 0 to PMQ |
| TZX | Transfer 0 to PIN |
| TAB | Transfer PAC to PMQ |
| TBA | Transfer PMQ to PAC |
| IXR | Increment PIN |
| CPA | Complement PAC |
| CPB | Complement PMQ |
| DXR | Decrement PIN |
| ROF | Reset noisy mode |
| SOF | Set noisy mode |
| EXC 1 | Absolute value of PAC |
| EXC 2 | Square root of PAC |
| INA | Input to PAC |
| INB | Input to PMQ |
| OAR | Output from PAC |
| OBR | Output from PMQ |

### Double word

| | | |
|---|---|---|
| JMP | REF1 | Jump unconditional |
| JAP | REF1 | Jump if PAC $\geq 0$ |
| JAN | REF1 | Jump if PAC $< 0$ |
| JAZ | REF1 | Jump if PAC $= 0$ |
| JBZ | REF1 | Jump if PMQ $= 0$ |
| JXZ | REF1 | Jump if PIN $= 0$ |
| JMPM | REF1 | Jump and mark unconditional |
| LDAI | 12345 | Load PAC immediate |
| LDAE | Q25 | Load PAC |
| LDBI | 5432 | Load PMQ immediate |
| LDBE | Q25 | Load PMQ |
| LDXI | 39 | Load PIN immediate |
| LDXE | K | Load PIN |
| STAE | Q25 | Store PAC |
| STBE | Q25 | Store PMQ |
| STXE | M | Store PIN |
| ADDI | 6789 | Add immediate to PAC |
| ADDE | Q25 | Add to PAC |
| SUBI | 16380 | Subtract immediate from PAC |
| SUBE | Q25 | Subtract from PAC |
| MULI | 7854 | Multiply immediate by PMQ |
| MULE | Q25 | Multiply by PMQ |
| DIVI | 88 | Divide immediate PAC |
| DIVE | Q25 | Divide PAC |
| IME | 1,Q25 | Input to storage |
| OME | 1,Q25 | Output from storage |

# Error Messages

Error: INVALID DIGIT IN OPERAND
Recovery: Digit is reduced modulo 10.
Error: UNNORMALIZED OPERAND
Recovery: Operand is normalized.
Error: OPERAND EXPONENT UNDERFLOW
Recovery: Operand is set to 0.
Error: INVALID INSTRUCTION
Recovery: Instruction is ignored.
Error: EXPONENT OVERFLOW
Recovery: Result is set to $\pm 9.99999 \ldots E + 16383$.
Error: EXPONENT UNDERFLOW
Recovery: Result is set to 0.
Error: ZERO DIVISOR
Recovery: Result is set to $\pm 9.99999 \ldots E + 16383$.
Error: NEGATIVE SQUARE ROOT
Recovery: Square root of absolute value is taken.
Error: REMAINDER EXPONENT UNDERFLOW
Recovery: Remainder is set to 0.

All error messages, which occur during execution, include the octal address of the pseudo-instruction being interpreted. After printing the error message, the machine is halted; to effect the stated recovery and continue, RUN must be pressed.

The error INVALID DIGIT IN OPERAND can occur if a packed number is operated on outside the interpretive system, to produce a binary coded decimal bit configuration greater than 9. The same sort of improper action can produce the error UNNORMALIZED OPERAND and OPERAND EXPONENT UNDERFLOW. Other than improper action taken outside the interpretive system, the error OPERAND EXPONENT UNDERFLOW will occur only on recovery from the error UNNORMALIZED OPERAND.

The error INVALID INSTRUCTION assumes that the invalid instruction was a single word; if it was not, an attempt is made to execute the second word as a separate instruction (which usually triggers the error message a second time).

Following the program for the 96 digit interpretive package is the complete code for the lake/fence problem: It is desired to fence in a rectangular field next to a lake of 1 mile radius, using 500 feet of fencing, with the field to have the maximum area.

The situation of this problem is shown in Figure A5.1 (the field is "rectangular" except for the side along the lake). The solution given in the code is by bracketing.

To calculate the area involved, it is necessary to calculate an arctangent. A subroutine in the program does this by series expansion. Within the subroutine, the argument is reduced to lie in the range from 0 to less than 1 (for an argument of precisely 1, the arctangent can be returned immediately). With the argument less than 1, it is further reduced by the identity

$$\tan Y = \frac{1 \pm \sqrt{1 + \tan^2 2X}}{-\tan 2X}$$

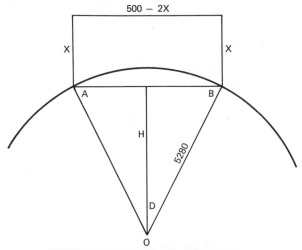

**FIGURE A5.1    The lake/fence problem.**

which the user may also invoke to speed up convergence. For example, suppose that it is known that the value of the tangent is .8 and the arctangent is needed. By the reduction

$$\tan B = \frac{1 \pm \sqrt{1 + (.8)^2}}{-.8}$$

$$\tan B = .35078106$$

we can enter the subroutine with the value .35078106 . . . (this calculation is extended to 96 digits, of course), and the result returned by the subroutine is then doubled.

```
*  *  *  *  *  *  *  *  *  *  *  *  *  *  *  *  *  *  *  *  *  *  *
*                                                                 *
*                                                                 *
*        96-DIGIT FLOATING DECIMAL INTERPRETER                    *
*                                                                 *
*                                                                 *
*        VERSION:   1              DATE:    8/21/72               *
*                                                                 *
*                                                                 *
*        REVISION:  A              DATE:    8/21/72               *
*                                                                 *
*                                                                 *
*  *  *  *  *  *  *  *  *  *  *  *  *  *  *  *  *  *  *  *  *  *  *

*
*        LINKAGE
*
         ,ORG    ,010
         ,DATA   ,FINT
         ,DATA   ,PI
         ,DATA   ,E
*
*        INTERPRETER
*
         ,ORG    ,030000
FINT     ,ENTR   ,
         ,LDAE   ,FINT        INITIALIZE PSEUDO IC
         ,STAE   ,PIC
         ,TZA    ,            RESET NOISY MODE
         ,STAE   ,FILL
FETC     ,LDXE   ,PIC         FETCH NEXT INSTRUCTION
         ,LDA    ,0,1
         ,STAE   ,INST
         ,LDA    ,1,1
         ,JAP    ,*+8
         ,ANAI   ,077777
         ,TAX    ,
         ,LDA    ,0,1
         ,JAN    ,*-4
         ,STAE   ,INST+1
         ,LDXI   ,(ENDT-TAB1)
SRCH     ,LDAE   ,TAB1-1,1    SEARCH TABLE FOR INSTRUCTION
         ,SUBE   ,INST
         ,JAZ    ,VALD
         ,DXR    ,
         ,JXZ    ,*+4
         ,JMP    ,SRCH
         ,ROF    ,            INVALID INSTRUCTION
         ,LDXI   ,(ERO4)
         ,CALL   ,ERR
```

```
         ,INRE   ,PIC
         ,JMP    ,FETC
VALD     ,ROF    ,              LINK TO SUBROUTINE
         ,LDAE   ,TAB2-1,1
         ,STA    ,*+2
         ,CALL   ,(000000)
         ,JMP    ,FETC
*
*        INSTRUCTION TABLES
*
TAB1     ,DATA   ,0000000   HLT
         ,DATA   ,0005000   NOP
         ,DATA   ,0005001   TZA
         ,DATA   ,0005002   TZB
         ,DATA   ,0005004   TZX
         ,DATA   ,0005012   TAB
         ,DATA   ,0005021   TBA
         ,DATA   ,0005144   IXR
         ,DATA   ,0005211   CPA
         ,DATA   ,0005222   CPB
         ,DATA   ,0005344   DXR
         ,DATA   ,0007400   ROF
         ,DATA   ,0007401   SOF
         ,DATA   ,0100001   EXC1
         ,DATA   ,0100002   EXC2
         ,DATA   ,0102100   INA
         ,DATA   ,0102200   INB
         ,DATA   ,0103100   OAR
         ,DATA   ,0103200   OBR
         ,DATA   ,0001000   JMP
         ,DATA   ,0001002   JAP
         ,DATA   ,0001004   JAN
         ,DATA   ,0001010   JAZ
         ,DATA   ,0001020   JBZ
         ,DATA   ,0001040   JXZ
         ,DATA   ,0002000   JMPM
         ,DATA   ,0006010   LDAI
         ,DATA   ,0006017   LDAE
         ,DATA   ,0006020   LDBI
         ,DATA   ,0006027   LDBE
         ,DATA   ,0006030   LDXI
         ,DATA   ,0006037   LDXE
         ,DATA   ,0006057   STAE
         ,DATA   ,0006067   STBE
         ,DATA   ,0006077   STXE
         ,DATA   ,0006120   ADDI
         ,DATA   ,0006127   ADDE
         ,DATA   ,0006140   SUBI
         ,DATA   ,0006147   SUBE
         ,DATA   ,0006160   MULI
```

```
        ,DATA   ,0006167   MULE
        ,DATA   ,0006170   DIVI
        ,DATA   ,0006177   DIVE
        ,DATA   ,0102001   IME
        ,DATA   ,0103001   OME
ENDT    ,EQU    ,*
TAB2    ,DATA   ,HLT
        ,DATA   ,NOP
        ,DATA   ,TZA
        ,DATA   ,TZB
        ,DATA   ,TZX
        ,DATA   ,TAB
        ,DATA   ,TBA
        ,DATA   ,IXR
        ,DATA   ,CPA
        ,DATA   ,CPB
        ,DATA   ,DXR
        ,DATA   ,ROF
        ,DATA   ,SOF
        ,DATA   ,EXC1
        ,DATA   ,EXC2
        ,DATA   ,INA
        ,DATA   ,INB
        ,DATA   ,OAR
        ,DATA   ,OBR
        ,DATA   ,JMP
        ,DATA   ,JAP
        ,DATA   ,JAN
        ,DATA   ,JAZ
        ,DATA   ,JBZ
        ,DATA   ,JXZ
        ,DATA   ,JMPM
        ,DATA   ,LDAI
        ,DATA   ,LDAE
        ,DATA   ,LDBI
        ,DATA   ,LDBE
        ,DATA   ,LDXI
        ,DATA   ,LDXE
        ,DATA   ,STAE
        ,DATA   ,STBE
        ,DATA   ,STXE
        ,DATA   ,ADDI
        ,DATA   ,ADDE
        ,DATA   ,SUBI
        ,DATA   ,SUBE
        ,DATA   ,MULI
        ,DATA   ,MULE
        ,DATA   ,DIVI
        ,DATA   ,DIVE
        ,DATA   ,IME
```

```
          ,DATA    ,OME
*
*        EXIT INTERPRETER
*
HLT      ,ENTR    ,
         ,LDAE    ,PIC
         ,IAR     ,
         ,STA     ,*+2
         ,RETU    ,(000000)
*
*        NO-OPERATION
*
NOP      ,ENTR    ,
         ,INRE    ,PIC
         ,RETU*   ,NOP
*
*        TRANSFER ZERO TO A
*
TZA      ,ENTR    ,
         ,TZA     ,
         ,LDXI    ,98
         ,STAE    ,PAC-1,1
         ,DXR     ,
         ,JXZ     ,*+4
         ,JMP     ,*-5
         ,INRE    ,PIC
         ,RETU*   ,TZA
*
*        TRANSFER ZERO TO B
*
TZB      ,ENTR    ,
         ,TZA     ,
         ,LDXI    ,98
         ,STAE    ,PMQ-1,1
         ,DXR     ,
         ,JXZ     ,*+4
         ,JMP     ,*-5
         ,INRE    ,PIC
         ,RETU*   ,TZB
*
*        TRANSFER ZERO TO X
*
TZX      ,ENTR    ,
         ,TZA     ,
         ,STAE    ,PIN
         ,INRE    ,PIC
         ,RETU*   ,TZX
*
*        TRANSFER A TO B
*
```

```
TAB      ,ENTR    ,
         ,LDXI    ,98
         ,LDAE    ,PAC-1,1
         ,STAE    ,PMQ-1,1
         ,DXR     ,
         ,JXZ     ,*+4
         ,JMP     ,*-7
         ,INRE    ,PIC
         ,RETU*   ,TAB
*
*        TRANSFER B TO A
*
TBA      ,ENTR    ,
         ,LDXI    ,98
         ,LDAE    ,PMQ-1,1
         ,STAE    ,PAC-1,1
         ,DXR     ,
         ,JXZ     ,*+4
         ,JMP     ,*-7
         ,INRE    ,PIC
         ,RETU*   ,TBA
*
*        INCREMENT X
*
IXR      ,ENTR    ,
         ,INRE    ,PIN
         ,INRE    ,PIC
         ,RETU*   ,IXR
*
*        COMPLEMENT A
*
CPA      ,ENTR    ,
         ,LDAE    ,PAC+2
         ,JAZ     ,*+8
         ,LDAE    ,PAC
         ,ERAI    ,0100000
         ,STAE    ,PAC
         ,INRE    ,PIC
         ,RETU*   ,CPA
*
*        COMPLEMENT B
*
CPB      ,ENTR    ,
         ,LDAE    ,PMQ+2
         ,JAZ     ,*+8
         ,LDAE    ,PMQ
         ,ERAI    ,0100000
         ,STAE    ,PMQ
         ,INRE    ,PIC
         ,RETU*   ,CPB
```

```
*
*       DECREMENT X
*
DXR     ,ENTR   ,
        ,LDAE   ,PIN
        ,DAR    ,
        ,STAE   ,PIN
        ,INRE   ,PIC
        ,RETU*  ,DXR
*
*       RESET NOISY MODE
*
ROF     ,ENTR   ,
        ,TZA    ,
        ,STAE   ,FILL
        ,INRE   ,PIC
        ,RETU*  ,ROF
*
*       SET NOISY MODE
*
SOF     ,ENTR   ,
        ,LDAI   ,9
        ,STAE   ,FILL
        ,INRE   ,PIC
        ,RETU*  ,SOF
*
*       ABSOLUTE VALUE
*
EXC1    ,ENTR   ,
        ,TZA    ,
        ,STAE   ,PAC
        ,INRE   ,PIC
        ,RETU*  ,EXC1
*
*       SQUARE ROOT
*
EXC2    ,ENTR   ,
        ,LDAE   ,PAC
        ,JAP    ,EX21
        ,LDXI   ,(ER08)
        ,CALL   ,ERR
        ,TZA    ,
        ,STAE   ,PAC
EX21    ,LDAE   ,PAC+2
        ,JAZ    ,EX23
        ,LDAE   ,PIC
        ,STA    ,EX25
        ,LDAE   ,PAC+1
        ,LSRA   ,1
        ,STA    ,EX27
```

**253**

```
            ,LDAE    ,PAC+1
            ,ANAI    ,1
            ,LDBE    ,PAC+2
            ,JAZ     ,*+10
            ,LLRL    ,19
            ,ADDE    ,PAC+2
            ,ADDE    ,PAC+2
            ,ADDE    ,PAC+3
            ,TAB     ,
            ,LDAE    ,EX24-1,2
            ,STA     ,EX27+1
            ,TZA     ,
            ,LDXI    ,23
            ,STAE    ,EX27+1,1
            ,DXR     ,
            ,JXZ     ,*+4
            ,JMP     ,*-5
            ,CALL    ,FINT
            ,STAE    ,EX28
            ,STBE    ,EX29
            ,STXE    ,EX26
            ,LDXI    ,8
EX22        ,LDAE    ,EX28
            ,DIVE    ,EX27
            ,TBA     ,
            ,ADDE    ,EX27
            ,TAB     ,
            ,MULE    ,HALF
            ,STAE    ,EX27
            ,DXR     ,
            ,JXZ     ,*+4
            ,JMP     ,EX22
            ,LDBE    ,EX29
            ,LDXE    ,EX26
            ,HLT     ,
            ,LDA     ,EX25
            ,STAE    ,PIC
EX23        ,INRE    ,PIC
            ,RETU*   ,EXC2
DIG         ,FORM.   ,4,12
EX24        ,DIG     ,1,0
            ,DIG     ,1,0
            ,DIG     ,1,0
            ,DUP     ,5
            ,DIG     ,2,0
            ,DUP     ,7
            ,DIG     ,3,0
            ,DUP     ,9
            ,DIG     ,4,0
            ,DUP     ,11
```

```
              ,DIG    ,5,0
              ,DUP    ,13
              ,DIG    ,6,0
              ,DUP    ,15
              ,DIG    ,7,0
              ,DUP    ,17
              ,DIG    ,8,0
              ,DUP    ,19
              ,DIG    ,9,0
EX25    ,BSS    ,1
EX26    ,BSS    ,1
EX27    ,BSS    ,25
EX28    ,BSS    ,25
EX29    ,BSS    ,25
*
*       INPUT  A
*
INA     ,ENTR   ,
        ,CALL   ,IN
        ,LDXI   ,98
        ,LDAE   ,POP-1,1
        ,STAE   ,PAC-1,1
        ,DXR    ,
        ,JXZ    ,*+4
        ,JMP    ,*-7
        ,INRE   ,PIC
        ,RETU*  ,INA
*
*       INPUT  B
*
INB     ,ENTR   ,
        ,CALL   ,IN
        ,LDXI   ,98
        ,LDAE   ,POP-1,1
        ,STAE   ,PMQ-1,1
        ,DXR    ,
        ,JXZ    ,*+4
        ,JMP    ,*-7
        ,INRE   ,PIC
        ,RETU*  ,INB
*
*       OUTPUT A
*
OAR     ,ENTR   ,
        ,LDXI   ,98
        ,LDAE   ,PAC-1,1
        ,STAE   ,POP-1,1
        ,DXR    ,
        ,JXZ    ,*+4
        ,JMP    ,*-7
```

```
                ,CALL    ,OUT
                ,INRE    ,PIC
                ,RETU*   ,OAR
*
*       OUTPUT  B
*
OBR     ,ENTR    ,
        ,LDXI    ,98
        ,LDAE    ,PMQ-1,1
        ,STAE    ,POP-1,1
        ,DXR     ,
        ,JXZ     ,*+4
        ,JMP     ,*-7
        ,CALL    ,OUT
        ,INRE    ,PIC
        ,RETU*   ,OBR
*
*       JUMP
*
JMP     ,ENTR    ,
        ,LDAE    ,INST+1
        ,STAE    ,PIC
        ,RETU*   ,JMP
*
*       JUMP A POSITIVE
*
JAP     ,ENTR    ,
        ,LDAE    ,PAC
        ,JAP     ,JAP1
        ,INRE    ,PIC
        ,INRE    ,PIC
        ,RETU*   ,JAP
JAP1    ,LDAE    ,INST+1
        ,STAE    ,PIC
        ,RETU*   ,JAP
*
*       JUMP A NEGATIVE
*
JAN     ,ENTR    ,
        ,LDAE    ,PAC
        ,JAN     ,JAN1
        ,INRE    ,PIC
        ,INRE    ,PIC
        ,RETU*   ,JAN
JAN1    ,LDAE    ,INST+1
        ,STAE    ,PIC
        ,RETU*   ,JAN
*
*       JUMP A ZERO
*
```

256

```
JAZ      , ENTR    ,
         , LDAE    , PAC+2
         , JAZ     , JAZ 1
         , INRE    , PIC
         , INRE    , PIC
         , RETU*   , JAZ
JAZ 1    , LDAE    , INST+1
         , STAE    , PIC
         , RETU*   , JAZ
*
*        JUMP B ZERO
*
JBZ      , ENTR    ,
         , LDBE    , PMQ+2
         , JBZ     , JBZ 1
         , INRE    , PIC
         , INRE    , PIC
         , RETU*   , JBZ
JBZ 1    , LDAE    , INST+1
         , STAE    , PIC
         , RETU*   , JBZ
*
*        JUMP X ZERO
*
JXZ      , ENTR    ,
         , LDXE    , PIN
         , JXZ     , JXZ 1
         , INRE    , PIC
         , INRE    , PIC
         , RETU*   , JXZ
JXZ 1    , LDAE    , INST+1
         , STAE    , PIC
         , RETU*   , JXZ
*
*        JUMP AND MARK
*
JMPM     , ENTR    ,
         , LDAE    , PIC
         , ADDI    , 2
         , LDXE    , INST+1
         , STA     , 0, 1
         , IXR     ,
         , STXE    , PIC
         , RETU*   , JMPM
*
*        LOAD A IMMEDIATE
*
LDAI     , ENTR    ,
         , CALL    , IMO
         , LDXI    , 98
```

257

```
            ,LDAE    ,POP-1,1
            ,STAE    ,PAC-1,1
            ,DXR     ,
            ,JXZ     ,*+4
            ,JMP     ,*-7
            ,INRE    ,PIC
            ,INRE    ,PIC
            ,RETU*   ,LDAI
*
*       LOAD A EXTENDED
*
LDAE    ,ENTR    ,
            ,CALL    ,UNPK
            ,LDXI    ,98
            ,LDAE    ,POP-1,1
            ,STAE    ,PAC-1,1
            ,DXR     ,
            ,JXZ     ,*+4
            ,JMP     ,*-7
            ,INRE    ,PIC
            ,INRE    ,PIC
            ,RETU*   ,LDAE
*
*       LOAD B IMMEDIATE
*
LDBI    ,ENTR    ,
            ,CALL    ,IMO
            ,LDXI    ,98
            ,LDAE    ,POP-1,1
            ,STAE    ,PMQ-1,1
            ,DXR     ,
            ,JXZ     ,*+4
            ,JMP     ,*-7
            ,INRE    ,PIC
            ,INRE    ,PIC
            ,RETU*   ,LDBI
*
*       LOAD B EXTENDED
*
LDBE    ,ENTR    ,
            ,CALL    ,UNPK
            ,LDXI    ,98
            ,LDAE    ,POP-1,!
            ,STAE    ,PMQ-1,1
            ,DXR     ,
            ,JXZ     ,*+4
            ,JMP     ,*-7
            ,INRE    ,PIC
            ,INRE    ,PIC
            ,RETU*   ,LDBE
```

```
*
*       LOAD X IMMEDIATE
*
LDXI    ,ENTR   ,
        ,LDXE   ,PIC
        ,LDX    ,1,1
        ,STXE   ,PIN
        ,INRE   ,PIC
        ,INRE   ,PIC
        ,RETU*  ,LDXI
*
*       LOAD X EXTENDED
*
LDXE    ,ENTR   ,
        ,LDXE*  ,INST+1
        ,STXE   ,PIN
        ,INRE   ,PIC
        ,INRE   ,PIC
        ,RETU*  ,LDXE
*
*       STORE A EXTENDED
*
STAE    ,ENTR   ,
        ,LDXI   ,98
        ,LDAE   ,PAC-1,1
        ,STAE   ,POP-1,1
        ,DXR    ,
        ,JXZ    ,*+4
        ,JMP    ,*-7
        ,CALL   ,PACK
        ,INRE   ,PIC
        ,INRE   ,PIC
        ,RETU*  ,STAE
*
*       STORE B EXTENDED
*
STBE    ,ENTR   ,
        ,LDXI   ,98
        ,LDAE   ,PMQ-1,1
        ,STAE   ,POP-1,1
        ,DXR    ,
        ,JXZ    ,*+4
        ,JMP    ,*-7
        ,CALL   ,PACK
        ,INRE   ,PIC
        ,INRE   ,PIC
        ,RETU*  ,STBE
*
*       STORE X EXTENDED
*
```

```
STXE    ,ENTR   ,
        ,LDXE   ,PIN
        ,STXE*  ,INST+1
        ,INRE   ,PIC
        ,INRE   ,PIC
        ,RETU*  ,STXE
*
*       ADD IMMEDIATE
*
ADDI    ,ENTR   ,
        ,CALL   ,IMO
        ,CALL   ,ADSB
        ,INRE   ,PIC
        ,INRE   ,PIC
        ,RETU*  ,ADDI
*
*       ADD EXTENDED
*
ADDE    ,ENTR   ,
        ,CALL   ,UNPK
        ,CALL   ,ADSB
        ,INRE   ,PIC
        ,INRE   ,PIC
        ,RETU*  ,ADDE
*
*       SUBTRACT IMMEDIATE
*
SUBI    ,ENTR   ,
        ,CALL   ,IMO
        ,LDAE   ,POP
        ,ERAI   ,0100000
        ,STAE   ,POP
        ,CALL   ,ADSB
        ,INRE   ,PIC
        ,INRE   ,PIC
        ,RETU*  ,SUBI
*
*       SUBTRACT EXTENDED
*
SUBE    ,ENTR   ,
        ,CALL   ,UNPK
        ,LDAE   ,POP
        ,ERAI   ,0100000
        ,STAE   ,POP
        ,CALL   ,ADSB
        ,INRE   ,PIC
        ,INRE   ,PIC
        ,RETU*  ,SUBE
*
*       MULTIPLY IMMEDIATE
```

```
*
MULI    ,ENTR   ,
        ,CALL   ,IMO
        ,CALL   ,MUL
        ,INRE   ,PIC
        ,INRE   ,PIC
        ,RETU*  ,MULI
*
*       MULTIPLY EXTENDED
*
MULE    ,ENTR   ,
        ,CALL   ,UNPK
        ,CALL   ,MUL
        ,INRE   ,PIC
        ,INRE   ,PIC
        ,RETU*  ,MULE
*
*       DIVIDE IMMEDIATE
*
DIVI    ,ENTR   ,
        ,CALL   ,IMO
        ,CALL   ,DIV
        ,INRE   ,PIC
        ,INRE   ,PIC
        ,RETU*  ,DIVI
*
*       DIVIDE EXTENDED
*
DIVE    ,ENTR   ,
        ,CALL   ,UNPK
        ,CALL   ,DIV
        ,INRE   ,PIC
        ,INRE   ,PIC
        ,RETU*  ,DIVE
*
*       INPUT MEMORY
*
IME     ,ENTR   ,
        ,CALL   ,IN
        ,CALL   ,PACK
        ,INRE   ,PIC
        ,INRE   ,PIC
        ,RETU*  ,IME
*
*       OUTPUT MEMORY
*
OME     ,ENTR   ,
        ,CALL   ,UNPK
        ,CALL   ,OUT
        ,INRE   ,PIC
```

```
            ,INRE   ,PIC
            ,RETU*  ,OME
*
*       PACK OPERAND
*
PACK    ,ENTR   ,
        ,LDAE   ,INST+1      GET OPERAND ADDRESS
        ,STA    ,PAC9
        ,LDXI   ,(POP+2)
        ,LDBI   ,25
        ,LDAE   ,POP+1       PACK SIGN AND EXPONENT
        ,ANAI   ,077777
        ,ORAE   ,POP
PAC1    ,STAE*  ,PAC9        SAVE A WORD
        ,INRE   ,PAC9
        ,DBR    ,
        ,JBZ*   ,PACK        RETURN IF DONE
        ,LDA    ,0,1         PACK FOUR DIGITS
        ,IXR    ,
        ,LRLA   ,4
        ,ORA    ,0,1
        ,IXR    ,
        ,LRLA   ,4
        ,ORA    ,0,1
        ,IXR    ,
        ,LRLA   ,4
        ,ORA    ,0,1
        ,IXR    ,
        ,JMP    ,PAC1
PAC9    ,BSS    ,1           OPERAND ADDRESS
*
*       UNPACK OPERAND
*
UNPK    ,ENTR   ,
        ,LDAE   ,INST+1      GET OPERAND ADDRESS
        ,STA    ,UNP9
        ,LDAI   ,-24
        ,STA    ,UNP8
        ,LDXI   ,(POP+2)
        ,LDAE*  ,UNP9        UNPACK SIGN AND EXPONENT
        ,INR    ,UNP9
        ,TAB    ,
        ,ANAI   ,0100000
        ,STAE   ,POP
        ,LRLB   ,1
        ,ASRB   ,1
        ,STBE   ,POP+1
UNP1    ,LDBE*  ,UNP9        UNPACK FOUR DIGITS
        ,INR    ,UNP9
        ,TZA    ,
```

```
          ,LLRL    ,4
          ,STA     ,0,1
          ,IXR     ,
          ,TZA     ,
          ,LLRL    ,4
          ,STA     ,0,1
          ,IXR     ,
          ,TZA     ,
          ,LLRL    ,4
          ,STA     ,0,1
          ,IXR     ,
          ,TZA     ,
          ,LLRL    ,4
          ,STA     ,0,1
          ,IXR     ,
          ,INR     ,UNP8
          ,LDA     ,UNP8
          ,JAN     ,UNP1
          ,LDXI    ,96
UNP2      ,LDAE    ,POP+1,1    CHECK FOR VALID DIGITS
          ,SUBI    ,10
          ,JAN     ,UNP3
          ,STA     ,UNP9       A BAD DIGIT
          ,STX     ,UNP8
          ,LDXI    ,(ER01)
          ,CALL    ,ERR
          ,LDX     ,UNP8
          ,LDA     ,UNP9
          ,STAE    ,POP+1,1
UNP3      ,DXR     ,
          ,JXZ     ,*+4
          ,JMP     ,UNP2
          ,LDAE    ,POP+2      CHECK IF NORMALIZED
          ,JAZ     ,*+4
          ,RETU*   ,UNPK       OK - RETURN
          ,LDXI    ,-95
UNP4      ,LDAE    ,POP+98,1   CHECK IF ZERO
          ,JAZ     ,*+4
          ,JMP     ,UNP5
          ,IXR     ,
          ,JXZ     ,*+4
          ,JMP     ,UNP4
          ,TZA     ,           OK - RETURN
          ,STAE    ,POP
          ,STAE    ,POP+1
          ,RETU*   ,UNPK
UNP5      ,STX     ,UNP8       NOT NORMALIZED
          ,LDXI    ,(ER02)
          ,CALL    ,ERR
          ,LDAI    ,-96        ADJUST EXPONENT
```

**263**

```
          ,SUB    ,UNP8
          ,ADDE   ,POP+1
          ,STAE   ,POP+1
          ,ADDI   ,16383
          ,JAP    ,UNP6
          ,LDXI   ,(ER03)      EXPONENT UNDERFLOW
          ,CALL   ,ERR
          ,TZA    ,
          ,LDXI   ,98
          ,STAE   ,POP-1,1
          ,DXR    ,
          ,JXZ*   ,UNPK
          ,JMP    ,*-5
UNP6      ,LDBI   ,-96         NORMALIZE
          ,LDX    ,UNP8
          ,LDAE   ,POP+98,1
          ,STAE   ,POP+98,2
          ,IBR    ,
          ,IXR    ,
          ,JXZ    ,*+4
          ,JMP    ,*-8
          ,LDAE   ,FILL
          ,STAE   ,POP+98,2
          ,IBR    ,
          ,JBZ*   ,UNPK        RETURN WHEN DONE
          ,JMP    ,*-5
UNP8      ,BSS    ,1           TEMPORARY
UNP9      ,BSS    ,1           OPERAND ADDRESS
*
*         IMMEDIATE OPERAND
*
IM0       ,ENTR   ,
          ,TZA    ,            ZERO POP
          ,LDXI   ,98
          ,STAE   ,POP-1,1
          ,DXR    ,
          ,JXZ    ,*+4
          ,JMP    ,*-5
          ,LDAI   ,(POP+2)
          ,STA    ,IM09
          ,LDXE   ,PIC         GET OPERAND
          ,LDA    ,1,1
          ,JAZ*   ,IM0         CHECK FOR ZERO
          ,JAP    ,IM01        CHECK FOR NEGATIVE
          ,CPA    ,
          ,IAR    ,
          ,LDBI   ,0100000
          ,STBE   ,POP
IM01      ,LDXI   ,4           COMPUTE EXPONENT
          ,LLSR   ,16
```

264

```
        ,DIVE   ,IM08,1
        ,JBZ    ,IM03
        ,STXE   ,POP+1
IM02    ,STBE*  ,IM09           COMPUTE DIGITS
        ,INR    ,IM09
        ,DXR    ,
        ,JAZ*   ,IM0            RETURN WHEN DONE
        ,LLSR   ,16
        ,DIVE   ,IM08,1
        ,JMP    ,IM02
IM03    ,DXR    ,
        ,JMP    ,IM01+2
IM08    ,DATA   ,1,10,100,1000,10000    DECIMAL POWERS
IM09    ,BSS    ,1              OPERAND POINTER
*
*       ADD/SUBTRACT
*
ADSB    ,ENTR   ,
        ,LDAE   ,POP+2          CHECK FOR ZERO OPERAND
        ,JAZ*   ,ADSB
        ,LDAE   ,PAC+2          CHECK FOR ZERO ACCUMULATOR
        ,JAZ    ,ADS3
        ,TZA    ,               ZERO CARRY
        ,STA    ,AD99
        ,LDAE   ,PAC+1          COMPARE EXPONENTS
        ,SUBE   ,POP+1
        ,STA    ,AD98
        ,JAZ    ,ADS4           PAC(E) = POP(E)
        ,JAN    ,ADS2           PAC(E) < POP(E)
        ,SUBI   ,97             PAC(E) > POP(E)
        ,JAP*   ,ADSB
        ,LDAI   ,96             SHIFT POP RIGHT
        ,SUB    ,AD98
        ,TAB    ,
        ,LDXI   ,96
        ,LDAE   ,POP+2,2
        ,SUBI   ,5
        ,JAN    ,*+3
        ,INR    ,AD99
        ,JBZ    ,ADS1
        ,LDAE   ,POP+1,2
        ,STAE   ,POP+1,1
        ,DBR    ,
        ,DXR    ,
        ,JMP    ,*-8
ADS1    ,TZA    ,
        ,STAE   ,POP+1,1
        ,DXR    ,
        ,JXZ    ,ADS4
        ,JMP    ,*-5
```

```
ADS2    ,ADDI    ,96
        ,JAN     ,ADS3
        ,LDAE    ,POP+1
        ,STAE    ,PAC+1
        ,LDAI    ,96              SHIFT PAC RIGHT
        ,ADD     ,AD98
        ,TAB     ,
        ,LDXI    ,96
        ,LDAE    ,PAC+2,2
        ,SUBI    ,5
        ,JAN     ,*+3
        ,INR     ,AD99
        ,JBZ     ,*+10
        ,LDAE    ,PAC+1,2
        ,STAE    ,PAC+1,1
        ,DBR     ,
        ,DXR     ,
        ,JMP     ,*-8
        ,TZA     ,
        ,STAE    ,PAC+1,1
        ,DXR     ,
        ,JXZ     ,ADS4
        ,JMP     ,*-5
ADS3    ,LDXI    ,98              MOVE POP TO PAC
        ,LDAE    ,POP-1,1
        ,STAE    ,PAC-1,1
        ,DXR     ,
        ,JXZ*    ,ADSB
        ,JMP     ,*-7
ADS4    ,LDAE    ,PAC             ADD OR SUBTRACT?
        ,ERAE    ,POP
        ,JAN     ,ADS7
        ,LDXI    ,96              ADD
        ,LDB     ,AD99
ADS5    ,TBA     ,
        ,ADDE    ,PAC+1,1
        ,ADDE    ,POP+1,1
        ,STAE    ,PAC+1,1
        ,TZB     ,
        ,SUBI    ,10
        ,JAN     ,*+5
        ,STAE    ,PAC+1,1
        ,IBR     ,
        ,DXR     ,
        ,JXZ     ,*+4
        ,JMP     ,ADS5
        ,JBZ*    ,ADSB
        ,INRE    ,PAC+1           NORMALIZE
        ,LDAE    ,PAC+1
        ,SUBI    ,16384
```

```
         , JAN    , ADS6
         , LDXI   , (ER05)      EXPONENT OVERFLOW
         , CALL   , ERR
         , LDAI   , 16383
         , STAE   , PAC+1
         , LDAI   , 9
         , LDXI   , 96
         , STAE   , PAC+1, 1
         , DXR    ,
         , JXZ*   , ADSB
         , JMP    , *-5
ADS6     , LDAE   , PAC+97
         , STA    , AD99
         , LDXI   , 95
         , LDAE   , PAC+1, 1
         , STAE   , PAC+2, 1
         , DXR    ,
         , JXZ    , *+4
         , JMP    , *-7
         , INCR   , 1
         , STAE   , PAC+2
         , LDA    , AD99        ROUND
         , SUBI   , 5
         , JAN*   , ADSB
         , LDXI   , 96
         , INRE   , PAC+1, 1
         , LDAE   , PAC+1, 1
         , SUBI   , 10
         , JAN*   , ADSB
         , STAE   , PAC+1, 1
         , DXR    ,
         , JMP    , *-11
ADS7     , LDXI   , 96          SUBTRACT
         , LDB    , AD99
ADS8     , LDAE   , PAC+1, 1
         , SUBE   , POP+1, 1
         , JBZ    , *+4
         , DAR    ,
         , TZB    ,
         , JAP    , *+5
         , ADDI   , 10
         , IBR    ,
         , STAE   , PAC+1, 1
         , DXR    ,
         , JXZ    , *+4
         , JMP    , ADS8
         , JBZ    , ADS9
         , INCR   , 2           RECOMPLEMENT
         , LDXI   , 96
         , TBA    ,
```

```
          , TZB     ,
          , ADDI    , 9
          , SUBE    , PAC+1, 1
          , STAE    , PAC+1, 1
          , SUBI    , 10
          , JAN     , *+5
          , STAE    , PAC+1, 1
          , IBR     ,
          , DXR     ,
          , JXZ     , *+4
          , JMP     , *-18
          , LDAE    , POP
          , STAE    , PAC
ADS9      , LDAE    , PAC+2
          , JAZ     , *+4
          , RETU*   , ADSB
          , LDBE    , PAC+1        NORMALIZE
          , LDXI    , -96
          , LDAE    , PAC+98, 1
          , JAZ     , *+4
          , JMP     , AD10
          , DBR     ,
          , IXR     ,
          , JXZ     , AD11
          , JMP     , *-10
AD10      , STBE    , PAC+1
          , TBA     ,
          , ADDI    , 16383
          , JAP     , AD12
          , LDXI    , (ER06)       EXPONENT UNDERFLOW
          , CALL    , ERR
AD11      , TZA     ,              ZERO RESULT
          , LDXI    , 98
          , STAE    , PAC-1, 1
          , DXR     ,
          , JXZ*    , ADSB
          , JMP     , *-5
AD12      , LDBI    , -96
          , LDAE    , PAC+98, 1
          , STAE    , PAC+98, 2
          , IBR     ,
          , IXR     ,
          , JXZ     , *+4
          , JMP     , AD12+2
          , LDAE    , FILL
          , STAE    , PAC+98, 2
          , IBR     ,
          , JBZ*    , ADSB
          , JMP     , *-5
AD98      , BSS     , 1            TEMPORARY
```

```
AD99    ,BSS    ,1              CARRY
*
*       MULTIPLY
*
MUL     ,ENTR   ,
        ,TZA    ,               ZERO PRODUCT
        ,LDXI   ,98
        ,STAE   ,PAC-1,1
        ,DXR    ,
        ,JXZ    ,*+4
        ,JMP    ,*-5
        ,LDAE   ,PMQ+2          RETURN IF MULTIPLIER ZERO
        ,JAZ*   ,MUL
        ,LDAE   ,POP+2          RETURN IF MULTIPLICAND ZERO
        ,JAZ*   ,MUL
        ,LDAE   ,PMQ            COMPUTE SIGN
        ,ERAE   ,POP
        ,STAE   ,PAC
        ,LDAE   ,PMQ+1          COMPUTE EXPONENT
        ,ADDE   ,POP+1
        ,STAE   ,PAC+1
        ,JAN    ,MUL2
        ,SUBI   ,16384
        ,JAN    ,MUL3
MUL1    ,LDXI   ,(ER05)         EXPONENT OVERFLOW
        ,CALL   ,ERR
        ,LDAI   ,16383
        ,STAE   ,PAC+1
        ,LDAI   ,9
        ,LDXI   ,96
        ,STAE   ,PAC+1,1
        ,DXR    ,
        ,JXZ*   ,MUL
        ,JMP    ,*-5
MUL2    ,ADDI   ,16383
        ,JAP    ,MUL3
        ,LDXI   ,(ER06)         EXPONENT UNDERFLOW
        ,CALL   ,ERR
        ,RETU*  ,MUL
MUL3    ,LDXI   ,96
        ,STX    ,MU99
        ,TZA    ,
        ,STA    ,MU98
MUL4    ,LDAE   ,PMQ+1,1        GET A MULTIPLIER DIGIT
        ,JAZ    ,MUL6
        ,STA    ,MUL5+5
        ,LDA    ,MU98
        ,LDXI   ,96
MUL5    ,ADDE   ,PAC+1,1        MULTIPLY BY CURRENT DIGIT
        ,LDBE   ,POP+1,1
```

**269**

```
            ,MULI    ,(0)
            ,DIVI    ,10
            ,STAE    ,PAC+1,1
            ,TBA     ,
            ,DXR     ,
            ,JXZ     ,MUL6
            ,JMP     ,MUL5
     MUL6   ,STA     ,MU97        PREPARE FOR NEXT DIGIT
            ,LDX     ,MU99
            ,DXR     ,
            ,STX     ,MU99
            ,JXZ     ,MUL7
            ,TZB     ,
            ,LDAE    ,PAC+97
            ,SUBI    ,5
            ,JAN     ,*+3
            ,IBR     ,
            ,STB     ,MU98
            ,LDXI    ,95
            ,LDAE    ,PAC+1,1
            ,STAE    ,PAC+2,1
            ,DXR     ,
            ,JXZ     ,*+4
            ,JMP     ,*-7
            ,LDA     ,MU97
            ,STAE    ,PAC+2
            ,LDX     ,MU99
            ,JMP     ,MUL4
     MUL7   ,JAZ*    ,MUL         OVERFLOW
            ,INRE    ,PAC+1
            ,LDAE    ,PAC+1
            ,SUBI    ,16384
            ,JAP     ,MUL1
            ,TZB     ,            ROUND
            ,LDAE    ,PAC+97
            ,SUBI    ,5
            ,JAN     ,*+3
            ,IBR     ,
            ,LDXI    ,95
     MUL8   ,TBA     ,
            ,TZB     ,
            ,ADDE    ,PAC+1,1
            ,STAE    ,PAC+2,1
            ,SUBI    ,10
            ,JAN     ,*+5
            ,STAE    ,PAC+2,1
            ,IBR     ,
            ,DXR     ,
            ,JXZ     ,*+4
            ,JMP     ,MUL8
```

```
          , TBA      ,
          , ADD      , MU97
          , STAE     , PAC+2
          , RETU*    , MUL
MU97      , BSS      , 1           OVERFLOW
MU98      , BSS      , 1           CARRY
MU99      , BSS      , 1           COUNTER
*
*         DIVIDE
*
DIV       , ENTR     ,
          , LDAE     , PAC+2       CHECK FOR ZERO DIVIDEND
          , JAZ      , DIV7
          , LDAE     , POP+2       CHECK FOR ZERO DIVISOR
          , JAZ      , *+4
          , JMP      , DIV2
          , LDXI     , (ER07)
DIV1      , CALL     , ERR
          , LDAE     , PAC
          , STAE     , PMQ
          , LDAI     , 16383
          , STAE     , PAC+1
          , STAE     , PMQ+1
          , LDAI     , 9
          , LDXI     , 96
          , STAE     , PAC+1, 1
          , STAE     , PMQ+1, 1
          , DXR      ,
          , JXZ*     , DIV
          , JMP      , *-7
DIV2      , LDAE     , PAC         COMPUTE QUOTIENT SIGN
          , ERAE     , POP
          , STAE     , PMQ
          , LDAE     , PAC+1       COMPUTE QUOTIENT EXPONENT
          , SUBE     , POP+1
          , STAE     , PMQ+1
          , JAN      , DIV3
          , SUBI     , 16384
          , JAN      , DIV4
          , LDXI     , (ER05)      EXPONENT OVERFLOW
          , JMP      , DIV1
DIV3      , ADDI     , 16383
          , JAP      , DIV4
          , LDXI     , (ER06)      EXPONENT UNDERFLOW
          , CALL     , ERR
          , TZA      ,
          , LDXI     , 98
          , STAE     , PAC-1, 1
          , STAE     , PMQ-1, 1
          , DXR      ,
```

```
            ,JXZ*   ,DIV
            ,JMP    ,*-7
DIV4        ,LDAE   ,PAC+1       COMPUTE REMAINDER EXPONENT
            ,SUBI   ,95
            ,STAE   ,PAC+1
            ,LDXI   ,-96
            ,CALL   ,DTST        CALCULATE FIRST DIGIT
            ,JAZ    ,*+4
            ,JMP    ,DIV6
            ,LDAE   ,PMQ+1       ADJUST QUOTIENT EXPONENT
            ,DAR    ,
            ,STAE   ,PMQ+1
            ,ADDI   ,16383
            ,JAN    ,DIV3+4
            ,LDAE   ,PAC+1       ADJUST REMAINDER EXPONENT
            ,DAR    ,
            ,STAE   ,PAC+1
DIV5        ,LDAE   ,PAC+2       SHIFT PAC LEFT
            ,ASLA   ,3
            ,ADDE   ,PAC+2
            ,ADDE   ,PAC+2
            ,ADDE   ,PAC+3
            ,STAE   ,PAC+2
            ,LDBI   ,-94
            ,LDAE   ,PAC+98,2
            ,STAE   ,PAC+97,2
            ,IBR    ,
            ,JBZ    ,*+4
            ,JMP    ,*-7
            ,TZA    ,
            ,STAE   ,PAC+97
            ,CALL   ,DTST
DIV6        ,STAE   ,PMQ+98,1    STORE QUOTIENT DIGIT
            ,IXR    ,
            ,JXZ    ,*+4
            ,JMP    ,DIV5
            ,LDAE   ,PAC+2
            ,JAZ    ,DIV8
            ,LDAE   ,PAC+1       CHECK REMAINDER EXPONENT
            ,ADDI   ,16383
            ,JAP*   ,DIV
            ,LDXI   ,(ER09)      REMAINDER EXPONENT UNDERFLOW
            ,CALL   ,ERR
            ,TZA    ,
            ,LDXI   ,98
            ,STAE   ,PAC-1,1
            ,DXR    ,
            ,JXZ*   ,DIV
            ,JMP    ,*-5
DIV7        ,TZA    ,            ZERO QUOTIENT
```

```
        ,LDXI    ,98
        ,STAE    ,PMQ-1,1
        ,DXR     ,
        ,JXZ*    ,DIV
        ,JMP     ,*-5
DIV8    ,TZA     ,            ZERO REMAINDER
        ,STAE    ,PAC
        ,STAE    ,PAC+1
        ,RETU*   ,DIV
*
*       DIVIDE TEST
*
DTST    ,ENTR    ,
        ,STX     ,DTS9        INITIALIZE VARIABLES
        ,TZA     ,
        ,STA     ,DTS8
DTS1    ,LDAE    ,PAC+2       IS SUBTRACTION POSSIBLE?
        ,SUBE    ,POP+2
        ,JAN     ,DTS4        NO - RETURN
        ,TZB     ,            MAYBE - TRY IT
        ,LDXI    ,96
DTS2    ,LDAE    ,PAC+1,1
        ,SUBE    ,POP+1,1
        ,JBZ     ,*+4
        ,DAR     ,
        ,TZB     ,
        ,JAP     ,*+5
        ,ADDI    ,10
        ,IBR     ,
        ,STAE    ,PAC+1,1
        ,DXR     ,
        ,JXZ     ,*+4
        ,JMP     ,DTS2
        ,JBZ     ,DTS5        MADE IT - TRY AGAIN
        ,TZB     ,            MISSED - RESTORE
        ,LDXI    ,96
DTS3    ,TBA     ,
        ,ADDE    ,PAC+1,1
        ,ADDE    ,POP+1,1
        ,STAE    ,PAC+1,1
        ,TZB     ,
        ,SUBI    ,10
        ,JAN     ,*+5
        ,STAE    ,PAC+1,1
        ,IBR     ,
        ,DXR     ,
        ,JXZ     ,DTS4
        ,JMP     ,DTS3
DTS4    ,LDA     ,DTS8        RETURN
        ,LDX     ,DTS9
```

```
          , RETU*   , DTST
DTS5    , INR      , DTS8         INCREMENT QUOTIENT DIGIT
        , JMP      , DTS1
DTS8    , BSS      , 1            QUOTIENT DIGIT
DTS9    , BSS      , 1            TEMPORARY
*
*       INPUT
*
IN      , ENTR     ,
        , TZA      ,              INTIALIZE VARIABLES
        , LDXI     , 98
        , STAE     , POP-1,1
        , DXR      ,
        , JXZ      , *+4
        , JMP      , *-5
        , STA      , IN7
        , STA      , IN8
        , STAE     , ITS8
        , DECR     , 1
        , STAE     , POP+1
        , INCR     , 1
        , STA      , IN9
        , STAE     , ITS9
        , STAE     , ITS9+1
        , STAE     , ITS9+2
        , LDXI     , -96
        , LDAI     , 0215         OUTPUT CR/LF/BELL
        , CALL     , TOT
        , LDAI     , 0212
        , CALL     , TOT
        , LDAI     , 0207
        , CALL     , TOT
IN1     , CALL     , ITST         IGNORE LEADING ZEROES
        , JAZ      , IN1
        , SUBI     , 10           NON-ZERO DIGIT
        , JAN      , IN4
        , DAR      ,
        , JAP      , *+18
        , CALL     , ITST         DECIMAL POINT
        , JAZ      , *+7
        , TZA      ,
        , STA      , IN9
        , TBA      ,
        , JMP      , IN5+2
        , LDAE     , POP+1        IGNORE ZEROES
        , DAR      ,
        , STAE     , POP+1
        , JMP      , *-14
        , DAR      ,
        , JAP      , IN2
```

274

```
            ,LDAI   ,0100000    NEGATIVE
            ,STAE   ,POP
            ,JMP    ,IN1
IN2         ,CALL   ,ITST       EXPONENT
            ,SUBI   ,10
            ,JAN    ,*+7
            ,LDAI   ,0100000    NEGATIVE
            ,STA    ,IN7
            ,JMP    ,IN2
            ,STB    ,*+6
            ,LDA    ,IN8
            ,ASLA   ,3
            ,ADD    ,IN8
            ,ADD    ,IN8
            ,ADDI   ,0
            ,STA    ,IN8
            ,SUBI   ,16384
            ,JAN    ,IN2
            ,LDA    ,IN7
            ,JAN    ,IN3
            ,LDXI   ,(ER05)     EXPONENT OVERFLOW
            ,CALL   ,ERR
            ,LDAI   ,16383
            ,STAE   ,POP+1
            ,LDAI   ,9
            ,LDXI   ,96
            ,STAE   ,POP+1,1
            ,DXR    ,
            ,JXZ*   ,IN
            ,JMP    ,*-5
IN3         ,LDXI   ,(ER06)     EXPONENT UNDERFLOW
            ,CALL   ,ERR
            ,TZA    ,
            ,LDXI   ,98
            ,STAE   ,POP-1,1
            ,DXR    ,
            ,JXZ*   ,IN
            ,JMP    ,*-5
IN4         ,JXZ    ,*+5        STORE THE DIGIT
            ,STBE   ,POP+98,1
            ,IXR    ,
            ,LDAE   ,POP+1      ADJUST EXPONENT
            ,ADD    ,IN9
            ,STAE   ,POP+1
IN5         ,CALL   ,ITST
            ,SUBI   ,10
            ,JAN    ,IN4
            ,DAR    ,
            ,JAP    ,IN2
            ,TZA    ,           DECIMAL POINT
```

```
          ,STA    ,IN9
          ,JMP    ,IN5
IN7       ,BSS    ,1           SIGN OF EXPONENT
IN8       ,BSS    ,1           EXPONENT
IN9       ,BSS    ,1           EXPONENT INCREMENT
*
*         INPUT TEST
*
ITST      ,ENTR   ,
          ,CALL   ,TIN         READ A CHARACTER
          ,STA    ,ITS7
          ,TAB    ,            CARRIAGE RETURN?
          ,SUBI   ,0215
          ,JAZ    ,ITS1
          ,TBA    ,            DIGIT?
          ,SUBI   ,0260
          ,JAN    ,*+6
          ,SUBI   ,10
          ,JAN    ,ITS2
          ,TBA    ,            DECIMAL POINT?
          ,SUBI   ,0256
          ,JAZ    ,ITS3
          ,TBA    ,            PLUS?
          ,SUBI   ,0253
          ,JAZ    ,ITS4
          ,TBA    ,            MINUS?
          ,SUBI   ,0255
          ,JAZ    ,ITS5
          ,TBA    ,            E?
          ,SUBI   ,0305
          ,JAZ    ,ITS6
          ,JMP    ,ITST+1      INVALID CHARACTER - IGNORE
ITS1      ,LDAE   ,POP+2       CARRIAGE RETURN
          ,JAZ    ,*+20
          ,LDAE   ,IN7         ADJUST EXPONENT
          ,JAP    ,*+8
          ,LDAE   ,POP+1
          ,SUBE   ,IN8
          ,JMP    ,*+6
          ,LDAE   ,POP+1
          ,ADDE   ,IN8
          ,STAE   ,POP+1
          ,JMP    ,*+7
          ,TZA    ,
          ,STAE   ,POP
          ,STAE   ,POP+1
          ,LDAI   ,0215        OUTPUT CR/LF
          ,CALL   ,TOT
          ,LDAI   ,0212
          ,CALL   ,TOT
```

276

```
          ,RETU*  ,IN        RETURN
ITS2      ,TBA    ,          DIGIT
          ,SUBI   ,0260
          ,TAB    ,
          ,TZA    ,
          ,STA    ,ITS9+1
          ,LDA    ,ITS7      ECHO CHARACTER
          ,CALL   ,TOT
          ,INR    ,ITS8
          ,LDA    ,ITS8      END OF LINE?
          ,SUBI   ,72
          ,JAN    ,*+12
          ,TZA    ,          YES - NEW LINE
          ,STA    ,ITS8
          ,LDAI   ,0215
          ,CALL   ,TOT
          ,LDAI   ,0212
          ,CALL   ,TOT
          ,TBA    ,
          ,JAN    ,ITST+1
          ,RETU*  ,ITST      RETURN
ITS3      ,LDA    ,ITS9      DECIMAL POINT
          ,JAZ    ,ITST+1
          ,LDBI   ,10
          ,TZA    ,
          ,STA    ,ITS9
          ,STA    ,ITS9+1
          ,JMP    ,ITS2+6    ECHO CHARACTER
ITS4      ,LDA    ,ITS9+1    PLUS
          ,JAZ    ,ITST+1
          ,LDBI   ,-1
          ,TZA    ,
          ,STA    ,ITS9+1
          ,JMP    ,ITS2+6    ECHO CHARACTER
ITS5      ,LDA    ,ITS9+1    MINUS
          ,JAZ    ,ITST+1
          ,LDBI   ,11
          ,TZA    ,
          ,STA    ,ITS9+1
          ,JMP    ,ITS2+6    ECHO CHARACTER
ITS6      ,LDA    ,ITS9+2    E
          ,JAZ    ,ITST+1
          ,LDBI   ,12
          ,TZA    ,
          ,STA    ,ITS9
          ,STA    ,ITS9+2
          ,INCR   ,1
          ,STA    ,ITS9+1
          ,JMP    ,ITS2+6    ECHO CHARACTER
ITS7      ,BSS    ,1         INPUT CHARACTER
```

**277**

```
ITS8    ,BSS    ,1          CHARACTER COUNT
ITS9    ,BSS    ,3          TRIGGERS
*
*       OUTPUT
*
OUT     ,ENTR   ,
        ,LDAI   ,0215       OUTPUT CR/LF
        ,CALL   ,TOT
        ,LDAI   ,0212
        ,CALL   ,TOT
        ,LDAI   ,0253       OUTPUT SIGN
        ,LDBE   ,POP
        ,JBZ    ,*+4
        ,LDAI   ,0255
        ,CALL   ,TOT
        ,LDAE   ,POP+2      OUTPUT FIRST DIGIT
        ,ADDI   ,0260
        ,CALL   ,TOT
        ,LDAI   ,0256       OUTPUT '.'
        ,CALL   ,TOT
        ,LDXI   ,(POP+3)
        ,LDBI   ,10
OUT1    ,LDA    ,0,1        OUTPUT GROUPS OF FIVE DIGITS
        ,ADDI   ,0260
        ,CALL   ,TOT
        ,LDA    ,1,1
        ,ADDI   ,0260
        ,CALL   ,TOT
        ,LDA    ,2,1
        ,ADDI   ,0260
        ,CALL   ,TOT
        ,LDA    ,3,1
        ,ADDI   ,0260
        ,CALL   ,TOT
        ,LDA    ,4,1
        ,ADDI   ,0260
        ,CALL   ,TOT
        ,LDAI   ,0240
        ,CALL   ,TOT
        ,TXA    ,
        ,ADDI   ,5
        ,TAX    ,
        ,DBR    ,
        ,JBZ    ,*+4
        ,JMP    ,OUT1
        ,SUBI   ,(POP+98)
        ,JAZ    ,OUT2
        ,LDAI   ,0215       OUTPUT CR/LF
        ,CALL   ,TOT
        ,LDAI   ,0212
```

```
        ,CALL   ,TOT
        ,LDAI   ,0240        OUTPUT '  '
        ,CALL   ,TOT
        ,CALL   ,TOT
        ,CALL   ,TOT
        ,LDBI   ,9           OUTPUT REMAINING DIGITS
        ,JMP    ,OUT1
OUT2    ,LDAI   ,0305        OUTPUT 'E'
        ,CALL   ,TOT
        ,LDBI   ,0253        OUTPUT EXPONENT SIGN
        ,LDAE   ,POP+1
        ,JAP    ,*+8
        ,CPA    ,
        ,IAR    ,
        ,STAE   ,POP+1
        ,LDBI   ,0255
        ,TBA    ,
        ,CALL   ,TOT
        ,LDAI   ,(OUT5)      OUTPUT EXPONENT
        ,STA    ,OUT4+1
        ,LDBE   ,POP+1
        ,LDXI   ,4
OUT3    ,TZA    ,
        ,DIVE   ,OUT9-1,1
        ,LLRL   ,16
OUT4    ,JAZ    ,OUT5
        ,ADDI   ,0260
        ,CALL   ,TOT
        ,LDAI   ,(OUT4+2)
        ,STAE   ,OUT4+1
OUT5    ,DXR    ,
        ,JXZ    ,*+4
        ,JMP    ,OUT3
        ,TBA    ,
        ,ADDI   ,0260
        ,CALL   ,TOT
        ,LDAI   ,0215        OUTPUT CR/LF
        ,CALL   ,TOT
        ,LDAI   ,0212
        ,CALL   ,TOT
        ,RETU*  ,OUT         RETURN
OUT9    ,DATA   ,10,100,1000,10000   DECIMAL POWERS
*
*       ERROR PRINT
*
ERR     ,ENTR   ,
        ,STX    ,ERR9        SAVE MESSAGE ADDRESS
        ,LDAI   ,0215        OUTPUT CR/LF
        ,CALL   ,TOT
        ,LDAI   ,0212
```

```
          ,CALL    ,TOT
          ,LDBE    ,PIC          GET INSTRUCTION ADDRESS
          ,LRLB    ,1
          ,LDXI    ,5
ERR1      ,LDAI    ,026          PRINT INSTRUCTION ADDRESS
          ,LLRL    ,3
          ,CALL    ,TOT
          ,DXR     ,
          ,JXZ     ,*+4
          ,JMP     ,ERR1
          ,LDAI    ,0240         OUTPUT ' - '
          ,CALL    ,TOT
          ,LDAI    ,0255
          ,CALL    ,TOT
          ,LDAI    ,0240
          ,CALL    ,TOT
          ,LDX     ,ERR9         GET MESSAGE ADDRESS
          ,LDB     ,0,1          GET MESSAGE LENGTH
ERR2      ,IXR     ,             PRINT ERROR MESSAGE
          ,LDA     ,0,1
          ,LRLA    ,8
          ,CALL    ,TOT
          ,DBR     ,
          ,JBZ     ,ERR3
          ,LRLA    ,8
          ,CALL    ,TOT
          ,DBR     ,
          ,JBZ     ,ERR3
          ,JMP     ,ERR2
ERR3      ,LDAI    ,0215         OUTPUT CR/LF
          ,CALL    ,TOT
          ,LDAI    ,0212
          ,CALL    ,TOT
          ,HLT     ,             HALT
          ,RETU*   ,ERR          RETURN
ERR9      ,BSS     ,1            MESSAGE ADDRESS
*
*         ERROR MESSAGES
*
ERO1      ,DATA    ,24,'INVALID DIGIT IN OPERAND'
ERO2      ,DATA    ,20,'UNNORMALIZED OPERAND'
ERO3      ,DATA    ,26,'OPERAND EXPONENT UNDERFLOW'
ERO4      ,DATA    ,19,'INVALID INSTRUCTION'
ERO5      ,DATA    ,17,'EXPONENT OVERFLOW'
ERO6      ,DATA    ,18,'EXPONENT UNDERFLOW'
ERO7      ,DATA    ,12,'ZERO DIVISOR'
ERO8      ,DATA    ,20,'NEGATIVE SQUARE ROOT'
ERO9      ,DATA    ,28,'REMAINDER EXPONENT UNDERFLOW'
*
*         TELETYPE INPUT
```

```
*
TIN     ,ENTR   ,
        ,SEN    ,0201,*+5  WAIT UNTIL TTY IS READY
        ,NOP    ,
        ,JMP    ,*-3
        ,CIA    ,1          INPUT ONE CHARACTER
        ,RETU*  ,TIN        RETURN
*
*       TELETYPE OUTPUT
*
TOT     ,ENTR   ,
        ,SEN    ,0101,*+5  WAIT UNTIL TTY IS READY
        ,NOP    ,
        ,JMP    ,*-3
        ,OAR    ,1          OUTPUT ONE CHARACTER
        ,RETU*  ,TOT        RETURN
*
*       VARIABLES
*
PIC     ,BSS    ,1          PSEUDO INSTRUCTION COUNTER
INST    ,BSS    ,2          INSTRUCTION
PAC     ,BSS    ,98         PSEUDO ACCUMULATOR
PMQ     ,BSS    ,98         PSEUDO MULTIPLIER/QUOTIENT
POP     ,BSS    ,98         PSEUDO OPERAND
PIN     ,BSS    ,1          PSEUDO INDEX
FILL    ,BSS    ,1          FILL DIGIT FOR NORMALIZATION
*
*       CONSTANTS
*
DEC     ,FORM   ,4,4,4,4
HALF    ,PZE    ,-1
        ,DEC    ,5,0,0,0
        ,DUP    ,23
        ,DEC    ,0,0,0,0
PI      ,PZE    ,0
        ,DEC    ,3,1,4,1
        ,DEC    ,5,9,2,6
        ,DEC    ,5,3,5,8
        ,DEC    ,9,7,9,3
        ,DEC    ,2,3,8,4
        ,DEC    ,6,2,6,4
        ,DEC    ,3,3,8,3
        ,DEC    ,2,7,9,5
        ,DEC    ,0,2,8,8
        ,DEC    ,4,1,9,7
        ,DEC    ,1,6,9,3
        ,DEC    ,9,9,3,7
        ,DEC    ,5,1,0,5
        ,DEC    ,8,2,0,9
        ,DEC    ,7,4,9,4
```

```
           ,DEC    ,4,5,9,2
           ,DEC    ,3,0,7,8
           ,DEC    ,1,6,4,0
           ,DEC    ,6,2,8,6
           ,DEC    ,2,0,8,9
           ,DEC    ,9,8,6,2
           ,DEC    ,8,0,3,4
           ,DEC    ,8,2,5,3
           ,DEC    ,4,2,1,1
     E     ,PZE    ,0
           ,DEC    ,2,7,1,8
           ,DEC    ,2,8,1,8
           ,DEC    ,2,8,4,5
           ,DEC    ,9,0,4,5
           ,DEC    ,2,3,5,3
           ,DEC    ,6,0,2,8
           ,DEC    ,7,4,7,1
           ,DEC    ,3,5,2,6
           ,DEC    ,6,2,4,9
           ,DEC    ,7,7,5,7
           ,DEC    ,2,4,7,0
           ,DEC    ,9,3,6,9
           ,DEC    ,9,9,5,9
           ,DEC    ,5,7,4,9
           ,DEC    ,6,6,9,6
           ,DEC    ,7,6,2,7
           ,DEC    ,7,2,4,0
           ,DEC    ,7,6,6,3
           ,DEC    ,0,3,5,3
           ,DEC    ,5,4,7,5
           ,DEC    ,9,4,5,7
           ,DEC    ,1,3,8,2
           ,DEC    ,1,7,8,5
           ,DEC    ,2,5,1,6
           ,END    ,
```

```
* * * * * * * * * * * * * *
*                           *
*      LAKE/FENCE  PROBLEM  *
*                           *
* * * * * * * * * * * * * *


*
*      LINKAGE
*
        ,ORG    ,010
FINT    ,BSS    ,1
PI      ,BSS    ,1
E       ,BSS    ,1
DEC     ,FORM   ,4,4,4,4
EXIT    ,OPSY   ,HLT
*
*      MAIN PROGRAM
*
        ,ORG    ,04000
LAKE    ,CALL*  ,FINT        LINK TO INTERPRETER
        ,LDAI   ,100         INITIALIZE VARIABLES
        ,STAE   ,X
        ,LDAI   ,10
        ,STAE   ,D
        ,TZA    ,
        ,STAE   ,0A
        ,STAE   ,00A
        ,LDXI   ,95
        ,STXE   ,K
REF2    ,LDAE   ,X           ADD D TO X
        ,ADDE   ,D
        ,STAE   ,X
        ,TAB    ,            COMPUTE H
        ,MULE   ,X
        ,STAE   ,TEM1
        ,LDBE   ,X
        ,MULI   ,500
        ,ADDE   ,CON1
        ,SUBE   ,TEM1
        ,EXC    ,2
        ,STAE   ,H
        ,LDAI   ,250         COMPUTE T
        ,SUBE   ,X
        ,STAE   ,TEM2
        ,DIVE   ,H
        ,TBA    ,
        ,CALL   ,ATAN
        ,STAE   ,T
        ,TAB    ,            COMPUTE A
        ,MULE   ,CON2
```

```
            ,STAE   ,TEM1
            ,LDBE   ,TEM2
            ,MULE   ,H
            ,STAE   ,TEM2
            ,LDAI   ,500
            ,SUBE   ,X
            ,SUBE   ,X
            ,TAB    ,
            ,MULE   ,X
            ,SUBE   ,TEM1
            ,ADDE   ,TEM2
            ,STAE   ,A
REF3        ,SUBE   ,0A          A:0A
            ,JAN    ,REF4
            ,LDAE   ,0A          A>=0A  MOVE 0A TO 00A
            ,STAE   ,00A
            ,LDAE   ,A                  MOVE A TO 0A
            ,STAE   ,0A
            ,JMP    ,REF2               DO IT AGAIN
REF4        ,LDAE   ,X           A<0A  BACK UP
            ,SUBE   ,D
            ,SUBE   ,D
            ,STAE   ,X
            ,LDAE   ,D                  CUT D BY 1/10
            ,DIVI   ,10
            ,STBE   ,D
            ,LDAE   ,00A                MOVE 00A TO 0A
            ,STAE   ,0A
            ,LDXE   ,K                  DECREMENT LOOP COUNTER
            ,DXR    ,
            ,STXE   ,K
            ,JXZ    ,*+4
            ,JMP    ,REF2               REPEAT FOR ANOTHER DIGIT
            ,OME    ,1,X         PRINT X
            ,EXIT   ,            EXIT INTERPRETER
            ,HLT    ,            HALT
*
*       CONSTANTS AND VARIABLES
*
CON1        ,PZE    ,7           CONSTANT 5280†2 - 250†2
            ,DEC    ,2,7,8,1
            ,DEC    ,5,9,0,0
            ,DUP    ,22
            ,DEC    ,0,0,0,0
CON2        ,PZE    ,7           CONSTANT 5280†2
            ,DEC    ,2,7,8,7
            ,DEC    ,8,4,0,0
            ,DUP    ,22
            ,DEC    ,0,0,0,0
K           ,BSS    ,1           LOOP COUNTER
```

```
X        ,BSS  ,25        X
D        ,BSS  ,25        DIFFERENCE
A        ,BSS  ,25        AREA
OA       ,BSS  ,25        OLD AREA
OOA      ,BSS  ,25        OLD OLD AREA
H        ,BSS  ,25        HEIGHT OF TRIANGLE
T        ,BSS  ,25        HALF-ANGLE OF SECTOR
TEM1     ,BSS  ,25        TEMPORARIES
TEM2     ,BSS  ,25
*
*        ARC-TANGENT
*
ATAN     ,ENTR ,
         ,JAZ* ,ATAN      RETURN IF ARGUMENT ZERO
         ,TZX  ,          STRIP OFF SIGN
         ,JAP  ,ATA1
         ,IXR  ,
         ,EXC  ,1
ATA1     ,STAE ,AT99
         ,STXE ,AT94
         ,SUBI ,1         X:1
         ,JAZ  ,ATA6      X=1  SPECIAL CASE
         ,TZX  ,
         ,JAN  ,ATA2      X<1  LEAVE IT ALONE
         ,IXR  ,          X>1  SOLVE FOR COMPLEMENTARY
         ,LDAI ,1                          ANGLE
         ,DIVE ,AT99
         ,STBE ,AT99
ATA2     ,STXE ,AT93
         ,LDXI ,4         REDUCE ARGUMENT USING
         ,LDBE ,AT99              GRUENBERGER METHOD
         ,MULE ,AT99
         ,ADDI ,1
         ,EXC  ,2
         ,SUBI ,1
         ,DIVE ,AT99
         ,STBE ,AT99
         ,DXR  ,
         ,JXZ  ,*+4
         ,JMP  ,ATA2+6
         ,MULE ,AT99      INITIALIZE VARIABLES
         ,CPA  ,
         ,STAE ,AT98
         ,TZA  ,
         ,STAE ,AT95
         ,LDAI ,1
         ,STAE ,AT97
ATA3     ,LDAE ,AT99      COMPUTE NEW TERM
         ,DIVE ,AT97
         ,STBE ,AT96
```

```
        ,TBA    ,
        ,ADDE   ,AT95       ADD IT TO SERIES' SUM
        ,STAE   ,AT95
        ,LDBE   ,AT99       FORM NEXT NUMERATOR
        ,MULE   ,AT98
        ,STAE   ,AT99
        ,LDAE   ,AT97       FORM NEXT DENOMINATOR
        ,ADDI   ,2
        ,STAE   ,AT97
        ,EXIT   ,           COMPARE SUM AND TERM
        ,LDAE   ,AT95
        ,LRLA   ,1
        ,ASRA   ,1
        ,STA    ,*+6
        ,LDAE   ,AT96
        ,LRLA   ,1
        ,ASRA   ,1
        ,ADDI   ,(0)
        ,ADDI   ,97
        ,JAN    ,ATA4
        ,CALL*  ,FINT       TERM STILL SIGNIFICANT
        ,JMP    ,ATA3           DO IT AGAIN
ATA4    ,CALL*  ,FINT       TERM NO LONGER SIGNIFICANT
        ,LDBE   ,AT95           COMPUTE TRUE ANGLE
        ,MULI   ,16
        ,LDXE   ,AT93       RECOMPLEMENT IF NECESSARY
        ,JXZ    ,ATA5
        ,STAE   ,AT95
        ,LDAE*  ,PI
        ,DIVI   ,2
        ,TBA    ,
        ,SUBE   ,AT95
ATA5    ,LDXE   ,AT94       ATTACH PROPER SIGN & RETURN
        ,JXZ*   ,ATAN
        ,CPA    ,
        ,RETU*  ,ATAN
ATA6    ,LDAE*  ,PI         SPECIAL CASE - ANGLE=PI/4
        ,DIVI   ,4
        ,TBA    ,
        ,JMP    ,ATA5
AT93    ,BSS    ,1          COMPLEMENTARY ANGLE TRIGGER
AT94    ,BSS    ,1          SIGN
AT95    ,BSS    ,25         FUNCTION VALUE (ANGLE)
AT96    ,BSS    ,25         TERM
AT97    ,BSS    ,25         DENOMINATOR
AT98    ,BSS    ,25         ARGUMENT↑2
AT99    ,BSS    ,25         NUMERATOR
        ,END    ,LAKE
```

# INDEX

**287**